Heaven, Hell and the Resurrection

Darrell Mowat

WESTBOW
PRESS®
A DIVISION OF THOMAS NELSON
& ZONDERVAN

WestBow Press books may be ordered through booksellers or by contacting:

WestBow Press
A Division of Thomas Nelson & Zondervan
1663 Liberty Drive
Bloomington, IN 47403
www.westbowpress.com
844-714-3454

ISBN: 978-1-6642-5844-0 (sc)
ISBN: 978-1-6642-5843-3 (e)

Print information available on the last page.

WestBow Press rev. date: 2/25/2022

Table of Contents

Preface

The idea for this book came from the desire to "better" understand God's plan for all of us in "eternity" or after this earthly life. As a child I was baptized and confirmed in the Anglican Church, I have attended worship services in various other denominations especially in my young grownup years. And when I began studying and writing, the ideas and various doctrines of these churches and even church denominations that I had never attended started to come together for me in my writing and understanding. It is interesting that there are so many different denominations of Christianity and even religion in general, but the Holy Bible says that things are here a little and there a little (Isa. 28:10). And I think God may have done the same thing in the differing denominations. That being said, one of the ideas that came into my mind even before I knew it was a doctrine of one of the denominations of Christianity was the idea of living on a planet like Adam and Eve did, some day after the final resurrection.

Of course the Holy Bible does talk about this as a possibility, in the "new heavens and the new earth", and Jesus said, "In my Father's house are many mansions…" (John 14:2, Rev. 21:1-5). I will go into greater detail about this in chapters two and three of this book. The point is that just because we think we might know something, does not really mean that we understand it fully (1 Cor. 13:9). The Holy Bible says, "Prove all things; hold fast that which is good." (1 Thess. 5:21). And God says of Himself, "For as the heavens are higher than the earth, so are my ways higher than your ways, and my thoughts than your thoughts." (Isa. 55:9). The reality is God is a Creator, and He desires His creation to grow, increase, and expand (Gen. 1:27, 28; Isa. 9:7). God is an abundant God and a loving God, He is a God of life, and an everlasting God, a God of infinite understanding, and as the Holy Bible says, He "… inhabiteth eternity…" (Ps. 147:5, Isa. 57:15). His works are everlasting and so are we if we accept the blood of His only begotten Son, Jesus Christ of Nazareth for the forgiveness of our sins. This requires that we humble ourselves and admit that we have sinned at least once, turn to God in repentance, ask for His forgiveness and receive the free gift of the Holy Spirit in the name of His only begotten Son, Jesus Christ of Nazareth, whom died on the cross for the forgiveness of our sins and was resurrected to give us the hope and promise of eternal life in His Holy name (Eph. 2:8, 9; 1 Pet. 5:6). Alleluia and praise the LORD. Amen and Amen.

I could not possibly encapsulate the description of "eternity" and God's plan for all of mankind in this book entirely. But at the least, it may be a means of opening up the Biblical Scriptures and the promises "hidden" within to a new generation. The prophets from the beginning have all likely seen at least a glimpse of all that God has planned for mankind (1 Pet. 1:10-12). Some have written in greater detail about it than others, but when searching through all of the scriptures, a full picture begins to unfold. Read on to learn more about the possibilities for you and others in this life and in the "world to come", eternal life (Mark 10:30). Alleluia and praise the LORD. And keep in mind, that it is the Holy Bible of God, with God, the Father, and His only begotten Son, Jesus Christ of Nazareth, through His Holy Spirit that reveals to us all things ultimately. So put your trust in Him first and foremost for understanding in reading this book and in your life in general. Alleluia and praise the LORD. Amen and Amen.

Acknowledgements

This book is written for the glory of God and His only begotten Son, Jesus Christ of Nazareth, and in acknowledgement of all throughout history who have kept the testimony of Jesus Christ of Nazareth. To God be the glory. Alleluia and praise the LORD. Amen and Amen.

Introduction

Jesus came to earth to give us life, and life more abundantly (John 10:10). It is life more abundantly because He gave us eternal salvation in His Holy name. In Romans 8 it speaks of believers in Christ being sons of God, we are "sons of God" if we are led by the Spirit of God (Rom. 8:14). This same Spirit is the Spirit of adoption (Rom. 8:15). Although we have all been born into this earth through earthly parents, God is calling us into His Holy and Eternal family through adoption, in the name and blood sacrifice of His only begotten Son, Jesus Christ of Nazareth. It does not matter your family background, what you have done in this life or what colour your skin is. God is calling mankind to Him, in the name of Jesus Christ of Nazareth. God loves you and desires that you live forever like His only begotten Son, Jesus Christ of Nazareth. This requires repentance, that is, recognizing that we have sinned and desiring earnestly to change, then we can turn to God in prayer and ask Him for forgiveness in the name of Jesus Christ of Nazareth, and ask that His Holy Spirit come into our life to guide us and keep us. To lead us in the righteous path of eternal life in the name of Jesus Christ of Nazareth, not by works, but by faith, this is a free gift from God (Eph. 2:8, 9). Alleluia and praise the LORD. Have you accepted His gift of eternal life yet? If not, what are you waiting for? Ask Him to come into your life and forgive you of your sins. He will and you will not regret it. I promise you that. Alleluia and praise the LORD. Amen and Amen.

That all being said let us talk a little about our existence before we get into the greater details of what the Bible says about heaven and hell. A human being, from God's perspective is made up of three parts; the body, the soul and the spirit (1 Thess. 5:23). Our spirit is not to be confused with God's Spirit, the Holy Spirit. God has given us our own spirit (Rom. 8:16). This is why the question and topic of salvation is so important. God has said in the Holy Bible that we are "gods"; this is not to be confused with the eternal God, the Father, Almighty, who came to earth in the person of Jesus Christ of Nazareth (Ps. 82:6, John 10:34, 35). The reason I say this is that, God, the Father, Almighty has given us a tremendous gift, we through our ancestors were created in His likeness and were made in His image (Gen. 1:26, 27). So the question then we must ask ourselves, is what does it mean to be like God, what does it mean to be a child of the living God, made in the image of God? If we screw up the answer to this one simple question, we might very well fail at our quest for eternal life and salvation. The Good News is, we are not alone in this "quest", we have the Holy Spirit, we have Jesus Christ of Nazareth as our example and we have fellow believers to help us along on this journey. Alleluia and praise the LORD. So take heart and read on to learn more about your place in God's eternal plan for us in this world and in the "world to come" (Mark 10:30). Alleluia and praise the LORD. Amen and Amen.

Last, the interpretations in this book may hinge on the correct interpretations of other end-time events spoken about in previous books. My interpretation and explanation of what heaven may be like is not likely going to compare with a child's simplicity of their description, i.e. "Heaven is for real". That being said, I will try my best according to Scriptural revelation, life experience and some open mindedness. Most important is to remember a personal relationship with your Lord and Saviour, Jesus Christ of Nazareth. He is the only name who can save under heaven (Acts 4:12). Anyone else, including myself, can at best, try and help point you in the correct direction. That is to Christ and God, the Holy Bible of God, a healthy prayer life and regular fellowship with other believers for the ultimate answers for what comes next in this life and in eternity. So, this book's main purpose or focus will be on three common topics, Salvation, Peculiarity, and Marriage. The salvation plan of God, the peculiar role we each play in God's greater common salvation plan for all of mankind, and His plans and purposes for marriage in this life and eternity. Alongside of these three main topics will be discussed the "darker" things of the Holy Bible, regarding, judgement, hell and death in general. It would be hard to discuss the one without the other, at least in considering all that must take place in this life, as the Holy Bible says, "…it is appointed unto men once to die, but after this the judgment…" (Heb. 9:27). So read on to learn more about what God, in Christ, may have instore for you in this life and into eternity.

Chapter 1: Heaven – Heaven on earth

"… accounted worthy to obtain that world, and the resurrection from the dead…"
- Luke 20:35

Introduction

The reality of heaven on earth is as simple as accepting God's Holy Spirit into your life; body, mind and soul, living for Him. We do this by accepting Jesus Christ of Nazareth as our Saviour. Isaiah 26:3 says "Thou wilt keep *him* in perfect peace, *whose* mind *is* stayed *on thee:* because he trusteth in thee.". The New Testament says something similar, in 2 Timothy 1:7 it says, "For God hath not given us the spirit of fear; but of power, and of love, and of a sound mind.". Jesus said, "…The kingdom of God cometh not with observation: Neither shall they say, Lo here! or, lo there! for, behold, the kingdom of God is within you." (Luke 17:20, 21). He sent the Holy Spirit to the New Testament Church of God, on Pentecost 31 A.D. and the kingdom of God has been growing here on earth ever since (Acts 2). There is prophecy of the "woman going into the wilderness", the Church of God until about the late 1500's A.D. (Rev. 12:6). But with the advent of the printing press and the translation of the Holy Scriptures into English and other tongues, the gospel message has flourished and will continue to flourish (Isa. 9:7, Matt. 16:18). The point is that God's Holy Spirit is what brings peace; our action of obedience to Him first and foremost in the mind is what brings us perfect peace. The remainder of this chapter will discuss this "spiritual" state of mind, the realities of peace on earth and what God may very likely have planned for planet earth in this age and in the world to come. Alleluia and praise the LORD. Amen and Amen.

Spiritual state of mind and the Messianic Age

During my early years of conversion there was a time where people would suggest that I was born again. And certainly there is a so called "movement" within the Christian realm of being so called "born again" believers. The reality of the matter is that to truly be born again, we must be born of the Holy Spirit (John 3:1-7, 1 Pet. 1:22, 23). The issue with being called a "born again" believer is that conversion does not happen overnight, it takes a life time and Isaiah 46 describes this idea thoroughly (Isa. 46:3, 4). Isaiah 46:3 and 4 say, "Hearken unto me, O house of Jacob, and all the remnant of the house of Israel, which are born *by me* from the belly, which are carried from the womb: And *even* to *your* old age I *am* he; and *even* to hoar hairs will I carry *you:* I have made, and I will bear; even I will carry, and will deliver *you*.". God describes us as being in the womb and being carried during our life here on earth by Him. He is taking care of us now! He goes on to talk about carrying us into old age, and still the birthing is not described yet. The truth of the matter is that as I had said conversion takes a lifetime, and we will not truly be "born again", better put born of the Holy Spirit until we shed this corruptible flesh (1 Cor. 15:42-58). If we are truly following Jesus, for better or for worse, we need to die someday, as the Holy Bible says, "And as it is appointed unto men once to die, but after this the judgment: So Christ was once offered to bear the sins of many; and unto them that look for him shall he appear the second time without sin unto salvation." (Heb. 9:27, 28). We can die to our old nature daily, but eventually we are all going to have to shed this fleshly life and it's corruptness in order to receive our glorified bodies like Jesus did (2 Pet. 1:14). If Jesus is the example to follow then we must also, lose our lives, or "give up the ghost" someday like He did (Matt. 16:24). Isaiah 46:3 and 4 describe Jesus' life giving offering as well. He desires us to dwell in Him and Him in us (John 6:53-56, 14:20, 15:5). He desires to carry us so to speak (Isa. 40:11). He desires to be our strength and our life provider, our protection and our refuge (Ps. 18:1, 2; 27:1). One Old Testament word used for compassion, "racham", can also be used to describe a womb, Strong's number 7356 (Gen. 43:14, 49:25, 1 Kings 8:50). Jesus Christ of Nazareth is full of compassion, and this was shown throughout His ministry, healing, feeding and dying on the cross for the forgiveness of our sins (Matt. 9:35, 36; 14:14, 15:32, 20:34, Mark 1:41, 5:19, 20; 6:34, 8:2, 3; Luke 7:13-15). His life giving blood flowed down the cross for forgiveness of our sins, He died and was buried, and the third day He arose to give us the hope and promise of eternal life in His life giving name, Jesus Christ of Nazareth (Acts 4:12). That being said, Jesus came to give us life and life more abundantly (John 10:10). He also said, "…And whosoever liveth and believeth in me shall never die…." (John 11:25, 26). This is the life giving promise we all have in Jesus Christ of Nazareth's Holy name, life and life more abundantly, life everlasting. Alleluia and Praise the Lord. Amen and Amen.

Another prophecy spoken of in the Holy Bible is the "Messianic Age", where God's peace and righteousness will reign on earth, although the phrase is not actually used as such in the Holy Bible. Revelation 19:7-9 says, "Let us be glad and rejoice, and give honour to him: for the marriage of the Lamb is come, and his wife hath made herself ready. And to her was granted that she should be arrayed in fine linen, clean and white: for the fine linen is the righteousness of saints. And he saith unto me, Write, Blessed are they which are called unto the marriage supper of the Lamb. And he saith unto me, These are the true sayings of God.". This likely speaks of the marriage supper of the "Messianic Age", with Christ and His resurrected saints ruling over the inhabitants of earth, of those whom survive the "Great Tribulation", spoken of in many places in the Holy Bible (Matt. 24:21, Rev. 2:22, 7:14). Mark 13:20 says, "And except that the Lord had shortened those days, no flesh should be saved: but for the elect's sake, whom he hath chosen, he hath shortened the days.". Proof there is an earthly existence after the "Great Tribulation", spoken of by Jesus in His parables of the time of the end (Matt. 24, Rev. 2:22). Days are shortened and flesh is saved, that means there is life here on earth after this time of great trouble here on earth. I have written another book on the subject, but the Holy Bible speaks of it in Ezekiel 40-48 and in Revelation 20:4 it says, "And I saw thrones, and they sat upon them, and judgement was given unto them: and I *saw* the souls of them that were beheaded for the witness of Jesus, and for the word of God, and which had not worshipped the beast, neither his image, neither had received *his* mark upon their foreheads, or in their hands; and they lived and reigned with Christ a thousand years.". This has no doubt, not yet taken place. Although much of this book will speak about earth's final "end", and the "New Heavens and New Earth", the reader should be forewarned, that there is likely an "age" here on earth, one thousand years to be exact, where God's peace will reign unimpeded, before the very "end" and the final judgement (Ezek. 40-48, Rev. 20:4). I will speak of this "age", the "Messianic Age" a few more times throughout this book, so now you have a little better idea of what I am speaking of. I do honestly believe this is to be literal and not spiritual in perspective only. The main reason for this belief is understanding and knowing God's nature is love, and peace and righteousness, and He has sovereignty over all things (John 1:1-3, 1 John 4:8, Rev. 4:11). Not only this but God desires us to live at peace with Him, so why would He not show us how this works for an extended period of time here on earth, as a testimony to His peace and righteousness, before the final judgement of all mankind? I will leave the answer up to you. But I know that there is still an age to come before the final judgement, for God, Christ, His saints' and mankind's sake (Rom. 11:29).

Praise be to God Almighty and His only begotten Son, Jesus Christ of Nazareth. Alleluia and praise the LORD. Amen and Amen.

God desires to give us a new spirit in us. Ezekiel 11:19 and 20 says, "And I will give them one heart, and I will put a new spirit within you; and I will take the stony heart out of their flesh, and will give them an heart of flesh: That they may walk in my statutes, and keep mine ordinances, and do them: and they shall be my people, and I will be their God.". Ezekiel 18:31 says, "Cast away from you all your transgressions, whereby ye have transgressed; and make you a new heart and a new spirit: for why will ye die, O house of Israel?". Ezekiel 36:26 says, "A new heart also will I give you, and a new spirit will I put within you: and I will take away the stony heart out of your flesh, and I will give you an heart of flesh.". The key to understanding these verses is that we as humans are made up of a physical body, like Adam was made from the dust of the earth, we are a living soul, just like God breathed life into Adam, and we have a spirit that was given to us at conception. In Jesus Christ of Nazareth's name through the forgiveness of our sins we are given a new heart and spirit, that come from God through repentance and the forgiveness of our sins, by the healing power of the blood of Jesus Christ of Nazareth spilt on the cross for the forgiveness of our sins. Alleluia and praise the LORD. Amen and Amen. Hebrews 4:12 says, "For the word of God is quick, and powerful, and sharper than any twoedged sword, piercing even to the dividing asunder of soul and spirit, and of the joints and marrow, and is a discerner of the thoughts and intents of the heart.". God's Holy Spirit is very much related to our physical bodies and the soul and spirit are related and in agreement but not the same (1 John 5:8). Our soul is what holds us together and what makes us humans, but the spirit is what relates us with God's Holy Spirit. Our bodies are the physical side that accomplishes things and feels pleasure and pain. In Jesus Christ of Nazareth, we can have healing; a new spirit in us, God's Holy Spirit, our souls can be cleansed of evil, decay and sin, and our bodies can be made anew. This is how we can receive our resurrection, both spiritually and physically, and it is through Jesus Christ of Nazareth's Holy name that we receive this eternal life and the body that comes with it. Our body is considered God's temple, and He desires that we treat it as a holy temple, not defiling it physically or spiritually (1 Cor. 3:16, 17). Matthew 6:22 and 23 says, "The light of the body is the eye: if therefore thine eye be single, thy whole body shall be full of light. But if thine eye be evil, thy whole body shall be full of darkness. If therefore the light that is in thee be darkness, how great is that darkness!". Jesus Christ of Nazareth is the true light, and when we put our trust in Him, obey Him and follow Him, He reveals more to us, He gives us of His Holy Spirit, and this Spirit is life and life everlasting (John 8:12, 1 John 4:13). Jesus said of God, the Father, and Himself, "And this is life eternal, that they might know thee the only true God, and Jesus Christ, whom thou hast sent." (John 17:3). Alleluia and praise the LORD. Amen and Amen.

New Jerusalem, and the New Heavens and New Earth

Some have suggested that the "New Heavens and New Earth" will be like a "new" Garden of Eden type scenario, you can see one reference book for this idea in appendix A. And in chapter three I will go into greater detail of the "new Jerusalem" that may help the reader understand this idea better. Revelation 3:12 says, "Him that overcometh will I make a pillar in the temple of my God, and he shall go no more out: and I will write upon him the name of my God, and the name of the city of my God, which is new Jerusalem, which cometh down out of heaven from my God: and I will write upon him my new name.". 1 Corinthians 15:45-49 says, "And so it is written, The first man Adam was made a living soul; the last Adam *was made* a quickening spirit. Howbeit that *was* not first which is spiritual, but that which is natural; and afterward that which is spiritual. The first man *is* of the earth, earthy; the second man *is* the Lord from heaven. As *is* the earthy, such *are* they also that are earthy: and as *is* the heavenly, such *are* they also that are heavenly. And as we have born the image of the earthy, we shall also bear the image of the heavenly.". Isaiah 41:4 says, "Who hath wrought and done *it*, calling the generations from the beginning? I the LORD, the first, and with the last, I *am* he.". Revelation 19:11-13 says, "And I saw heaven opened, and behold a white horse; and he that sat upon him *was* called Faithful and True, and in righteousness he doth judge and make war. His eyes *were* as a flame of fire, and on his head *were* many crowns; and he had a name written, that no man knew, but he himself. And he *was* clothed with a vesture dipped in blood: and his name is called The Word of God.". Revelation 21:4 says, "And God shall wipe away all tears from their eyes; and there shall be no more dearth, neither sorrow, nor crying, neither shall there be any more pain: for the former things are passed away.". The point in all of this is that God has and is preparing a place for us that is not of this world (John 14:2). Jesus said this, and I will speak of it in greater detail throughout this book. But we must remember first and foremost that God's kingdom is spiritual. As Jesus said, God is a Spirit (John 4:24). Our salvation and redemption come from Jesus Christ of Nazareth, by the offering of His life on the cross for the forgiveness of our sins. He has given us the hope for a future in His Holy name, because there is no other name under heaven by which we can be saved (Acts 4:12). Praise the LORD God Almighty, and His only begotten Son, Jesus Christ of Nazareth. Alleluia and praise the LORD. Amen and Amen.

Revelation 2:7 says, "He that hath an ear, let him hear what the Spirit saith unto the churches; To him that overcometh will I give to eat of the tree of life, which is in the midst of the paradise of God.". See Appendix A – Resources for more on "Garden of Eden" references, as mentioned earlier. Israel is referred to as a tree of life. Isaiah 27:6 says, "He shall cause them that come of Jacob to take root: Israel shall blossom and bud, and fill the face of the world with fruit.". Compare this with the tree of life mentioned in the book of Revelation and similar trees mentioned in Ezekiel 47 (Ezek. 47:7, 12; Rev. 2:7, 22:2, 14). Genesis 2:9 says, "And out of the ground made the LORD God to grow every tree that is pleasant to the sight, and good for food; the tree of life also in the midst of the garden, and the tree of knowledge of good and evil.". Ezekiel 47:12 says, "And by the river upon the bank thereof, on this side and on that side, shall grow all trees for meat, whose leaf shall not fade, neither shall the fruit thereof be consumed: it shall bring forth new fruit according to his months, because their waters they issued out of the sanctuary: and the fruit thereof shall be for meat, and the leaf thereof for medicine.". Revelation 22:2 says, "In the midst of the street of it, and on either side of the river, *was there* the tree of life, which bare twelve *manner of* fruits, *and* yielded her fruit every month: and the leaves of the tree *were* for the healing of the nations.". Isaiah 61:3 says, "To appoint unto them that mourn in Zion, to give unto them beauty for ashes, the oil of joy for mourning, the garment of praise for the spirit of heaviness; that they might be called trees of righteousness, the planting of the LORD, that he might be glorified.". Jeremiah 17:8 says, "For he shall be as a tree planted by the waters, and *that* spreadeth out her roots by the river, and shall not see when heat cometh, but her leaf shall be green; and shall not be careful in the year of drought, neither shall cease from yielding fruit.". Proverbs 3:18 says, "She *is* a tree of life to them that lay hold upon her: and happy *is every one* that retaineth her."; Solomon here is speaking of wisdom and understanding as a tree of life (Prov. 3:13). Proverbs 11:30 says, "The fruit of the righteous *is* a tree of life; and he that winneth souls *is* wise.". Isaiah 48:3 says, "I have declared the former things from the beginning; and they went forth out of my mouth, and I shewed them; I did *them* suddenly, and they came to pass.". Compare this with "evolution" or even the ideas of the seven day creation week being figurative, which I have heard been suggested. The reality is that God said He did it "suddenly". Ultimately, our tree of life is the cross of Jesus Christ of Nazareth, He gave himself up to be hung on a tree, to die for the forgiveness of our sins and He was resurrected to give us the hope and promise of eternal life in His Holy name (1 Pet. 2:24). Jesus Christ of Nazareth is the true "Shepherd and Bishop" of our souls (1 Pet. 2:25). Alleluia and praise the LORD. Amen and Amen.

God commands us to "forget" the past, Isaiah 43:18 says, "Remember ye not the former things, neither consider the things of old.". This is likely regarding preparing us first and foremost for the "new covenant" in Jesus Christ of Nazareth. As the writer continues, "Behold, I will do a new thing; now it shall spring forth; shall ye not know it? I will even make a way in the wilderness, *and* rivers in the desert." (Isa. 43:19). God forgets the past. Isaiah 65:17 says, "For, behold, I create new heavens and a new earth: and the former shall not be remembered, nor come into mind.". Isaiah 66:22 says, "For as the new heavens and the new earth, which I will make, shall remain before me, saith the LORD, so shall your seed and your name remain.". Revelation 21:1 says, "And I saw a new heaven and a new earth: for the first heaven and the first earth were passed away; and there was no more sea.". This is the "bigger" picture to the wedding supper and marriage of the Lamb I spoke of associated with the "Messianic Age" in the previous section. The "bigger" picture is that God has an eternal plan for all of us and it does not only include our life here on earth today. It is an eternal plan, God willing, that lasts forever. You can look at appendices B and C for some insight into the possible future of life here on earth, in the short term and long term for more detail and ultimately the Holy Bible of God does the best job of describing things that have been, are and are to come, forever. Alleluia and praise the LORD. Amen and Amen. Nevertheless we must continually keep our eye on the truth of God, that is, in Jesus Christ of Nazareth. He was and is the, Son of God, the Word of God, and the Creator of the Universe and everything in it (John 1:1-3 14, 34). He was with God in the beginning and is God (John 1:2). He desires us to "forsake" all and follow Him, although He promises one hundred fold in this life and in the "world to come" eternal life if we do (Matt. 19:27-30, Luke 14:33). This is the truth of life in Jesus Christ of Nazareth, life and life more abundantly (John 10:10). Alleluia and praise the LORD. Amen and Amen. That being said, He also promised in this life we would have troubles, but not to fear, because He has overcome the world (John 16:33). Alleluia and praise the LORD. Jesus Christ of Nazareth came into this world, conceived by the Holy Ghost in the virgin Mary, born of the virgin, Mary, espoused to Joseph (Matt. 1:18-25). He was raised a child of Israel, of the tribe of Judah (Luke 2:41-52, Rev. 5:5). He taught, fed, healed and forgave all of our sins (Matt. 5:5, 14:16-21, 15:30, 31; 18:21-35). And ultimately He showed us all of His Holy love, by dying on the cross for the forgiveness of our sins, spilling His Holy and righteous blood on the cross, He was buried and the third day He arose to give us the hope and promise of eternal life in His Holy name. Alleluia and praise the LORD. Amen and Amen. There is still much knowledge in the Holy Bible to be learned, and all of it is righteous and true, but our reality is in Jesus Christ of Nazareth, and Salvation is in His Holy name alone (Acts 4:12). Alleluia and praise the LORD. Amen and Amen.

Restoration of all things

The Elijah, Restitution and Restoration of all things (Mal. 4:5, 6, Matt. 17:11, Acts 3:21). Jesus called John the Baptist, Elias, that is Elijah, and John pointed everything right back to Jesus (Matt. 3:11,

12; John 3:30). The coming Elijah according to Malachi was to "…turn the heart of the fathers to the children, and the heart of the children to their fathers, lest I come and smite the earth with a curse.". And in the New Testament it says of John the Baptist, "And he shall go before him in the spirit and power of Elias, to turn the hearts of the fathers to the children, and the disobedient to the wisdom of the just; to make ready a people prepared for the Lord." (Mal. 4:5, 6; Luke 1:17). Again, John the Baptist said of Jesus and himself, "He must increase, but I *must* decrease." (John 3:30). He also said, "I indeed baptize you with water unto repentance: but he that cometh after me is mightier than I, whose shoes I am not worthy to bear: he shall baptize you with the Holy Ghost, and *with* fire: Whose fan *is* in his hand, and he will throughly purge his floor, and gather his wheat into the garner; but he will burn up the chaff with unquenchable fire." (Matt. 3:11, 12). Two of Jesus' disciples, James and John, not John the Baptist, at one point asked Him if they ought to call down fire from heaven upon some whom did not receive Jesus in a Samaritan village, like Elias, that is Elijah did similarly, and He rebuked them for it because His face was set toward Jerusalem for His judgement, crucifixion and resurrection (Luke 9:51-56). Acts 3:19-21 says, "Repent ye therefore, and be converted, that your sins may be blotted out, when the times of refreshing shall come from the presence of the Lord; And he shall send Jesus Christ, which before was preached unto you: Whom the heaven must receive until the times of the restitution of all things, which God hath spoken by the mouth of all his holy prophets since the world began.". Acts 1:11 says, "…Ye men of Galilee, why stand ye gazing up into heaven? this same Jesus, which is taken up from you into heaven, shall so come in like manner as ye have seen him go into heaven.". And Jesus says in John 14:3, "…if I go and prepare a place for you, I will come again, and receive you unto myself; that where I am, *there* ye may be also.". How could this be unless it was at the very end of earth's history? Is it not possible then that the restoration of ALL things is a New Heaven and a New Earth, with a New Jerusalem!? Jesus says in John 6:38-40, "For I came down from heaven, not to do mine own will, but the will of him that sent me. And this is the Father's will which hath sent me, that of all which he hath given me I should lose nothing, but should raise it up again at the last day. And this is the will of him that sent me, that every one which seeth the Son, and believeth on him, may have everlasting life: and I will raise him up at the last day.". Alleluia and praise the LORD. Amen and Amen.

The following is an example of Elijah and the prophets of Baal (1 Kings 18). Elijah, told the prophets of Baal to prepare an offering of a bullock for their "gods" (1 Kings 18:23, 24). And Elijah did the same for his God, the God of Israel (1 Kings 18:23, 24). He told them to call on their "gods" to consume the offering, if their "gods" were the true God (1 Kings 18:24, 25). They entreated their "gods", cut themselves, stomped on the offering, but nothing came of it (1 Kings 18:26-29). So Elijah repaired the altar of the LORD that was broken down, that may represent the cross of Christ (1 Kings 18:30). He took twelve stones for the twelve tribes of Israel and built an altar for his offering (1 Kings 18:31, 32). He made a trench in the earth around it all, like God's protection around us, God's people (1 Kings 18:32). He put the wood in order, cut the bullock in pieces and laid them on the wood, that may represent Christ offering of His life for us on the cross, specifically during the parting of His garments (1 Kings 18:33, Matt. 27:35). Then some of the Israelites with him poured four barrels of water, three times, on all of this, filling the trenches as well, which again represents Christ Jesus, as "living waters", poured out on all, like rain, "God is not a respecter of persons" (1 Kings 18:33-35; John 4:10-26, 7:37-39; Acts 10:34). Also the people involved with the pouring shows our part in sharing the gospel of Jesus Christ, through the Holy Spirit in us and through us and with us. Last, Elijah calls on the God of Israel and down comes the consuming fire of God, that consumes the altar, wood, offering and water, including the dust, licking the last bit of water from the trenches, and the people repent (1 Kings 18:36-39). This shows God's ultimate authority over all of us, even over His only begotten Son, Jesus Christ of Nazareth, whom died on the cross for the forgiveness of our sins, He was buried and the third day He arose to give us the hope and promise of eternal life in His Holy name. After all of this, Elijah called the people to bind the four hundred and fifty prophets of Baal, whose offering was not consumed and he slew them all (1 Kings 18:40). This account is a good example of God's ability, especially in the "end" of earth's history as we know it (2 Pet. 3:10-13, Rev. 20:9-21:1). He has the ability to consume everything and destroy the wicked, and this may very well be the case, in order to establish the "New Heavens and New Earth", along with the "New Jerusalem", that will be spoken of more in later chapters of this book. Now we have the example of Elijah, the king and the whirlwind (2 Kings 1, 2). Elijah was approached twice by a group of fifty soldiers (2 Kings 1:9-12). The first and second time they requested of him to speak to the king, referring to him as a "man of God", and he said, "…If I *be* a man of God, then let fire come down from heaven, and consume thee and thy fifty…." and it did (2 Kings 1:10). After the second time this happened, a third group of fifty was sent, but this time they bowed down to him, calling him lord, and pleaded with him that he not speak out against them also (1 Kings 1:13, 14). So the angel of the LORD told him to go with them, not to be afraid (1 Kings 1:15). After this and some time, he was speaking with Elisha, his successor, asking what Elisha would have before he was taken, and Elisha asked for a double portion of the his spirit, the Holy Spirit (1 Kings 2:9). He said it was a hard thing he asked, but if he saw Elijah being taken up he would receive what he asked, soon after God took him up in a whirlwind to heaven, which Elisha saw, and he was not with him any longer (1 Kings 2:10-12). These two accounts are a good example of God's ability to "consume" the wicked and "take up" or "save" the righteous. These comparisons along with the account of Daniel's colleagues in the furnace may be the best example for what will happen to "mankind" here on earth at the "end" of earth's history (Dan. 3). That is, the "wicked" will be consumed, and the "righteous" will be saved to participate in the "New Heavens and New Earth", in the "New Jerusalem", forever more, with God Almighty and His only begotten Son, Jesus Christ of Nazareth, through the Holy Spirit of God. Alleluia and praise the LORD. Amen and Amen.

The City; Hebrews 11:14-16 says, "For they that say such things declare plainly that they seek a country. And truly, if they had been mindful of that *country* from whence they came out, they might have had opportunity to have returned. But now they desire a better *country*, that is, an heavenly: wherefore God is not ashamed to be called their God: for he hath prepared for them a city.". Jesus was born in Bethlehem, it is also known as the city of David, according to Luke (Matt. 2:1, Luke 2:4). In chapter three I will go into greater detail about the "New Jerusalem" and how it may be associated with our life here on earth today and in the "world to come" (Rev. 21, 22). The heavenly city is just that the Spirit of God. We can experience that far off place where we are today, that city that we are looking to be a part of, the Garden of Eden, that most holy place. It was made attainable to all through the life and love of Jesus Christ of Nazareth. Alleluia and praise the LORD. Amen and Amen. As mentioned in section one of this chapter, our body is, a tabernacle, a temple of God's Holy Spirit (1 Cor. 3:16, 17). One part of this great purpose for us in this life is marriage and producing godly seed (Mal. 2:14-16). Deuteronomy 17:14-20 speaks of a true king; not multiplying horses and wives to himself, nor greatly multiplying gold and silver to himself, but diligent in studying the word of God and obeying His commandments. And the reality is in Jesus Christ of Nazareth as He is that perfect husbandman and head of the body (Col. 1:18). He has come for His bride in the flesh and continues to sojourn with us through His Holy Spirit until the end. And on that final day, God willing, we will stand before Him without condemnation and will be with Him forever more in the New Heaven and New Earth (Rom. 8:1, 1 John 3:20). Marriage is between one man and one woman, and according to the Holy Bible a prudent wife, spouse, comes from the LORD (Gen. 2:24, Prov. 19:14). God calls us to be fruitful and multiply (Gen. 1:28). Children are a blessing (Ps. 127:3). And in marriage there is opportunity for godly fellowship, help, enjoyment and pleasure (Gen. 2:18, 20-24; 1 Cor. 7:3, 14:35; 1 Pet. 3:1-7). Obedience to God brings prosperity and pleasure (Job 36:11). All pleasure is at God's right hand, where Jesus Christ of Nazareth sits (Ps. 16:11, Luke 22:69, Rev. 4:11). Salvation comes from God in Christ Jesus of Nazareth alone by His Holy Spirit freely given to all whom receive Him, but God can use the spouse to bring the other to the knowledge of salvation in Jesus Christ of Nazareth, by His Holy Spirit working in and through them (Proverbs 12:4, James 1:12, 1 Pet. 3:1, 2; Rev. 2:10, 3:11). Alleluia and praise the LORD. Amen and Amen. 1 Peter 3:7 speaks of the husband and wife saying they are "…heirs together of the grace of life…". Proverbs 18:22 says, "*Whoso* findeth a wife findeth a good *thing*, and obtaineth favour of the LORD.". The epistle to Titus has advice on maintaining family dynamic, and so does other epistles and the entire Holy Bible in general. I have expanded on the subject of family in appendix D, and will speak of the subject in greater detail in the coming chapters, but our reality is in Christ Jesus of Nazareth. Alleluia and praise the LORD. Amen and Amen.

Conclusion

Although we look for a new heaven and new earth, we must remember that our bodies are temples of the Holy Spirit. In order to prepare for a resurrection and eternal life, we need to practice that "holy" way of living now. We need to focus daily on our relationship with our Creator, through prayer, study, praise and fellowship with other believers. Communication is the key to growth here on earth with God Almighty and others. Alleluia and praise the LORD. Amen and Amen. You can look at appendix B, for a more in depth discussion on the concept of being "born again" for your interest. No matter, we must remember that Jesus came to teach us about the kingdom of God (Matt. 6:33, 12:28; Mark 1:14, 15; 10:14, 15; Luke 16:16). That is God's sovereignty over all things, and His desire for us to receive forgiveness of our sins, by the blood of His beloved son, Jesus Christ of Nazareth, through the spilling of Jesus' Holy and righteous blood on the cross for the forgiveness of our sins. Then His death, burial and resurrection three days later to give us the hope and promise of eternal life in His Holy name. Alleluia and praise the LORD. Amen and Amen. The Holy Bible in a couple places references the "…world without end." (Isa. 45:17, Eph. 3:21). The Holy Bible says in various places that the earth will not come to an end completely, that it seems to be everlasting (Gen. 17:8, 48:4, 49:26). This is where Peter's writing comes in regarding the "dissolving" of things, and the regeneration and renewing that Paul also speaks of, even Moses in Psalm 90 speaks of "…everlasting to everlasting…" (Ps. 90:2, Isa. 24:1-6, 2 Pet. 3:10-13, 2 Cor. 5:1; Tit. 3:4-7). Because likely as will be spoken of in later chapters this earth will likely go through a trial by literal fire, that will purge the earth of sin completely, that is, the records of our former and present habitation in this current Biblical account of life and history here on earth, see appendix C for more detail on this subject (2 Pet. 3:10-13, Rev. 20:9-21:5). But if we believe and live in the Holy Spirit of God, our life will not come to an "end" in Christ Jesus of Nazareth's Holy name, Jesus and God are everlasting, and His kingdom is everlasting (Ps. 41:13, 93:2, 145:13; Isa. 9:6, 40:28; John 11:25-27). However, we look for a "New Heaven and New Earth", as mentioned above and will be spoken of throughout this book. It is this "New Heaven and New Earth", that we will inhabit forever and in reality, as has been said and will be said, God's kingdom is spiritual first and foremost, as God is a Spirit (Luke 17:20, 21; John 4:24). So we need not look further than the Holy

Spirit given to us through the knowledge of the forgiveness of our sin in Jesus Christ of Nazareth's Holy name. Because Jesus Christ of Nazareth died on the cross for the forgiveness of our sins, He shed His Holy and righteous blood on the cross for the forgiveness of our sins, He was buried and the third day He arose to give us the hope and promise of eternal life in His Holy name. Alleluia and praise the LORD. Amen and Amen. The next chapter will continue this discussion of the literal heavens going into more detail about the heavens that are above, read on to learn more.

Discussion: Salvation

> "The hill of God *is as* the hill of Basha; and high hill *as* the hill of Bashan. Why leap ye, ye high hills? *This is* the hill *which* God desireth to dwell in; yea, the LORD will dwell *in it* for ever. The chariots of God *are* twenty thousand, *even* thousands of angels: the Lord *is* among them, *as in* Sinai, in the holy *place.*"
> - Psalm 68:15-17

Some of us may never "see" or step foot in the "promised land", Moses saw it from a hill and many Israelites died in the wilderness without likely even seeing a glimpse of it literally. This may be a reality for many today who are not able to, for one reason or another, travel to these places of pilgrimage literally. But we must remember as Jesus said, "...I am with you alway, *even* unto the end of the world. Amen." (Matt. 28:20). And He said, "... the hour cometh, when ye shall neither in this mountain, nor yet at Jerusalem, worship the Father...the hour cometh, and now is, when the true worshippers shall worship the Father in spirit and in truth..." (John 4:21, 23). My point is God and Jesus Christ are with us no matter where we are here on earth, even to the "end", whether we "see" that far off "promised land" or not (Matt. 28:20). It is by faith we live in God and Christ, and this is a gift, not earned by merit of works, so that no man can boast (Eph. 2:8, 9). Glory be to God, the Father, Almighty and His only begotten Son, Jesus Christ of Nazareth. Alleluia and praise the LORD. King David lived in Jerusalem, and he still felt like a stranger from time to time (Ps. 39:12, 69:8). The apostles wrote about being a stranger on the earth, and a pilgrim (Matt. 25:35, Eph. 2:12, 13, 19-22; 1 Pet. 2:11, 12). And Jesus said Himself, that His kingdom was not of this world, or else His servants would fight for Him, albeit Peter did cut off the ear of a high priests servant, but Jesus healed the servant's ear, and Jesus spoke those words after that event (Matt. 18:10, 11, 36; Luke 22:50, 51). We must remember as Jesus Christ, Himself said, that God is a Spirit (John 4:24). So this means that His kingdom is a spiritual kingdom first and foremost. He inhabits our praise (Ps. 22:3). Righteousness and judgment are the habitation of His throne (Ps. 97:2). He inhabits eternity (Isa. 57:15). This is a God much greater than us, but merciful and loving enough to send His only begotten Son, Jesus Christ of Nazareth, to die on the cross for the forgiveness of our sins and to show us the way to salvation in His Holy name. It is by grace that we are saved, not by works, so that no man can boast (Eph. 2:8, 9). Praise the LORD God Almighty, and His only begotten Son, Jesus Christ of Nazareth. Alleluia and Praise the LORD. Jesus also said that God's kingdom does not come by observation, but that His kingdom is within us (Luke 17:20, 21). That is because God is a Spirit and all of creation exists by, through and for Him (John 1:1-3, Rev. 4:11). When reading through this chapter's discussion questions and meditating on any answers, consider that great gift God has given us in His only begotten Son, Jesus Christ of Nazareth, whom died on the cross for the forgiveness of our sins, He was buried and arose three days later to give us the hope and promise of everlasting life in His Holy and precious name. Glory, thanks and praise be to our God, in Jesus Christ of Nazareth's Holy name. Alleluia and praise the LORD. Amen and Amen.

Discussion Questions

1. What do you believe about salvation and being "born again"? Read Isaiah 46:3 & 4 and some other Biblical verses that may help you with your understanding of being born again.

   _____

   _____

   _____

2. Have you accepted Christ's sacrifice for your sins yet?

   _____

   _____

   _____

3. How seriously do you take your conversion, and what are some changes you can make today to better follow God's path for you in this life?

   _____

   _____

   _____

Chapter 2: Heaven – Outer Space

"And after the earthquake a fire; *but* the LORD *was* not in
the fire: and after the fire a still small voice."
- 1 Kings 19:12

Introduction

The concepts in this chapter are meant to expand the understanding of the reader's mind, and address some of the ideas of aliens, angels and other theories of earth's inhabitants as well as what is "out there". God created everything we see and everything we cannot see (Col. 1:12-17). At night under the right lighting and clarity we can see constellations, the milky way galaxy, etc. and scientists have been able to peer further into the universe using technology with high powered telescopes on earth and in space, albeit I have heard that what we see through a telescope is actually history, because it takes time for light to travel. Nevertheless, the Holy Bible says, "…with God all things are possible." (Matt. 19:26). The question of whether or not we are alone in this universe is not new and to this day it would seem that the discussion is not resolved, as of the date of writing this book in 2018 A.D.. But from a follower of Christ's perspective the answer is easy, of course we are not alone (Heb. 13:5). God makes this clear time and again in the Holy Bible, that He lives, Jesus Christ of Nazareth lives and He has given us of His Holy Spirit to dwell with and in us all, to teach, comfort and guide us in all things (Gen. 1:26, Ex. 3:14, Matt. 28:20, John 14:16-18, 1 John 4:13). Nevertheless in the remainder of this chapter we will discuss the deeper things of God in reference to the universe and the possibilities for mankind in it, read on to learn more.

Planets, Solar systems and "Spaceship Earth"

The inspiration behind this chapter is a lifetime of watching television shows, movies, documentaries and school lessons about space travel. Early on in doing the research for this book I found out that the astronaut, Buzz Aldrin, took communion on the moon. Also, there is video on the internet of the Apollo 8 astronauts reading from the book of Genesis while they orbit the moon, see appendix A for references to these two subjects.[1] So I ask, who is really in control of our space exploration? Matthew 6:33 says, "But seek ye first the kingdom of God, and his righteousness; and all these things shall be added unto you.". I am not sure if they decided to take this literally and seek out God's kingdom, or not, but I can tell you that God's kingdom is spiritual first and foremost (John 4:24). As Jesus said, God is a Spirit, and we are to worship him in spirit and in truth (John 4:23). He created the heavens and the earth and all that are in them, but He was before all things, the beginning of creation (Col. 1:17, 1 John 2:13, 14). The idea of "super heroes" or multiple saviours can also be addressed in the Holy Bible, but this is likely speaking of the "saints", or "elect", of God, many of which are likely the people whom have written and are written about in the Holy Bible, e.g. Noah, Abraham, Isaac, Jacob, Joseph, Moses, Deborah, David, and the list will go on, that being said, God spoke to Ezekiel and stated if He were to punish the land only Noah, Job and Daniel would be saved alive out of it by their righteousness (Neh. 9:27, Obad. 1:21, Ezek. 14:12-20). This may be part of the reason why we

---

[1] https://www.youtube.com/watch?v=9BEULHeAHWo, reading of Genesis 1:1-10, by Bill Anders, Jim Lovell and Frank Borman, starting about 29:10 minutes into the video, retrieved 02/04/2018

have multiple world religions and in some religions multiple "gods", as the Holy Bible says we are all "gods", but the reality is in Jesus Christ of Nazareth (Ps. 82:6, 96:5; John 10:34-36, 1 Cor. 8:5, 6). Jesus Christ of Nazareth is the only true Saviour of the whole world, Creator of the heavens and the earth and all that are in them, and Redeemer of all mankind (Hos. 13:4, John 1:1-3, Rev. 4:11). He is the Saviour of saviours, the Saviour of the elect or "saints", and all mankind (Neh. 9:27, Ob. 1:21, Eph. 2:19, 3:6). He works through, in and with all of us by His Holy Spirit (John 14:16-18, Eph. 2:19-22). This means you to. Job 15:17-19 says, "I will shew thee, hear me; and that *which* I have seen I will declare; Which wise men have told from their fathers, and have not hid *it:* Unto whom alone the earth was given, and no stranger passed among them.". This seems to be proof that there are no aliens from other planets that visit earth. God gave earth to mankind to be inhabited, not aliens from other planets. God is not a liar and His gifts and calling are without repentance (Num. 23:19, Rom. 11:29). Do not mistake the word alien, as a stranger from another family or tribe, with alien, the little green martian man depicted of in television shows, other media and the like. When I speak of aliens from other planets, I mean the fictitious ideas, depicted in movies, etc. Nevertheless, the Holy Bible does say, "…with God all things are possible." (Matt. 19:26). So I will let you be the judge of the truth of all of this. And let God receive the glory in the truth of all of these things. Alleluia and praise the LORD. Amen and Amen.

In chapter three, I will be referencing the idea of life on other "planets" and in other "solar systems" according to Biblical Scripture in greater detail, but simply put, as the Holy Bible says, "…with God all things are possible." (Mat.t. 19:26, Luke 20:35, Heb. 1:2, 11:3). That being said, I do not believe that we will be travelling to them or them to us, that is, planets already inhabited by people God created. As Jesus said, "…no man has ascended up to heaven, but he that came down from heaven, *even* the Son of man which is in heaven.", that is Jesus Christ of Nazareth (John 3:13). He is preparing a "New Heaven and New Earth" for us, and again, the book of Job makes mention that no strangers from outside earth have come amongst us (Job 15:17-19). God created us to inhabit earth physically (Gen. 1:26). He does say that His offspring will increase, as the children of God, in the kingdom of God, possibly into the "universe", God's "house" (John 14:1-4). But not by our own human effort, as salvation in Christ Jesus is a free gift; again this will be discussed with more clarity in the next chapter (Eph. 2:8, 9). It has been said that the next closest "solar system" is 4.3 light years away. That would require quite a long time to travel to, in comparison to our technology today. Genesis 1:26 says, "And God said, Let us make man in our image, after our likeness: and let them have dominion over the fish of the sea, and over the fowl of the air, and over the cattle, and over all the earth, and over every creeping thing that creepeth upon the earth.". There is no mention here of man having dominion over the "heavens", albeit the Holy Bible does say we will "inherit all things" in Christ Jesus of Nazareth's Holy name, in the "New Heaven and the New Earth" with the "New Jerusalem" (Rev. 21:7). Nevertheless, as I had said, Jesus Christ of Nazareth proved that God's kingdom is spiritual, and God is a Spirit first and foremost (John 3:3-7, 4:24). When the Holy Bible references aliens, it is often referring to people from foreign nations, outside of the children of Israel, but can be referring to the children of Israel when they are in lands and in situations foreign to them, we can even become alienated in our mind, which I will speak about in more detail in chapter four (Ex. 18:3, Deut. 14:21, Job 19:15, Ps. 69:8, Isa. 61:5, Lam. 5:2, Ezek. 23:17, 18, 22, 28). That being said, the Holy Bible says not to vex or oppress the "stranger", a more common word for alien, as we as the children of Israel were strangers in Egypt (Ex. 22:21). For more detail on the topic of aliens and other similar ideas spoken of in this chapter see appendix E near the end of this book. Nevertheless, the reality is in Jesus Christ of Nazareth, the

Saviour of the whole world (John 3:16, 17). Angels are also mentioned in scripture and are associated with people in some cases (Zech. 12:8, Acts 6:15, Rev. 21:17). The term angels used in the Holy Bible may be referring to both the human and the heavenly, see appendix F which goes into the topic of "angels" in greater detail (Ezek. 1, Matt. 1:20, Matt. 4:11, Rev. 21:17). As angel means "messenger" in some instances in Biblical references (Gen. 16:7, 32:3, Mal. 3:1). That being said, I do believe that God has a Spirit that dwells with us and in us, if we accept Him, known as the Holy Ghost, Holy Spirit and Comforter, and the Holy Bible makes clear there is a fallen "spirit" world as well, as mentioned above, as of the date of writing this book in 2018 A.D. (Luke 11:13, John 14:26, Rev. 12:9). This is why we need to put our faith and life in Jesus Christ of Nazareth's Holy name, because He has overcome the world (Matt. 28:18, John 16:33). And in Him is our life, and life everlasting. Alleluia and praise the LORD. Amen and Amen.

Some people have talked about this idea of having different ethnic origins of mankind, and numbering the different races. The reality is, all of mankind that we see today are descendants of our ancestors whom stepped off of Noah's ark of God, about 2348 B.C. (Gen. 8:14-19). One particular term used when people are speaking about these "ancient" races is the "blue" bloods. I suppose the reality of this has something to do with the caucasion race or others, I do not know, and our ability to see our veins that appear to have blue blood running through them. The colour no doubt can represent the living waters, that Jesus spoke of during His ministry in the early first century A.D., as the Holy Bible says, "...the blood *is* the life..." thereof (Deut. 12:23, John 4:10-15, 7:38). Other ideas of different skin colours can be seen in the changing of pigments of skin, through "albinos", and the skin condition "melanoma". Most common differences in skin colour have no doubt happened naturally through the environmental influences that our ancestors were living in. The Hamites living in generally places nearer to the equator, where the skin had a chance to darken, as the name Ham means "hot", and the Japhethites living in the East and North, where the sun rises and shines off of the snow, causing the eye lids to be slanted to protect from the brightness of the sun. The Caucasians are generally of Shemite descent, I would suggest. Now I realize there are various other tribes, and nations with varying colours of skin, one of them being known as "red". But in some instances this could be associated with Esau, one of Isaac's sons, as he was said to be red and hairy (Gen. 25:25). And Adam's name in the beginning meant "earth" or "red" (Gen. 2:7, 5:1, 2). The reality is that along with Biblical prophecy that is fulfilled in the colours of our skins, because of our locations that we live in and the diets that cause certain colours to come out in our skin throughout the centuries. We are not all that different, when it comes down to it. We may have different ancestors after the flood, but we all originated from Adam and Eve in the beginning, and we all have salvation in Jesus Christ of Nazareth alone, as there is no other name under heaven by which we can be saved (Acts 4:12). Also regarding modern technology, in general, Sir Isaac Newton, was an early pioneer of modern physics and part of the "enlightenment" era, about the 1600's to 1700's. He was the person whom is credited with discovering the concept of "gravity", mathematically speaking, with the apple falling from the tree. Newton was a follower of Christ and he can be easily attributed to much of the mathematical ground work and theoretical physics required to build the various dynamic moving parts of vehicles, ground, sea and air that we have today, not to mention the physics required to calculate the forces needed to overcome the natural law of gravity. This just goes to show, as in the astronauts traveling to the moon, how deep God's involvement goes into our desire and abilities to travel through space, here on earth and in the firmaments of heaven (Gen. 1:6-8, Rev. 4:11).

New Heavens and New Earth

John 14:2 says, "In my Father's house are many mansions: if *it were* not *so*, I would have told you. I go to prepare a place for you.". Our natural desire to live comfortably, be in control and increase are all God given desires, commanded from the beginning (Gen. 1:28). The Holy Bible even seems to indicate that we have the opportunity to inherit all things (Rev. 21:7). This would explain the growth of God's family into the "universe" with the possibility of the "mansions" in God's house being other "solar systems" with an inhabitable earth in each, and the "universe" being God's house (Isa. 66:1). The next chapter will go into this topic in greater detail using the "New Jerusalem" and it's representation in the greater detail of God's plan for mankind in the "New Heaven and New Earth" (Rev. 21:1-5). Revelation 19:12 says, "His eyes *were* as a blazing fire, and on his head *were* many crowns. And he had a name written, that no man knew, but he himself.". Is this possibly more confirmation of many kingdoms? Many earths or worlds? The Holy Bible says Jesus is the Lord of lords, King of kings, and God of gods (Deut. 10:17, Jos. 22:22, Ps. 136:2, Dan. 2:47, 11:36). In Isaiah 9:6 and 7 it says, "... the government shall be upon his shoulder: and his name shall be called Wonderful, Counselor, The mighty God, The everlasting Father, The Prince of Peace. Of the increase of *his* government and peace *there shall be* no end...". Gadal and Raba are two Hebrew words for "Greatness" or "Increase". The Hebrew word "marbeh" in the Isaiah 9 prophecy is more likely meaning "increase" or multiply, which is the root words meaning, Strong's number 4766 (Gen. 1:22, Isa. 9:7). Increase is spoken of often in the epistles to the Thessalonians (Col. 2:19, 1 Thess. 3:12, 4:10; 2 Thess. 1:3). Jesus spoke about increase in general, both in this life and storing up treasures in heaven (Matt. 6:20, 21; Mark 4:8). Jesus said, we will receive a hundredfold in this life and in the world to come eternal life if we follow Him (Matt. 19:29, Mark 10:30). The point is God is a God of abundance and increase, NOT a god of death, decrease, destruction and nothingness. However, He has authority over all that takes place, here on earth and in heaven, in this life and in eternity, in the name of Jesus Christ of Nazareth, God's only begotten Son, the Creator of us all. Whom died on the cross for the forgiveness of our sins, spilling His Holy and righteous blood for us, He was buried and the third day He arose to give us the hope and promise of eternal life in His Holy name. Alleluia and praise the LORD. Amen and Amen.

Jesus spoke of the ten virgins preparing for the bridegroom, but only five were ready for the wedding supper (Matt. 25:1). If we flip this and relate the verse with Revelation 20:2 that says, "...new Jerusalem, coming down from God out of heaven, prepared as a bride adorned for her husband.", than we have multiple "virgins" or more than one "new Jerusalem" (Eph. 5:27, 2 Cor. 11:2, Heb. 1:2, 11:3). I do not think Jesus is talking about polygamy in the literal sense here, so this leaves us with the concept of multiples of the "New Heaven and New Earth", with the "new Jerusalem" as spoken of above and in chapter one. Of course the other interpretation for the five virgins is those whom are preparing and will be prepared for Jesus Christ's rule with His saints in the "Messianic Age", that is prophesied to literally take place here on earth after the "Great Tribulation" and before the "Final Judgement", but I will not go into that further here. The point is that Jesus again, with the other scriptures used in this chapter and in other places in this book and more importantly the Holy Bible in general, is likely talking about expanding God's spiritual and physical kingdom into the "universe", by His chosen, the elect or "saints" in Christ Jesus of Nazareth's Holy name first and foremost through His Holy Spirit (Matt. 28:18, Rev. 7). To God be the glory in the truth of the interpretation of this idea. The Holy Bible also speaks of the "voice of many waters" and of "great thunder" speaking from heaven in Revelation 14:2. And in Ezekiel 43:2 it speaks of God coming in His glory from the east, and His voice was like "a noise of many waters" and the "earth shined with his glory.". Psalm 29:3 says, "The voice of the LORD *is* upon the waters: the God of glory thundereth: the LORD *is* upon many waters.". Jesus spoke of living waters coming out of us if we believe in Him, that is the living waters of His Holy Spirit (John 4:14). John 7:38 says, "He that believeth on me, as the scripture hath said, out of his belly shall flow rivers of living water.". If these "many waters" are people here on earth, whom have received the Holy Spirit and are following Jesus Christ as their Saviour, doing His will, then this could be part of God's way of speaking to this world, through each of us. Of course this would explain the many denominations of so called Christ following Churches, and the many congregations and ministers in each of these denominations. But no matter, our first priority in communication must be with God, the Father, in Christ Jesus of Nazareth's Holy name, through the Holy Ghost, the Holy Spirit in us, as we receive Him, praying, reading His Word, the Holy Bible, and then fellowship with others as God wills it. In Song of Solomon 8:7 it says, "Many waters cannot quench love, neither can the floods drown it: if a man would give all the substance of his house for love, it would utterly be contemned.". So we do not have to worry about all of these "voices", opinions and any general distractions from communing with the true God, through Jesus Christ of Nazareth, by His Holy Spirit, the Holy Ghost, because all the voices in the world cannot quench God's love for us. Alleluia and praise the LORD. Amen and Amen.

The apostle, Paul, speaks of Jesus Christ of Nazareth being the first fruits of all the saints (1 Cor. 15:23). Is it not then possible that we may all have the opportunity to be like Adam and Eve some day? Does this not relate our inner desire to explore space, travel and yearn for a "new home", with Biblical proof of starting a new heaven and new earth dominions as a sons and daughters of God under His authority? Like Adam and Eve did so long ago. Just look up into the stars if you can, and ask yourself, is there life outside of earth? Certainly the Creator exists out there and in us as we receive Him here, His throne is in the heaven and the earth is His footstool (Isa. 66:1, Acts 7:49). Nevertheless, becoming like Jesus Christ of Nazareth is our goal, today and tomorrow and forever (Col. 3:1-3, Rev. 3:21). Colossians 3:2 says, "Set your mind on things above, not on earthly things", similar to what Jesus admonished (Matt. 6:20, 21). 2 Thessalonians 1:10 says, "When he shall come to be glorified in his saints, and to be admired in all them that believe (because our testimony among you was believed) in that day.". God, the Father, in His only begotten Son, Christ Jesus of Nazareth's Holy name, through the spiritual birthing process of the Holy Ghost, the Holy Spirit, has given all of us the opportunity to be spiritually born sons and daughters of God, born of God's Holy Spirit, through accepting Jesus Christ of Nazareth as our Saviour, Redeemer and Deliverer for the forgiveness of our sins (Isa. 63:16, Mal. 2:10, Luke 3:38, John 3:3-7, 10:36). Alleluia and praise the LORD. Amen and Amen. The religious leaders of Jesus' earthly ministry seemed to have been ignorant of this, but God's children are not (John 5:18). David felt like a stranger on earth. Psalm 119:19 says, "I *am* a stranger in the earth: hide not thy commandments from me.". Hebrews 11:13 says, "These all died in faith, not having received the promises, but having seen them afar off, and were persuaded of *them*, and embraced *them*, and confessed that they were strangers and pilgrims on the earth.". This is the best explanation of the term alien in the human sense; it is the children of God, like Jesus, whom said of Himself, "...I am not of this world." (John 8:23, 15:19). This world became fallen after the beginning when Adam and Eve ate from the tree of knowledge of good and evil in the Garden of Eden (Gen. 3). But it is through Jesus Christ of Nazareth and salvation in His Holy name, through the shedding of His Holy and righteous blood on the cross for the forgiveness of our sins, that we have eternal life, and are adopted into the family of God forever. Alleluia and praise the LORD. He died on the cross for the forgiveness of our sins, He was buried and the third day He arose to give us the hope and promise of eternal life in His Holy name. Alleluia and praise the LORD. And now He sits on the right hand of the Father until all His enemies are made His footstool (Ps. 110:1, Heb. 10:13). Alleluia and praise the LORD. Amen and Amen. And He has given us of His Spirit, the Holy Ghost, to live with us and dwell in us, as a faithful promise that He will be with us always, even to the end of the world, and forever more in the "world to come" (Matt. 28:20, John 14:16-18, 1 John 4:13). Alleluia and praise the LORD. Amen and Amen.

God's kingdom here and our peculiarity in Christ

God's variety can be seen in His creation, even in the descriptions of the New Heavens and the New Earth (Rev. 21:9-22:7). Certainly we are peculiar in Christ and were created to be as such, even in the world to come and in eternity (Ex. 19:5, Deut. 14:2, 26:18; Ps. 135:4, Tit. 2:14, 1 Pet. 2:9). The Holy Bible says, "Thou shalt not revile the gods, nor curse the ruler of thy people." (Ex. 22:28). This is because we are created as "gods" by God Almighty, in Jesus Christ of Nazareth's Holy name (Ps. 82:6, John 10:34-36). God is saying to not curse Him, each other or ourselves for that matter, which is similarly what Jesus said, "…Thou shalt love the Lord thy God with all thy heart, and with all thy soul, and with all thy mind. This is the first and great commandment. And the second *is* like unto it, Thou shalt love thy neighbor as thyself." (Matt. 22:37-39). He said, "On these two commandments hang all the law and the prophets." (Matt. 22:40). Jesus also said not to blaspheme the Holy Ghost, which would be reviling the gods, that is we ought not to speak evil of God, or else we are in danger of eternal damnation (Mark 3:29, Luke 12:10). Galatians 5:16-25 says, "*This* I say then, Walk in the Spirit, and ye shall not fulfil the lust of the flesh. For the flesh lusteth against the Spirit, and the Spirit against the flesh: and these are contrary the one to the other: so that ye cannot do the things that ye would. But if ye be led of the Spirit, ye are not under the law. Now the works of the flesh are manifest, which are *these;* Adultery, fornication, uncleanness, lasciviousness, Idolatry, witchcraft, hatred, variance, emulations, wrath, strife, seditions, heresies, Envyings, murders, drunkenness, revellings, and such like: of the which I tell you before, as I have also told *you* in time past, that they which do such things shall not inherit the kingdom of God. But the fruit of the Spirit is love, joy, peace, longsuffering, gentleness, goodness, faith, meekness, temperance: against such there is no law. And they that are Christ's have crucified the flesh with the affections and lusts. If we live in the Spirit, let us also walk in the Spirit.". 1 Corinthians 12:4-11 says, "Now there are diversities of gifts, but the same Spirit. And there are differences of administrations, but the same Lord. And there are diversities of operations, but it is the same God which worketh all in all. But the manifestation of the Spirit is given to every man to profit withal. For to one is given by the Spirit the word of wisdom; to another the word of knowledge by the same Spirit; To another faith by the same Spirit; to another the gifts of healing by the same Spirit; To another the working of miracles; to another prophecy; to another discerning of spirits; to another *divers* kinds of tongues; to another the interpretation of tongues: But all these worketh that one and the selfsame Spirit, dividing to every man severally as he will.". These are the gifts of God we each have the opportunity to partake in, as God wills it, through accepting His only begotten Son, Jesus Christ of Nazareth, as our Saviour. Whom died on the cross for the forgiveness of our sins, spilling His Holy and righteous blood, He was buried and the third day He arose to give us the hope and promise of eternal life in His Holy name. Alleluia and praise the LORD. Amen and Amen.

The apostle, Paul, says, "For as the body is one, and hath many members, and all the members of that one body, being many, are one body: so also *is* Christ. For by one Spirit are we all baptized into one body, whether *we be* Jews or Gentiles, whether *we be* bond or free; and have been all made to drink into one Spirit. For the body is not one member, but many." (1 Cor. 12:12-14). That no doubt includes many gifts or talents, distributed throughout the members of the body, but one Christ, that works all in all (1 Cor. 12:12). A perfect example of this is the references I use for this book and others. I have knowledge God has given me, but I have also found knowledge that God gave to others, that I have researched about and read, and used as references for this book and others I have written, the Holy Bible of God being the main reference. Our gifts, trials, desires and experiences are not all the "exact" same, but we have a common salvation in Jesus Christ of Nazareth (Jude 1:3). The Holy Bible says, some are apostles, some prophets, some evangelists, some pastors, some teachers, some do miracles, some gifts of healing, some helps, some governments, and some diversities of tongues (1 Cor. 12:28, Eph. 4:11). These "jobs", speaking generally cover every task given to mankind here on earth, especially "helps", because this covers both volunteering and working in a paid job. If we are working for the kingdom of God all things are possible (Matt. 19:26). The Holy Bible says we are "called" to the vocation of being a minister of God (Matt. 20:26-28, Mark 10:43-45, 2 Cor. 3:5, 6; Eph. 3:7). This is not done by men, but by God (John 1:13, 6:44). If you believe you are being called to do "the work of God", then you must place your trust in Him, especially through Jesus Christ of Nazareth (John 6:29). You can no longer place your trust in men, and this world's reward systems, recognition ceremonies, etc. (John 2:24, 25; 1 Cor. 7:23, 1 John 2:15). As Jesus said, "… when ye shall have done all those things which are commanded you, say, We are unprofitable servants: we have done that which was our duty to do." (Luke 17:10). That being said, as God shines His light in your life, His works will be manifest, and as the Holy Bible says, you will receive favour with God and men, just as Jesus did (Luke 2:52, John 7:7, 8:12). But when persecution and trials come, do not think that they are some strange thing, as Jesus and the apostles warned that this would happen to us in this life (John 16:33, 1 Pet. 4:12). But He says, "…be of good cheer; I have overcome the world." (John 16:33). Psalm 96:5 says, "For all the gods of the nations *are* idols: but the LORD made the heavens.". There is One God, and One Jesus Christ of Nazareth, the life of Jesus Christ ought to be our example for daily living. Jesus said, "If any *man* will come after me, let him deny himself, and take up his cross, and follow me." (Matt. 16:24, Mark 8:34, Luke 9:23). This is our individual responsibility He has given to each and every one of us, to take up our own cross and follow Him. There is One common salvation in Christ Jesus of Nazareth, Jesus cannot be crucified again (Heb. 6:4-6). We need to accept the strait and narrow gate of salvation in Jesus Christ of Nazareth (Matt. 7:14). We cannot save ourselves, neither can anyone else, but Jesus Christ of Nazareth, because He died on the cross for the forgiveness of our sins, spilling His Holy and righteous blood on the cross, He was buried and the third day He arose to give us the hope and promise of eternal life in His Holy name. Alleluia and praise the LORD. This is the peculiarity that Jesus Christ of Nazareth has; He is the only true Saviour of all of mankind (Acts 4:12). Alleluia and praise the LORD. Amen and Amen.

Regarding alienation, Jesus said, "My kingdom is not of this world: if my kingdom were of this world, then would my servants fight, that I should not be delivered to the Jews: but now is my kingdom not from hence." (John 18:36). John 1:10-13 says, "He was in the world, and the world was made by him, and the world knew him not. He came unto his own, and his own received him not. But as many as received him, to them gave he power to become the sons of God, *even* to them that believe on his name: Which were born, not of blood, nor of the will of the flesh, nor of the will of man, but of God.". This may be the only evidence a person could use for Jesus being considered an alien. But the reality is we are all aliens in some sense. We are alienated from God by our sin (Isa. 59:2, Jer. 5:25). And

He is alienated from us because of our sins (Ezek. 23:18). This is what makes God an alien to those who do not know Him (John 6:46). But it is through the forgiveness of our sins that we are cleansed of this alienation from God's kingdom, and we are received into life everlasting (John 6:29, 47; 17:3; Col. 1:9-17). We are also alienated from other people because of our sin, and/or because of their sin (Ezek. 23:17, 1 Pet. 4:4). God separates us to protect us from the sins of others and the other way around (2 Thess. 3:14). He desires us to have a relationship with Him first, and then if He so wills it, other people here on earth. Jesus did say, "A new commandment I give unto you, That ye love one another; as I have loved you, that ye also love one another." (John 13:34). The reality is that following Christ can bring persecution and trials, but Jesus said these things would happen to us (John 16:33). The challenge is enduring these "fiery trials" unto the end (Matt. 10:22). Jesus said, "In your patience possess ye your souls." (Luke 21:19). This world is broken and very broken. Jesus said it would be this way in the "time of the end", especially before His coming again (Gen. 6:5-13, Matt. 24:37-39). If you are feeling like you are different or set apart, this does not have to be a "bad" thing. God may have done this according to His purposes (Acts 26:16-18, Rom. 8:28). As I have heard, God loves variety. Just read about the tree of life in the "New Jerusalem", it has "…twelve *manner of* fruits…" (Rev. 22:2). The foundations of the city are made with twelve different stones, representing the apostles, judges of the twelve tribes of Israel (Matt. 19:28, Luke 22:29, 30; Rev. 21:14, 19, 20). Read about the apostles of Christ, they all had their own view point of salvation in Christ, as I have spoken of some of them in my writing and they wrote the New Testament by inspiration of the Holy Spirit of God. But the simplicity of this variety is that we are all one in Christ Jesus of Nazareth, by His salvation of us through His death on the cross for the forgiveness of our sins, spilling His Holy and righteous blood, He was buried and the third day He arose to give us the hope and promise of eternal life in His Holy name. Alleluia and praise the LORD. That is our common salvation, regardless of skin colour, cultural background, the type of sin we have committed in the past, or otherwise. We are all one in the suffering of Jesus Christ of Nazareth on the cross and His resurrection unto life everlasting in Jesus Christ of Nazareth's Holy name. Alleluia and praise the LORD. Amen and Amen.

Conclusion

Ever expanding universe or imploding universe…You decide, it's your life. A New Testament apostle and writer, Paul, says in a letter to the Colossians, "And you, that were sometime alienated and enemies in *your* mind by wicked works, yet now hath he reconciled In the body of his flesh through death, to present you holy and unblameable and unreproveable in his sight: If ye continue in the faith grounded and settled, and *be* not moved away from the hope of the gospel, which ye have heard, *and* which was preached to every creature which is under heaven; whereof I Paul am made a minister; Who now rejoice in my sufferings for you, and fill up that which is behind of the afflictions of Christ in my flesh for his body's sake, which is the church: Whereof I am made a minister, according to the dispensation of God which is given to me for you, to fulfil the word of God; *Even* the mystery which hath been hid from ages and from generations, but now is made manifest to his saints: To whom God would make known what *is* the riches of the glory of this mystery among the Gentiles; which is Christ in you, the hope of glory: Whom we preach, warning every man, and teaching every man in all wisdom; that we may present every man perfect in Christ Jesus: Whereunto I also labour, striving according to his working, which worketh in me mightily." (Col. 1:21-29). Jesus also said, "But whosoever shall deny me before men, him will I also deny before my Father which is in heaven. Think not that I am come to send peace on earth: I came not to send peace, but a sword. For I am come to set a man at variance against his father, and the daughter against her mother, and the daughter in law against her mother in law. And a man's foes *shall be* they of his own household. He that loveth father or mother more than me is not worthy of me: and he that loveth son or daughter more than me is not worthy of me. And he that taketh not his cross, and followeth after me, is not worthy of me." (Matt. 10:33-38). This topic of division will be spoken of in greater detail in other chapters, but the main point here is that Jesus spoke about "variance" (Matt. 10:35). This Greek word "deekhadzo" according to Strong's concordance can also mean alienate, Strong's number 1369. We have the perfect example of this when Jesus said on the cross, "My God, my God, why hast thou forsaken me?", echoing words king David wrote in psalm about one thousand years before this (Ps. 22:1, Matt. 27:46, Mark 15:34). The point is that Jesus felt the wrath of God, the sword of God, the alienation from God, the Father, because Jesus took our sins upon Himself on the cross, shedding His Holy and righteous blood and dying for the forgiveness of our sins. Alleluia and praise the LORD. The good news is after He was buried the third day He arose to give us the hope and promise of eternal life in His Holy name. Alleluia and praise the LORD. Amen and Amen.

The universe as God's body; I had an idea in chemistry class in high school, where we had an opportunity to write an essay about a topic of our choice. The idea that came to mind was that of comparing the solar system, galaxies and universe to "atoms" and part of a larger "organism". I ended up writing about oil and its various products that come from it in refining. However, the Holy Bible does describe God's creation as a body in some respects. Here are just a few verses, "Hearken unto me, O house of Jacob, and all the remnant of the house of Israel, which are born *by me* from the belly, which are carried from the womb: And *even* to *your* old age I *am* he; and *even* to hoar hairs will I carry *you*: I have made, and I will bear; even I will carry, and will deliver *you*." (Isa. 46:3, 4). The Holy Bible speaks of us being in the loins of our fathers before we are born (Gen. 35:11, 46:26; Ex. 1:5, Heb. 7:5, 10). The apostle, Paul, refers to the Church as the "Body of Christ" (1 Cor. 12:27). Interesting ideas, but ultimately Jesus said that, God is a Spirit, and we are to dwell in Him and Him in us, which would explain this womb protected like existence in this life and forever more in Christ Jesus of Nazareth's Holy name, through His Holy Spirit (John 17:21-23). He was compassionate during His life here on earth, compassion in the Old Testament is also used to describe mercy, the bowels and the womb, Strong's number 7356 (Gen. 43:14, 43:30, 49:25; Matt. 9:36, 14:14, 15:32, 20:34). His blood flowed on the cross for the forgiveness of our sins and redemption of our souls (John 19:34). He truly is the One whom gave conception to our parents, carried us into this world, carries us in this world, and forever more in the "word to come", through His life giving name, Jesus Christ of Nazareth (Ruth 4:13, Isa. 46:3, 4; Matt. 28:20). Alleluia and praise the Lord. Now, Isaiah 55:6-9 says, "Seek ye the LORD while he may be found, call ye upon him while he is near: Let the wicked forsake his way, and the unrighteous man his thoughts: and let him return unto the LORD, and he will have mercy upon him; and to our God, for he will abundantly pardon. For my thoughts *are* not your thoughts, neither *are* your ways my ways, saith the LORD. For *as* the heavens are higher than the earth, so are my ways higher than your ways, and my thoughts than your thoughts.". This may be why I am now mentioning and writing about this example here. 1 John 3:2 says, "Beloved, now are we the sons of God, and it doth not yet appear what we shall be: but we know that, when he shall appear, we shall be like him; for we shall see him as he is.". So this is the reality of this book and my "interpretations" of some of the Scriptures and what they may have to do with the future of this world and the future of the "universe" and our part in it. However the reality is in Jesus Christ of Nazareth and His kingdom with God, the Father, and the Holy Spirit, is a spiritual one first and foremost. This is why it is important to accept the gift of Jesus Christ of Nazareth into our life, accepting His Holy Spirit, His life giving work and His forgiveness for our sins on the cross. Whom died on the cross for the forgiveness of our sins, shedding His Holy and righteous blood, He was buried and the third day He arose to give us the hope and promise of eternal life in His Holy name. Alleluia and praise the LORD. Amen and Amen.

Again, regardless of the truth of "other worlds" and other "sons" or "daughters" of God, we must remember that God is One and eternal, His sons and daughters are just that, children He created (John 10:30, 17:22, 23; Rom. 8:14-17). The eternal One, the Almighty God, is the Creator of the heavens and the earth, not the heaven only, but the heavens plural (Gen. 2:1, 4; Heb. 1:10, 2 Pet. 3:13). So no matter how many worlds, inhabited planets, etc. exist or could exist, our main focus here on earth ought to be working out our own salvation with fear and trembling, in the name of Jesus Christ of Nazareth, the only begotten Son of God that, I know of, and has been revealed to us through the Holy Bible and those whom testify to Jesus Christ's existence, and through true miracles, signs and wonders (Acts 4:12, Phil. 2:12). The Holy Bible of God is the ultimate revealer of the truth of God's universe and how it works (Ps. 147:5). He is the Creator of it all, after all, and He knows how it functions (Ps. 147:5). If we are truly seeking the truth of the workings of the heavens above and the "next life" our best option is to put our trust in Jesus Christ of Nazareth and God Almighty, the Father, through the indwelling of the Holy Spirit to reveal to us all things (John 14:26). If you have not made a decision to place your trust in and follow Jesus Christ of Nazareth yet in this life, consider it and receive the gift He gave us on the cross, which is eternal life in Jesus Christ of Nazareth's Holy name. Alleluia and praise the LORD. Amen and Amen. Deuteronomy 26:18 and 19 say, "And the LORD hath avouched thee this day to be his peculiar people, as he hath promised thee, and that *thou* shouldest keep all his commandments; And to make thee high above all nations which he hath made, in praise, and in name, and in honour; and that thou mayest be an holy people unto the LORD thy God, as he hath spoken.". And 1 Peter 2:9 and 10 say, "But ye *are* a chosen generation, a royal priesthood, an holy nation, a peculiar people; that ye should shew forth the praises of him who hath called you out of darkness into his marvellous light; Which in time past *were* not a people, but *are* now the people of God: which had not obtained mercy, but now have obtained mercy.". This is the wonderful gift we all have in the name of Jesus Christ of Nazareth, whom died on the cross for the forgiveness of our sins, spilling His Holy and righteous blood on the cross, He was buried and the third day He arose to give us the hope and promise of eternal life in His Holy name. Alleluia and praise the LORD. Amen and Amen.

Discussion: Peculiarity

"Prove all things, hold fast to that which is good."
- 1 Thessalonians 5:21

God does not desire us to be blind, cookie cutter people (Ex. 19:5, 6; 2 Pet. 2:9, 10). He created Adam from the dust, and then created Eve from one of Adam's ribs (Gen. 2:21-25). This is the first example of God using two different "methods" to bring about the same result, human life. God does say that He does not change, and I am not suggesting anything otherwise, but we must remember that God created us all (Mal. 3:6). This is where a discernment of spirits comes in (1 Cor. 12:10). The apostle, John, admonishes to "try the spirits", as not all "spirits" are in Christ Jesus of Nazareth (1 John 4:1). We must remember that we each have our own spirit that dwells in us, and this spirit without Christ Jesus of Nazareth is naturally fallen, and rebellious towards God, as we "inherited" this nature from our ancestors in Adam and Eve first, after they ate from the tree of knowledge of good and evil (Gen. 3, Job 32:8). That being said, we can be redeemed from this fallen "nature" by the blood of Jesus Christ of Nazareth. Alleluia and praise the LORD. It is by His Holy and righteous blood that we are saved from our sins and we have the hope of our own resurrection and eternal life in His Holy name. Jesus did many miracles and a variety of them as well, healing the sick, the blind, the lame, the dumb, He walked on water and cast out unclean spirits, He also multiplied fishes and loaves (Matt. 4:24, 9:27-30, 11:4, 5; 12:22; 14:24-33; Mark 1:23-27, 6:35-44). Not only this, but He said, we would do greater things than Him, in His Holy name, because He went to the Father (John 14:12). Is it any wonder we live in the world we do today with all of its miraculous inventions? I think not, all for the glory of God in the name of His only begotten Son, Jesus Christ of Nazareth. Alleluia and Praise the LORD. We must remember that God created us to be like Him, He gave us a mind to think up and invent incredible things, but this same mind can be deceived, and be used to do evil as well. This is why we need Jesus Christ of Nazareth in our life, accepting the Holy Spirit, as God's Spirit to fellowship with us and teach us, and help us in our thoughts, plans and to fulfil our desires and "dreams" (John 15:5). Without God and His Holy Spirit we are nothing more than brute beasts, and eventually dust (Gen. 3:19, 2 Pet. 2:12, Jude 1:10). But with Christ Jesus of Nazareth, we have eternal life in His Holy name. Praise the LORD God Almighty and His only begotten Son, Jesus Christ of Nazareth. Alleluia and praise the LORD. When reading through this section, consider the offering in Christ Jesus of Nazareth, God gave for your sins on the cross so that you can have life and life more abundantly, in Jesus Christ of Nazareth's Holy name. And how you can use this precious life God has given you to glorify Him, in Christ Jesus of Nazareth's Holy name, God's only begotten Son. Alleluia and praise the LORD. Amen and Amen.

Discussion Questions

1. What do you believe about your place in your relationship with God and others?

   _____

   _____

   _____

2. Are we all created like robots or is there something different about each of us in Christ Jesus of Nazareth?

   _____

   _____

   _____

3. There is a long list of "jobs" inside of the Church of God, what gifts do you think you might have that you can use to glorify God?

   _____

   _____

   _____

4. Does God place any favour for men over women or women over men in the salvation plan?

   _____

   _____

   _____

Chapter 3: Heaven – Spiritual Realm – "After Life"

"For thy Maker *is* thine husband; the LORD of hosts *is* his name; and thy Redeemer
the Holy One of Israel; The God of the whole earth shall he be called."
- Isaiah 54:5

Introduction

Psalm 96:11-13 says, "Let the heavens rejoice, and let the earth be glad; let the sea roar, and the fullness thereof. Let the field be joyful, and all that *is* therein: then shall all the trees of the wood rejoice before the LORD: for he cometh, for he cometh to judge the earth: he shall judge the world with righteousness, and the people with his truth.". Psalm 99:5 says, "Exalt ye the LORD our God, and worship at his footstool; *for* he *is* holy.". According to Scripture, the whole earth is His footstool and the inhabitants thereof (Ps. 110:1, Isa. 66:1, Matt. 5:35). Jesus said, "But the hour cometh, and now is, when the true worshippers shall worship the Father in spirit and in truth: for the Father seeketh such to worship him. For God *is* a spirit: and they that worship him must worship *him* in spirit and in truth." (John 4:23, 24). Jesus said we know the way to everlasting life (John 14:3, 4). John 14:3 and 4 say, "And if I go and prepare a place for you, I will come again, and receive you unto myself; that where I am, *there* ye may be also. And whither I go ye know, and the way ye know.". The apostle, Thomas, questioned Jesus about this saying, asking "…how can we know the way?" and Jesus said of Himself, "I am the way the truth and the life: no man cometh unto the Father, but by me." (John 14:5, 6). The remainder of this chapter will describe and "interpret" some of the seeming mysteries of the "resurrection" of the dead, the "New Jerusalem" and the "New Heavens and New Earth" according to John's vision and other scriptures in the Holy Bible, as well as the "theme" of marriage, throughout the Holy Bible of God. As Jesus admonishes, "…whither I go ye know, and the way ye know." (John 14:4). That means you and I. Praise the Lord God Almighty and His only begotten Son, Jesus Christ of Nazareth. We know the way to Him and we know where He is. Thanks be to God, and Jesus Christ of Nazareth, His only begotten Son, He lives and reigns forever. He died on the cross for the forgiveness of our sins, He was buried and the third day He arose to give us the hope and promise of eternal life in His Holy name. He lives. Alleluia and Praise the LORD. Amen and Amen.

Resurrection

"…Holy, holy, holy, Lord God Almighty, which was, and is, and is to come." (Rev. 4:8). This is spoken of in Revelation 4:8 by four beasts, I see this as representative of the glorification of God in the forgiveness of sin and the resurrection of the dead in the name of Jesus Christ of Nazareth. God has, is and will be glorified in the life of mankind, and all of His creation, especially through His only begotten Son, Jesus Christ of Nazareth, before the world was, in His life ministry, His death on the cross for the forgiveness of our sins, His burial and His miraculous resurrection three days later after Passover in 31 A.D. and forever more in His Holy name (John 13:31, 32; 14:13, 17:5, 10, 22-24). Alleluia and praise the LORD. God has and will be glorified in the lives and resurrection of the saints at the "first" resurrection, at the outset of the "Messianic Age", also known as the 1000 years of Christ's rule with His saints, albeit many of the saints whom slept arose out of their graves and were seen in Jerusalem after Jesus gave up the ghost on the cross at Passover 31 A.D. (Matt. 27:52,

53; 2 Thess. 1:10, Rev. 20:4, 6). Nevertheless, then finally God will be glorified at the "last great day", the final resurrection and judgement of all mankind at the end of the Messianic Age (John 6:44, 54; John 11:24-26, John 12:44-50, John 14:3, 4; Rev. 20:5, 11-15). These to me are the three "holies" that are spoken of by the four beasts in Revelation 4:8. These beasts are representative of God's creation, the "wild" beasts of the field, the lion, the domestic animals, the calf, mankind, the man faced beast, and the eagle, the beasts of the air and sea (Rev. 4:6-8). As throughout the Holy Bible, His creation is mentioned that it does indeed proclaim the wonderful works of God (Rom. 1:20). Isaiah 51:6 says, "Lift up your eyes to the heavens, and look upon the earth beneath: for the heavens shall vanish away like smoke and the earth shall wax old like a garment, and they that dwell therein shall die in like manner: but my salvation shall be for ever, and my righteousness shall not be abolished.". Revelation 4:1-6 says, "After this I looked, and, behold, a door was opened in heaven: and the first voice which I heard *was* as it were of a trumpet talking with me; which said, Come up hither, and I will shew thee things which must be hereafter. And immediately I was in the spirit: and, behold, a throne was set in heaven, and *one* sat on the throne. And he that sat was to look upon like a jasper and a sardine stone: and *there was* a rainbow round about the throne, in sight like unto an emerald. And round about the throne *were* four and twenty seats: and upon the seats I saw four and twenty elders sitting, clothed in white raiment; and they had on their heads crowns of gold. And out of the throne proceeded lightnings and thunderings and voices: and *there were* seven lamps of fire burning before the throne, which are the seven Spirits of God. And before the throne *there was* a sea of glass like unto crystal: and in the midst of the throne, and round about the throne, *were* four beasts full of eyes before and behind.". These seven lamps burning likely represent the seven churches mentioned in Revelation 1, 2 and 3. Revelation 5:6 speaks of the lamb with seven horns and seven eyes, showing the oneness of God's Church no matter where it is located here on earth or in heaven. This similarity again is mentioned in the Old Testament by the prophet Zechariah, speaking of a stone with seven eyes, and removing the iniquity of the land in one day, which no doubt speaks of Jesus Christ of Nazareth's sacrifice on the cross at Passover 31 A.D., dying for the forgiveness of our sins, shedding His Holy and righteous blood on the cross, He was buried and then arose the third day to give us the hope and promise of eternal life in His Holy name (Zech. 3:9). Alleluia and praise the LORD. Amen and Amen.

Daniel 7:9 and 10 say, "I beheld till the thrones were cast down, and the Ancient of days did sit, whose garment *was* white as snow, and the hair of his head like the pure wool: his throne *was like* the fiery flame, *and* his wheels *as* burning fire. A fiery stream issued and came forth from before him: thousand thousands ministered unto him, and ten thousand times ten thousand stood before him: the judgement was set, and the books were opened.". Revelation 20:11-15 says, "And I saw a great white throne, and him that sat on it, from whose face the earth and the heaven fled away; and there was found no place for them. And I saw the dead, small and great, stand before God; and the books were opened: and another book was opened, which is *the book* of life: and the dead were judged out of those things which were written in the books, according to their works. And the sea gave up the dead which were in it; and death and hell delivered up the dead which were in them: and they were judged every man according to their works. And death and hell were cast into the lake of fire. This is the second death. And whosoever was not found written in the book of life was cast into the lake of fire.". This describes a "great white throne judgement" that will not be here on earth physically. God is a Spirit, and it seems He will judge us in Spirit at the final resurrection first and foremost (John 4:24, Rev. 20:11-15). The final resurrection was described briefly by Jesus regarding judgment (Luke 11:31, 32). He said, "The queen of the south shall rise up in the judgment with the men of this generation, and condemn them:

for she came from the utmost parts of the earth to hear the wisdom of Solomon; and, behold, a greater than Solomon is here. The men of Nineve shall rise up in the judgment with this generation, and shall condemn it: for they repented at the preaching of Jonas; and, behold, a greater than Jonas *is* here." (Luke 11: 31, 32). Simply put we will be judged by our own words and works (Matt. 12:37, Titus 3:11). Every person has their specific time, 1 Corinthians 15:23 says, "But every man in his own order: Christ the firstfruits; afterward they that are Christ's at his coming.". 1 Corinthians 15 goes into detail about the resurrection, and 1 Corinthians 15:52 sums it up, saying, "In a moment, in the twinkling of an eye, at the last trump: for the trumpet shall sound, and the dead shall be raised incorruptible, and we shall be changed.". Again this may speak of the "Messianic age" harvest of saints, whom have not died of natural death or martyrdom during the "Great tribulation", but is also regarding the very end of earth's present history, as is spoken of in this book, "the last great day" (Matt. 24:31, 25:31-33). Chapter five will go into greater detail of the subject of change, and the Holy Bible of God should always be the main book to reveal the truth of these interpretations, and through the Holy Spirit of God, by Jesus Christ of Nazareth and God, the Father, the Revealers of all truth (John 14:26). Praise be to God, the Father, Almighty and His only begotten Son, Jesus Christ of Nazareth, the Saviour of the world, and Redeemer of all mankind. Alleluia and praise the LORD. Amen and Amen.

After studying the "new Jerusalem", as is described in the next section, I have come to the conclusion that Adam and Eve will highly likely receive life in the resurrection, if they have not already. The Tree of life representing an Adam and Eve like relationship, shows that this tree will not die, as it is firmly planted in the city of life, by the waters of life, that proceed out of the throne of God; that being said, that is just my interpretation (2 Pet. 1:20, Rev. 22:1, 2). I will leave it up to the reader to decide the truth of that and what you believe, as the Holy Bible says, "Prove all things; hold fast that which is good." (1 Thess. 5:21). No matter the truth of this we must remember that the "first" Adam sinned and Jesus Christ of Nazareth, the last Adam conceived by the Holy Spirit, the only begotten Son of God, is our true Saviour, whom we can also become like through accepting His blood offering made for us on the cross for the forgiveness of our sins (Luke 3:38, 1 Cor. 15:45, Rev. 21:7). 1 Corinthians 15:45-49 says, "And so it is written, The first man Adam was made a living soul; the last Adam *was made* a quickening spirit. Howbeit that *was* not first which is spiritual, but that which is natural; and afterward that which is spiritual. The first man *is* of the earth, earthy; the second man *is* the Lord from heaven. As *is* the earthy, such *are* they also that are earthy: and as *is* the heavenly, such *are* they also that are heavenly. And as we have born the image of the earthy, we shall also bear the image of the heavenly.". Isaiah 41:4 says, "Who hath wrought and done *it*, calling the generations from the beginning? I the LORD, the first, and with the last; I *am* he.". Genesis 2:7 says, "And the LORD God formed man *of* the dust of the ground, and breathed into his nostrils the breath of life; and man became a living soul.". John 5:21 says, "For as the Father raiseth up the dead, and quickeneth *them;* even so the Son quickeneth whom he will.". And Romans 5:14 says, "Nevertheless death reigned from Adam to Moses, even over them that had not sinned after the similitude of Adam's transgression, who is the figure of him that was to come.". It is this "last" Adam, Jesus Christ of Nazareth, conceived by the Holy Spirit of God, the Spiritual man, and Saviour of us all, that we need to accept, "believe on", and follow, unto eternal life in His Holy name. Alleluia and praise the LORD. Ephesians 2:19 and 20 say, "Now therefore ye are no more strangers and foreigners, but fellowcitizens with the saints, and of the household of God; And are built upon the foundation of the apostles and prophets, Jesus Christ himself being the chief corner *stone;*". Praise the Lord God Almighty, and His only begotten Son, Jesus Christ of Nazareth, Saviour of the whole world, and Redeemer of all mankind. Alleluia and praise the LORD. Amen and Amen.

The end is not to be a fearful time or experience. Psalm 51:10-12 says, "Create in me a clean heart, O God; and renew a right spirit within me. Cast me not away from thy presence; and take not thy Holy Spirit from me. Restore unto me the joy of thy salvation; and uphold me *with thy* free spirit.". Psalm 69:18 says, "Draw nigh unto my soul, *and* redeem it: deliver me because of mine enemies.". Redemption is the free gift of God in the Holy name of Jesus Christ of Nazareth. He has purchased us by the shedding of His Holy and righteous blood on the cross for the forgiveness of our sins (Isa. 55:1, 1 Cor. 6:20, 7:23). He died for our sins on the cross, He was buried and the third day He arose to give us a hope for life everlasting in His Holy name. Because there is no other name under heaven by which we can be saved (Acts 4:12). To put this all into perspective it says in Psalm 22:3, "But thou *art* holy, *O thou* that inhabitest the praises of Israel.". If you desire to have a relationship with the Almighty God in Jesus Christ of Nazareth's Holy name in this life and forever more, in the world to come, worship, praise, obey and follow Him and Him only. To God be the Glory in the name of His only begotten Son, Jesus Christ of Nazareth. Alleluia and praise the LORD. In the New Testament a derived word used for end is also used for perfection in some places. We are working toward a goal, that goal is to become like we were meant to be created in the beginning. God like beings, children of God, created in His image, His likeness, like Adam and Eve were created before the fall, and Jesus Christ of Nazareth was in the beginning, is today, and always will be (Gen. 1:26, 31; John 8:58, Rev. 1:8, 21:7). Jesus admonishes in Matthew 5:48, "Be ye therefore perfect, even as your Father which is in heaven is perfect.". Job 14:12 says, "So man lieth down, and riseth not: till the heavens *be* no more, they shall not awake, nor be raised out of their sleep.". This is one of the first indicators in the Holy Bible of what physical "death", will be like, and is like for those, awaiting their resurrection. Jesus confirmed this with Lazarus, and David mentioned this as well in a psalm, as well as other New Testament writers (Ps. 13:3, John 11:11, Acts 7:60, 13:36; 1 Cor. 15:6, 20). This topic will be spoken of in greater detail in chapter five and briefly in chapter four of this book. Nevertheless, we must remember what Jesus said about our "resurrection"; He said of Himself, "...whomsoever liveth and believeth in me shall never die." (John 11:26). This is the simplicity of life, death and our resurrection in Jesus Christ of Nazareth's Holy name. Praise the Lord God Almighty, and His only begotten Son, Jesus Christ of Nazareth. Alleluia and praise the LORD. Amen and Amen. John 3:17 says, "For God sent not his Son into the world to condemn the world; but that the world through him might be saved.". John 5:24-27 says, "Verily, verily, I say unto you, He that heareth my word, and believeth on him that sent me, hath everlasting life, and shall not come into condemnation; but is passed from death unto life. Verily, verily, I say unto you, The hour is coming, and now is, when the dead shall hear the voice of the Son of God: and they that hear shall live. For as the Father hath life in himself; so hath he given to the Son to have life in himself; And hath given him authority to execute judgment also, because he is the Son of man.". Romans 5:18 says, "Therefore as by the offense of one *judgment came* upon all men to condemnation; even so by the righteousness of one *the free gift came* upon all men unto justification of life.". 1 John 3:20 and 21 say, "For if our heart condemn us, God is greater than our heart, and knoweth all things. Beloved, if our heart condemn us not, *then* have we confidence toward God.". This is a simple way of looking at it. Jesus said, judge not lest you be judged, that means we ought not to judge ourselves either (Matt. 7:1). Praise the Lord God Almighty and His only begotten Son, Jesus Christ of Nazareth. Alleluia and praise the LORD. Amen and Amen.

New Jerusalem

The measure of a man, of the angel, the walls; the walls protect the city from unbelievers, that is the Holy Spirit of God physically and through the Holy Scriptures, the works and the testimonies of the saints, and all those whom have done the "work of God" (Gen. 3:24, Eph. 6:17, Rev. 21:17). Jesus said, "…This is the work of God, that ye believe on him whom he hath sent.", that is believe on the name of Jesus Christ of Nazareth (John 6:29). Alleluia and praise the LORD. The wall is of jasper, and this stone is used to describe the glory of God in the New Jerusalem coming down from heaven in Revelation 21:11, it is described as "clear" and the light of it is described as a precious stone of jasper. It seems that jasper is red in colour and this could represent the blood, sweat and tears of the prophets and the saints, namely of Jesus Christ of Nazareth (Luke 22:44, John 11:35, 19:34; Rev. 4:3). This was required for a testimony of the kingdom of God, and now protects the city, by their testimony, especially through the written word of God, the Holy Bible of God and the Holy Spirit of God (Matt. 8:4, 10:18; Mark 6:11, John 3:31-3, 8:17, 18; 21:24, Rev. 21:18). Before going too far, there seems to be three standards in the Holy Bible for being counted among those serving God, the first is being counted amongst the children of Israel at age twenty, the second is being counted to do service in the tabernacle at age twenty five, and then starting at age thirty, service and work in the tabernacle, ending at the age of fifty, then becoming ministers in the congregation, albeit these later two examples were attributed to the Levites, but no doubt they can serve as an example for all mankind (Ex. 30:14, 38:26; Lev. 27:3, Num. 1:3, 18; 4:3, 23, 30, 35, 39, 43, 47; 8:24-26). These three ages would be a good example and practically are in the societies we live in today as far as training goes for various vocations. A man can join the military, attend a higher education, or join the working world, in and around the age of twenty, and is considered a "man" in and around that age, as far as drinking, and other "age" appropriate laws go, as of the date of writing this book in 2018 A.D. (Ex. 30:14, 38:26; Lev. 27:3, Num. 1:3). By the age of twenty five a person usually has some descent trade, life or educational experience to use in service to God and his fellow man (Num. 8:24-26). And those whom are called to work in the tabernacle of God which should be everyone from a spiritual perspective, whether that is having children of our own to raise up the next generation, literally becoming a minister of God in a church, or starting a career or business (Num. 4:3, 23, 30, 35, 39, 43, 47). The point is that the Biblical standard of "growing" up seems to be followed with some margin of freedom in this world we live in today, and no doubt we will be following it in the "world to come", as God does not change (Ps. 51:12, Mal. 3:6). Nevertheless Jesus did say, "The kingdom of God cometh not with observation: …for, behold, the kingdom of God is within you." (Luke 17:20, 21). Also, He gave a parable of a man whom cast seed into the ground to grow, but did not know how it grew up (Mark 4:26, 27). So no matter my interpretation of things, the truth of the matter is in the Holy Bible of God, and through Jesus Christ of Nazareth, whom died on the cross for the forgiveness of our sins, He shed His Holy and righteous blood, He was buried and the third day He arose to give us the hope and promise of eternal life in His Holy name. Alleluia and praise the LORD. Amen and Amen.

In the "New Jerusalem", if the wall's thickness is compared with the height of a man, of an angel, let us do some calculations for this (Eph. 4:13-16, Col. 2:7, Rev. 21:17). The wall is 144 cubits thick and there are four sides to it, using the thickness of the wall and comparing it with the height of a man "laying down", as Jesus laid down His life for us and asks us to do the same (John 10:15, 15:13; Rev. 21:16, 17). This may also have something to do with resting, because generally when we are lying down we are resting (Matt. 8:24, 26:40, 43, 45). With this thought in mind, let us think about the thickness of the wall being related to working and/or resting time also, taking the average man to be about six feet tall. Doing some calculations, 4 walls x 144 cubits/wall x 21in/cubit x 1ft/12in x 1 rest day/6 ft. man = 168 rest days. This works out to be close to half of a year. And if we take the average day from sun up to sun down, then with the Sabbaths and Holydays, we would have the "average" workload on a man for a Biblical year (Ps. 68:19, John 11:9). It actually works out to about 8 hours a day, Sunday to Friday, with the seventh day Sabbath for rest, also with Holyday Sabbaths; the first and last day of the Feast of Unleavened bread, Pentecost, Feast of Trumpets, Day of Atonement, and the first and last day of the Feast of Tabernacles, off for rest, they are seven in total (Gen. 2:1-3, Lev 23:7, 8, 21, 24, 25, 27-32, 34-36). This is proof of God's perfect plan for mankind, as we are already somewhat following it, with our common eight hour workdays in this world. So these walls could very well represent the works that are given to man, by God, to maintain throughout his life here on earth, which from a practical perspective makes sense. Because the Holy Bible does say that we will be judged by our works, and that God has prepared our works for us ahead of time (Eph. 2:10, Rev. 20:12). But we receive eternal life, not by works, but by faith, which is a free gift (Matt. 10:8, Rom. 5:15, 16, 18; Eph. 2:8, 9; Rev. 21:6, 22:17). Alleluia and praise the Lord. This may also represent the "straightness" of our works given to us by God, as the measurement would be the thickness of the wall, pointed straight in towards the city, the throne of God and Lamb, Jesus Christ of Nazareth (Matt. 7:13, 14; Rev. 22:1). This is why Jesus says, "…seek ye first the kingdom of God, and his righteousness; and all these things shall be added unto you." (Matt. 6:33). All of our works in this life ought to be for the kingdom of God, through His beloved son, Jesus Christ of Nazareth, by His Holy Spirit working in, with and through us. We ought to be serving Him, in body, mind and soul, every day, even when we are lying down and resting, in meditation, prayer and rest (Matt. 22:37). A practical example of this would be the example of the building of the walls of Jerusalem during the second temple period, about 457 B.C. (Neh. 2, 3). While building these walls they had half of the man power building and the other half as "guards" (Neh. 4:13-23). This is a reality of the world we live in today, as of the date of writing this book in 2018 A.D., just as it was back then. As followers of Christ we are called to be on guard spiritually first and foremost through, as mentioned, prayer and praise, study of the Holy Bible of God, and fellowship with other believers, we are also called to watch (Matt. 24:42). Alleluia and praise the LORD. Amen and Amen.

Now let us do a simple calculation of the area of the wall using again the man as a standard. Using the number 144 000 as the number of people "in" the wall (Rev. 7:4). The walls are 12 000 furlong by 12 000 furlong and there are four walls (Rev. 21:16). Finding the "area" for one saint or "man", we would have 12 000 furlongs x 12 000 furlongs x 4 walls / 144 000 elect = 4000 furlongs squared = 63 furlongs x 63 furlongs. This is approximately equal to about 12 km x 12 km, and if the saints are to be husband and wife, "heirs together", this would leave them with a city or "territory" of 25 km x 25 km (Heb. 11:14-16, 1 Pet. 3:7). If we read what Jesus says about the parable of pounds, this is exactly what Jesus is speaking of, some having five cities and some having ten cities (Matt. 19:11-27). Jesus also spoke of the city set on a hill, he said, "Ye are the light of the world. A city that is set on an hill cannot be hid." (Matt. 5:14). The point in all of this is to show that God plans to reward mankind in the next life. We are not just going to be flying around in clouds or doing some other mysterious job, unless your job is an airplane pilot, astronaut or some other figurative job that involves "flying" in clouds. Of course exactly what we will be doing is a mystery, but God seems to speak through His Holy prophets, namely through Jesus Christ of Nazareth, in telling us what the "world to come", will be like, literally a "New Heaven and New Earth" with a "new Jerusalem" (Rev. 21:1-5). He says, "In my Father's house are many mansions: if *it were* not *so*, I would have told you. I go to prepare a place for you." (John 14:2). This would explain the growth of God's family into the "universe" as spoken of briefly in chapter two, with the possibility of the "mansions" in God's house being other "solar systems" with an inhabitable earth in each, and the "universe" being God's house (Acts 7:48, 49). He also said, "…Whither I go, thou canst not follow me now; but thou shalt follow me afterwards." (John 13:36). These promises God has made for us should be a comfort to all believers in Jesus Christ of Nazareth. He has a plan for us in this life and for eternity, we have no reason to fear Him in this life or in life eternal in His Holy name, because "There is no fear in love; but perfect love casteth out fear…" (1 John 4:18). He says, "A new commandment I give unto you, That ye love one another; as I have loved you, that ye also love one another." (John 13:34). 1 John 4:12 says, "No man hath seen God at any time. If we love one another, God dwelleth in us, and his love is perfected in us.". Alleluia and praise the LORD. Amen and Amen.

Last, let us consider the "territory" of this husband and wife and the managing of it. Let us say that you can fit five cities within this land area. Using Moses and his father in law's suggestion as an example for easing the burden of rule by putting men whom fear God, are truthful and whom hate covetousness as rulers of thousands, hundreds, fifties and tens (Ex. 18:19-26). And the seventy elders over the people with Moses, we would have fourteen elders in each of these five cities, or seven "couples" (Ex. 24:1, 9). If you consider the family unit, having two children, through the living generations, there would be two parents, with their two children and two spouses, and then four grandchildren with their four spouses; seven "couples". So in some respects these cities could very well represent the family structure as well. To God be the glory in the truth of these interpretations. Alleluia and praise the LORD. I realize that this thinking is in some respects abstract and they are estimations, as life as we see it today, does not always work out so "perfectly". But my point in writing these interpretations of the "New Jerusalem", its various dimensions and how it is made, and with what it is made, is to show the reader that God indeed does have a plan for mankind, and it involves, much like in the beginning, being fruitful and multiplying, throughout eternity (Gen. 1:28). The prophecies of Jesus and His government in the book of Isaiah are such that the INCREASE of his government shall have no end (Isa. 9:6, 7). This means that His family is going to continue to grow forever, God willing. And we have a wonderful and purposeful part in growing God's family, physically and spiritually, through teaching the next generation the gospel message of the kingdom of God Almighty, and His salvation message in Jesus Christ of Nazareth, His only begotten Son, including marrying and bearing children from our own loins, God willing and for God and Christ's sake (Gen. 1:28, Mal. 2:15). As children of our God in Christ Jesus of Nazareth's Holy name, adopted into the family of God by His Holy Spirit, through Holy baptism, receiving His Holy Spirit and our own testimony of Jesus Christ of Nazareth and God Almighty forever. Ultimately we do this by repenting of our sins, and accepting Jesus Christ of Nazareth as our Lord and Saviour, whom died on the cross for the forgiveness of our sins, He was buried and the third day He arose to give us the hope and promise of eternal life in His Holy name. Alleluia and praise the Lord God Almighty, in His only begotten Son, Jesus Christ of Nazareth's Holy name. Alleluia and praise the LORD. Amen and Amen.

The gates; the gates are said to be of pearls (Rev. 21:21). There are twelve of them, and they are associated with the twelve tribes of Israel, whose names are written on them (Rev. 21:12, 13; Ps. 24:7). Pearls are made up from a grain of sand or some other irritant that is caught in an oyster's shell and then the oyster slowly but surely covers it over with the pearl's mineral. This takes time of course, and likely represents the patience it takes to enter into the kingdom of our God. Alleluia and praise the LORD. The life God has given us here on earth is on average about seventy to eighty years long up to one hundred and twenty years if God so wills it (Gen. 6:3, Ps. 90:10). But the point is that it takes a lifetime however long it is to repent and be converted to following God's way and obey Him (Isa. 65:20). Accepting the offering of the sacrifice of the eternal Lamb of God, in Jesus Christ of Nazareth on the cross, whom died on the cross for the forgiveness of our sins, is the first and most important step (John 1:29, 36). Because He said of Himself, "…I am the door of the sheep….I am the door…" (John 10:7-9). We need to focus and continue following Jesus' example of a sacrificial life, a giving life, and "take up" our "cross daily, and follow" Him (Matt. 16:24, Mark 8:34, Luke 9:23). This again, requires a life time of, prayer, praise, Bible study, fellowship and as God gives us other "good works" to do (Eph. 2:10). That all being said, we ought not to fear this life that God has given us here on earth, or in the world to come (John 14:1, 27). God is love, and as the Holy Bible says, "Herein is love, not that we loved God, but that he loved us, and that he sent his Son *to be* a propitiation for our sins." (1 John 4:10). The apostle, John, said, "And this is love, that we walk after his commandments. This is the commandment, That, as ye have heard from the beginning, ye should walk in it." (2 John 1:6). How simple is it for us to obey God, follow Jesus Christ of Nazareth, and believe on Him, because God is love (1 John 4:8). The Holy Bibles says, "…This is the work of God, that ye believe on him whom he hath sent.", that is Jesus Christ of Nazareth (John 6:29). Alleluia and praise the LORD. We must also remember that we are "tabernacles" of God, created in His image, and Jesus is waiting at the door of our body, mind and soul and knocking, waiting for us to invite Him in to us (Luke 12:35, 36; Rev. 3:20). Last the Holy Bible says, "In your patience possess ye your souls." (Luke 21:19). This is the key, after accepting Christ as our Lord and Saviour, that we wait for Him, in this life and forever more, because we can do nothing without Him, we live, eat and breath by Jesus Christ of Nazareth (Luke 12:35, 36; John 15:5, 17:2). Repent and believe the gospel of the kingdom of God and His only begotten Son, Jesus Christ of Nazareth. Alleluia and praise the LORD. As well the gates are said to be open all of the time, and there is no night in the "new Jerusalem" (Rev. 3:8, 21:25). This is an invitation for you and I to accept Jesus Christ of Nazareth today, He has always and always will be with us, "…*even* unto the end of the world. Amen." (Matt. 28:20). And when we are resurrected, God willing, and stand before Him without guilt or shame, then He will take us where He is (John 14:3, Rom. 9:33, Col. 4:12). To His New Heaven and New Earth, in the living city of God, the New Jerusalem, coming down from Heaven for us (Rev. 3:12, 21:1-5). Just remember in this life, we can have a faithful and abundant life in Jesus Christ of Nazareth, before the "next" one, by God's merciful gift of eternal life in the name of His only begotten Son, Jesus Christ of Nazareth, by the gift of the Holy Spirit dwelling with, through and in us, forever more. Jesus said of Himself, "…whosoever liveth and believeth in me shall never die." (John 11:26). He proved this by His own resurrection three days after His burial, after His death on the cross for the forgiveness of our sins, death could not hold Him captive (Luke 4:17-19, Eph. 4:8). He lives. And so will you, if you repent and believe in the gospel of Jesus Christ of Nazareth and the kingdom of God Almighty. Praise the Lord God Almighty and His only begotten Son, Jesus Christ of Nazareth. Alleluia and praise the LORD. Amen and Amen.

The foundation and size; the foundation of the walls of the "new Jerusalem" are made up of twelve types of stone: jasper, sapphire, chalcedony, emerald, sardonyx, sardius, chrysolyte, beryl, topaz, chrysoprasus, jacinth and amethyst (Rev. 21:14, 19, 20). And the names in them are of the twelve apostles of the Lamb of God, Jesus Christ of Nazareth (Rev. 21:14). These stones are the same stones that are on the High Priest's breastplate, whom was the intercessor for God, between God and Israel in the tabernacle of God in the wilderness, and the temple of God built in Jerusalem, starting with Aaron, Moses' brother in about 1500 B.C., then other descendants of Aaron throughout the 1st millennia B.C. into Jesus Christ of Nazareth's physical ministry here on earth, in the first century A.D., with Caiaphas being the High Priest the year Jesus Christ of Nazareth was crucified, whom also prophesied of His death for the nation and to bring together in one the children of God scattered abroad (Ex. 28:17-21, John 11:49-52). These stones in the breastplate represented the weight and value of the children of Israel to God, which the High Priest was representing during his ministering to God in the tabernacle in the wilderness and temple in Jerusalem, the breastplate covering the heart of the High Priest also protecting his heart from the enemy (Deut. 32:9, 10). In the "New Jerusalem", these stones again, likely represent the tribes themselves, as the foundation of the city walls and how important God's chosen people are to him and possibly the one hundred and forty four thousand, as they are chosen out of the twelve tribes of Israel (Rev. 7). But as mentioned in this foundation was the names of the twelve apostles of Jesus Christ of Nazareth, so this also likely indicates that these twelve apostles have the same status as "High Priest" (Matt. 25:34, Luke 6:48, 11:50; Eph. 1:4, 2:20; 1 Tim. 6:19, 2 Tim. 2:19, Heb. 1:10, 4:3, 11:10; 1 Pet. 1:20, Rev. 21:14). This would also likely fulfill Jesus' promise to the twelve apostles to sit on twelve thrones judging the twelve tribes of Israel, as they are the foundation of the walls of the "New Jerusalem" (Matt. 19:29, Luke 22:30). Jesus Christ of course is of the tribe of Judah through His earthly mother, Mary, and He is the "chief corner stone", in our foundation of life in Him (Matt. 1:1-16, Luke 3:23-38, Eph. 2:20, 1 Pet. 2:6, Rev. 22:16). He also has taken on this weight on His breastplate, His chest, on the cross (Isa. 53:3-10, Matt. 11:28-30, Mark 13:33, 34). He took all of our sins upon Him, so that we can receive this very eternal life in His kingdom that is spoken of in the latter portion of the book of Revelation and throughout the Holy Bible (Isa. 53:4-10, John 3:16, 1 John 2:20). The Holy Bible of God speaks of the full armour of God, and putting on the "breastplate of righteousness" (Isa. 59:17, Eph. 6:13-18). It is by putting on the life of Jesus Christ of Nazareth and following Him, that we receive this "breastplate of righteousness" for ourselves (Isa. 59:17, Eph. 6:14, Col. 3:10, 11). I must emphasize, that it is not by our own works that we are saved, but by Him, by Jesus Christ of Nazareth offering up His life on the cross, as the eternal, Passover lamb for the forgiveness of our sins, that we are saved, forever (Eph. 2:8, 9; Heb. 10:10). As the Holy Bible says, "…This is the work of God, that ye believe on him whom he hath sent." (John 6:29). Alleluia and praise the LORD. Amen and Amen.

That being said, Jesus did say that not a jot or tittle would be removed from the law until all is fulfilled, and that heaven and earth would pass away before the law and commandments of God would pass away (Matt. 5:17, 18). John speaks about keeping God's commandments several times in his first epistle (1 John 2:3-5; 3:22, 24; 5:2, 3). Keeping the seventh day of the week for rest, as mentioned briefly earlier, is a command mentioned throughout the Holy Bible of God (Gen. 2:1-3, Heb. 4). That being said, Jesus Christ is Lord of the Sabbath, so keep this in mind, when seeking His rest in this life and forever more in the world to come (Matt. 12:8). Peace and rest begins in the mind first by God's Holy Spirit dwelling in us, through Jesus Christ of Nazareth's Holy name. Alleluia and praise the LORD. Also, calculating the size of the "New Jerusalem", using a comparison to our present earth, we can find that God, may be representing this "New Jerusalem" in a "New Heaven and New Earth", encompassing the earth, land, sea and air. The dimensions are 12000 furlongs by 12000 furlongs by 12000 furlongs (Rev. 21:16). This works out to be 1500 miles x 1500 miles x 1500 miles. And using these dimensions with the area of the present earth being about 195 million miles squared, we can find the approximate height of the "New Jerusalem", using the present earth's area, that works out to be about seventeen miles, above the earth, into the "stratosphere", where the "ozone" layer is. This all makes sense, because the ozone layer protects us from the harmful rays of the sun, as the Holy Bible says, "The sun shall not smite thee by day, nor the moon by night." (Ps. 121:6). It is very possible that God is showing us that the "New Heaven and New Earth", will be similar in shape and size to the heaven and earth we experience in this life, but without sin (Rev. 21:1-5). This would describe similarly the creation week in the beginning, concluding with the seventh day of rest for God and His creation after all of His work. First creating the light, dividing day and night, creating the firmament of heaven dividing the waters above and below the firmament, forming seas and the dry earth, the grass, herb yielding seed and fruit yielding trees, creating the lesser great and greater lights and the stars, creatures of the sea big and small and fowl of the air, and finally the beasts of the earth, cattle, creepy things, and man made in God's image, male and female He created them, to have dominion over the earth and all that dwells in it and to be fruitful and multiply like the rest of God's living creation, after this God rested on the seventh day as mentioned (Gen. 1:1-2:3). Alleluia and praise the LORD. Amen and Amen.

The city, river and tree of life; the city of pure gold, represents the people saved by refining in the "fiery furnace" of trials, in Jeremiah's lamentations, it compares the "precious sons of Zion" to gold (Lam. 4:2, Dan. 3, Rev. 21:18). Isaiah 62:12 says, "And they shall call them, The holy people, The redeemed of the LORD: and thou shalt be called, Sought out, A city not forsaken.". Alleluia and praise the LORD. The tree of life is said to be on either side of the river that is coming out of the throne of God and the Lamb (Rev. 22: 1, 2). To me this may represent the tree being of mankind, the male and the female, each on one side of the river. The river in between being the Holy Spirit that flows out of God, and Jesus Christ the Lamb of God, as it does freely today to us here on earth, since at least Pentecost 31 A.D. (Acts 2). The tree also has twelve manner of fruits, with fruit yielded each month, which likely represents the monthly opportunity for a wife to conceive a child, the fruit of her womb (Ps. 127:3, Rev. 22:2). No doubt the number is also related to the twelve tribes of Israel, and possibly, the creation of a new earthly kingdom, patterned by the twelve tribes, and twelve apostles in the New Heaven and New Earth (Jer. 10:16, Rev. 21:12-14). But the reality is that it also shows the conception cycle, with the potential of bearing fruit of the womb each month of the year. This is also related to our work, as mentioned in the wall, showing that we ought to bear fruit, every month of the year (John 15:8). Also the tree of life has leaves for healing, I think these leaves may be representative of the gentile nations whom are saved, as God can and does work through all of mankind, not just through the tribes of Israel and her descendants (Ps. 1:1-3, Rom. 2:14-16). Leaves are also used for shade, they convert light energy into useful energy for the growth and fruit of the tree and can be used as a sort of time keeper, as we know that the leaves grow in the spring, and wither away in the fall (Matt. 24:32, Mark 13:28). They are usually the first sign of growth out of a tree in spring and the last sign of growth, after harvest. This again would represent the life cycle continuing in the "New Heavens and New Earth", with possibly a "New Creation" type situation, like it was in the beginning with Adam and Eve (Gen. 1:1-2:3). It should be noted that all of this life comes from God Almighty and the Lamb, Jesus Christ of Nazareth, sitting on the throne in the center of the city, with the river of water proceeding from His throne (Rev. 22:1). This is very clearly representative of our life here on earth and in eternity proceeding from God, His only begotten Son, Jesus Christ of Nazareth, and the Holy Spirit, living waters of the river of life forever more (Rev. 22:1). Alleluia and praise the LORD. Amen and Amen.

General theme… Marriage

The apostle, Paul, said, "…Jerusalem which is above is free, which is the mother of us all." (Gal. 4:26). What was Paul talking about if Jesus was talking about marriage? Obviously we cannot marry our mother (Lev. 18:6-8). Paul could have been talking about the next spiritual birth of "firstfruits", in the world to come. Jesus Christ of Nazareth, and His elect, the saints, are the firstfruits in this life, but if there is to be a "New Heaven and Earth", and "New Jerusalem", there will likely be a New Biblical account of history. That being said, someone could also interpret this as leaving the Jerusalem "above", our mother and father, and cleaving to our spouse, the "New Jerusalem" (Gen. 2:24, Matt. 19:4-6). Where in this "New Jerusalem", we have a house, fully protected by God and Jesus Christ of Nazareth, with the foundation of the apostles and prophets, and walls of strength in "good works" and the streets of gold, the sons of Zion, family, friends, etc., tried by fire. With the living waters, the Holy Spirit, coming from the throne of God and the Lamb and the husband and wife as the tree of life, rooted by these "living waters", bearing fruit and leaves of healing for the nations (Eph. 3:17, Col. 2:7). That is, leaves of Biblical truth and teaching for the fruit, the "nations", and the children of God they conceive and bring forth into life, by the "living waters" of God and the Lamb (Ruth 4:13, John 17:1, 2). No matter the way this is all interpreted, we have eternal life in the Son of God, Jesus Christ of Nazareth; this is the most important thing to remember. He said, that in the resurrection we will be as the angels of God in heaven, neither marrying nor giving in marriage (Matt. 22:30). But in reality there must be a new life for us after this one, I have no doubt in my mind anyhow. A general theme of prophecy and simplified version throughout the Holy Bible is that God is coming with His angels and/or saints (Matt. 16:28, 24:27, 30, 31, 37-39; 1 Thess. 3:13). If we can keep just this one message in mind, then we know that God does have a goal in mind, and that is to bring justice to earth and to bring His purposes of His creation here on earth to pass, when and how He desires it. Not only this, but He is the Lord of hosts, so He is already not alone (1 Sam. 1:3). We have a very good future ahead of us if we believe in and follow the commandments of Jesus Christ of Nazareth and God Almighty, which is life everlasting (John 12:50). In John 11:25 and 26 it says, "Jesus said unto her, I am the resurrection, and the life: he that believeth in me, though he were dead, yet shall he live: And whosoever liveth and believeth in me shall never die. Believest thou this?". Jeremiah 29:11 says, "For I know the thoughts that I think toward you, saith the LORD, thoughts of peace, and not of evil, to give you an expected end.". End can mean goal, the goal being eternal life in Jesus Christ of Nazareth's Holy name with God and His creation, and in this life, God willing an undefiled marriage bed and fruit, children of our own loins, in Christ Jesus of Nazareth, with our fellow heir, our spouse, all by the life giving blood of Christ Jesus of Nazareth. Praise the Lord God Almighty and glory be to His Holy name, through Jesus Christ of Nazareth, His only begotten Son. Alleluia and praise the LORD. Amen and Amen.

Marriage Supper; Jesus had favour with God and man, His bride is the Church, the Body of Christ (Luke 2:52, Eph. 5:23-32). We have the same opportunity physically here on earth with a spouse and spiritually with God, through the indwelling of the Holy Spirit, by the name of Jesus Christ of Nazareth (John 14:16-18, Eph. 5:21-33). Proverbs 18:22 says of a wife, "*Whoso* findeth a wife findeth a good *thing*, and obtaineth favour of the LORD.". Hebrews 13:4 says of marriage, "Marriage *is* honourable in all, and the bed undefiled: but whoremongers and adulterers God will judge.". 1 Peter 3:7 says of husband and wife, "Likewise, ye husbands, dwell with *them* according to knowledge, giving honour unto the wife, as unto the weaker vessel, and as being heirs together of grace of life; that your prayers be not hindered.". There are many other verses about husband and wife relationship in the Holy Bible, these are just a few (Eph. 5:22-33, 1 Cor. 7:2-5, 10-17; 1 Tim. 3:1-11). Isaiah 62:5 says, "For *as* a young man marrieth a virgin…and as the bridegroom rejoiceth over the bride, so shall thy God rejoice over thee.". This seems to indicate the age appropriate time for marriage, that is, about the age of twenty years old. Anna, a prophetess whom met Jesus as a new born, was married seven years from her virginity but a widow of eighty four years old at the time, likely married at the age of twenty seven, another indication of the approximate age for appropriate courtship and marriage (Luke 2:36-38). Nevertheless the reality is in Jesus Christ of Nazareth, whom has authority over all these things (Matt. 28:18). Now commonly after marriage comes the opportunity to conceive, bear and raise up godly children, as commanded from the beginning (Gen. 1:28, Mal. 2:15). Matthew 18:1-5 says of children, "At the same time came the disciples unto Jesus, saying, Who is the greatest in the kingdom of heaven? And Jesus called a little child unto him, and set him in the midst of them, And said, Verily I say unto you, Except ye be converted, and become as little children, ye shall not enter into the kingdom of heaven. Whosoever therefore shall humble himself as this little child, the same is greatest in the kingdom of heaven. And whoso shall receive one such little child in my name receiveth me.". Matthew 19:14 says of children, "But Jesus said, Suffer little children, and forbid them not, to come unto me: for of such is the kingdom of heaven.". There are also many other verses about raising children in the Holy Bible, these are just a few (Deut. 4:9, 10; Eph. 6:4). The point in all of this is to explain that marriage, child bearing and child rearing are a solid part of God's plan for mankind from the beginning, read appendix D for more details on family and child rearing (Gen. 1:28). I should also mention that Jesus used many other parables to describe the kingdom of God, as I have mentioned some of them in my writing, nevertheless marriage, child bearing and child rearing seem to be the central purpose to God's plan for mankind, physically and spiritually speaking in Christ Jesus of Nazareth's Holy name, and Salvation through His name only by repentance and remission of our sins (Matt. 13:24-52, Luke 24:47, Acts 4:12). Alleluia and praise the LORD. Amen and Amen.

Hosea 2:16-23 says, "And it shall be at that day, saith the LORD, *that* thou shalt call me Ishi; and shalt call me no more Baali. For I will take away the names of Baalim out of her mouth, and they shall no more be remembered by their name. And in that day will I make a covenant for them with the beasts of the field and with the fowls of heaven, and *with* the creeping things of the ground: and I will break the bow and the sword and the battle out of the earth, and will make them to lie down safely. And I will betroth thee unto me for ever; yea, I will betroth thee unto me in righteousness, and in judgment, and in lovingkindness, and in mercies. I will even betroth thee unto me in faithfulness: and thou shalt know the LORD. And it shall come to pass in that day, I will hear, saith the LORD, I will hear the heavens, and they shall hear the earth; And the earth shall hear the corn, and the wine, and the oil; and they shall hear Jezreel. And I will sow her unto me in the earth; and I will have mercy upon her that had not obtained mercy; and I will say to *them which were* not my people, Thou *art* my people; and they shall say, *Thou art* my God.". This was fulfilled in Jesus Christ of Nazareth; He is and was a "Man", Ishi, and Baali, means "master". Jesus said, "Henceforth I call you not servants…but I have called you friends…" (John 15:15). This is why the book of Revelation likely speaks against the doctrine of "Balaam", albeit he was a foreign prophet (Num. 24, Rev. 2:14). Nevertheless, Jesus Christ of Nazareth is our friend, and God is our friend, He is merciful and full of truth (Luke 6:36, John 1:14, 14:6). He is love after all (1 John 4:8). This is also fulfilled in the covenant relationship between husband and wife, and will continue to be fulfilled spiritually in this world, between God and man, and God and the physical earth He created, continued unto the final resurrection, judgement, and the coming of the "New Heaven and New Earth", with the "New Jerusalem". Alleluia and praise the LORD. Amen and Amen. Nevertheless, we must remember that we can have and do have a relationship with God now, today, through our Lord and Saviour, Jesus Christ of Nazareth. This is the promise Jesus gives us that we can have life and life more abundantly (John 10:10). He expects us to leave all and follow Him, but He says that we will receive one hundred fold in this life, and in the world to come eternal life (Matt. 19:29, Mark 10:29, 30; Luke 18:29, 30). The point is that Jesus Christ of Nazareth came to save us, heal us and forgive us, and give us a new life in His Holy name. He desires to have a relationship with us, first and foremost, and then we can share in that fellowship with others, and a spouse and children as God wills it. Alleluia and praise the LORD. Because Jesus Christ of Nazareth came, born of the virgin, Mary, espoused to Joseph (Matt. 1:18-25). He was born, humbly, in a manger in Bethlehem, raised as a child of Israel, a son of a carpenter and carpenter by trade, Himself (Matt. 2:7, Matt. 13:55, Mark 6:3). He had brothers and sisters and other relatives (Matt. 13:55, 56; Mark 6:3, Luke 1:34-36). But He is the only begotten Son of God, because He was conceived by the Holy Ghost of God (Matt. 1:18, Luke 1:35). He taught of God and His kingdom, He healed, forgave, did miracles and ultimately He died on the cross for the forgiveness of our sins. He was buried and the third day He arose to give us the hope and promise of eternal life in His Holy name. Alleluia and praise the LORD. Amen and Amen.

Conclusion

As mentioned in the last section, the apostle, Paul, speaks of the "…Jerusalem which is above is free, which is the mother of us all." (Gal. 4:26). Could this be another Adam and Eve like scenario again? Eve was considered the "…mother of all living." (Gen. 3:20). Nevertheless, the most important idea to understand is that, God is a Spirit (John 4:24). Jesus admonishes us, not to think on things of this world (Matt. 6:24-34). Not to store up for ourselves treasures on earth but in heaven (Matt. 6:19-21). This is the key to living a life for Christ Jesus of Nazareth and God Almighty. This will take our entire life to live out these commands, but our reward will be in heaven. As the Holy Bible says, "Beloved, now are we the sons of God, and it doth not yet appear what we shall be: but we know that, when he shall appear, we shall be like him; for we shall see him as he is." (1 John 3:2). Revelation 22:10 says, "…Seal not the sayings of the prophecy of this book: for the time is at hand.". This is an invitation to all of us to understand and speak of the writings in these books of the Holy Bible of God, even the book of Revelation. God has commanded us to keep them open, that means we can understand His plans for mankind, in this life and the next. Alleluia and praise the LORD. This is the purpose of the writing of the book you are reading now and the others I have authored, by God's divine inspiration, God willing. All for the Glory of God, and His only begotten Son, Jesus Christ of Nazareth, whom died on the cross for the forgiveness of our sins, He was buried and the third day He was raised up to give us the hope and promise of eternal life in His Holy name. Alleluia and praise the LORD. That being said, do not believe my interpretations and understanding, search God's truth, the Holy Bible, for yourself. As the Holy Bible says, "Prove all things; hold fast that which is good." (1 Thess. 5:21). Remember only by the name of Jesus Christ of Nazareth can you or I be saved. There is no other name under heaven by which we can be saved (Acts 4:12). God loves you; He proved this and will continue to prove this by the life of His only begotten Son, Jesus Christ of Nazareth. Accept Him and His offering to you and you will be saved. Praise the Lord. Understanding that Jesus Christ of Nazareth is at the door to the New Jerusalem, is standing at the gates, will give us a better understanding of what is required of us to make it through those "pearly gates" (Rev. 3:20, Rev. 21:21). It will be Jesus Christ of Nazareth either welcoming us in or saying, "…I never knew you: depart from me…" (Matt. 7:23). The believer in Jesus Christ of Nazareth can rest assured that we have no reason to condemn others in this life or in eternity. Jesus has done ALL of the judging for us, through His words in the Holy Bible of God, and ultimately He has left the decision up to us whether or not we receive eternal life (John 12:44-48). This is the gift of free will, the freedom in Christ, and the freedom of eternal life in the Son of God, Jesus Christ of Nazareth. Glory be to our God and His Christ forever and ever. Jesus said that God's command is life everlasting (John 12:49, 50). Alleluia and praise the LORD. Amen and Amen.

Isaiah 60:18 says, "Violence shall no more be heard in thy land, wasting nor destruction within thy borders; but thou shalt call thy walls Salvation, and thy gates Praise.", because Jesus Christ of Nazareth is all in all (Matt. 28:18, John 1:1-3, 17:2; 1 Cor. 12:6, 15:28; Eph. 1:15-23, Rev. 4:11). He is in the "saints" of the walls of the "New Jerusalem", He is in the children of the twelve tribes of Israel in the gates, and He is in the foundation of His twelve apostles, the apostles of Jesus Christ of Nazareth and He is that light to the gentiles. He dwells on the throne with God Almighty, and He is the living waters, He is the tree of life, and He is a "son of Zion", Son of man, born of the virgin, Mary, tried by fire, and raised up to give us all the hope and promise of eternal life in His Holy name. Praise the Lord, Jesus Christ of Nazareth, and God, the Father, Almighty. A right foundation is built upon good works, it will last and the man will receive a reward, if another's works are burned up, he may suffer loss but the man may be saved (1 Cor. 3:12-15). This is the difference between the saints building the walls of the New Jerusalem, and those whom are attempting to do similar work, but may not be "saints", there works will burnt up, but they may be saved (1 Cor. 3:12-15). No matter what is to come of our works our foundation must start with the cornerstone of Jesus Christ of Nazareth (1 Cor. 3:11). We must remember that it is not by works that we are saved, but by grace through faith, and that faith is a free gift from God, in Christ Jesus of Nazareth's Holy name (Eph. 2:8, 9). John the Baptist spoke of himself as "…friend of the bride groom…" (John 3:29). So, who is Jesus coming to "marry"? The saints or the general assembly, the "people of the saints", the Body of Christ (Dan. 7:27, 1 Cor. 12:27, Heb. 12:23)? The saints are also the firstfruits of God, like Christ Jesus of Nazareth, but Jesus Christ of Nazareth is the first of the firstfruits, the sheaf of the wave offering shown at His resurrection (Ex. 23:19, Lev. 23:10-12, 1 Cor. 15:20, Jam. 1:18). The book of Revelation seems to speak of a first and second resurrection (Rev. 20:5, 6, 11-15). Jesus' marriage is spiritual first and foremost, but also there is that physical element, that exists here on earth and in the "New Heavens and New Earth" with the "New Jerusalem". The most important thing to understand is that Jesus has a bride, and that is His people, He also said, that I have other sheep not of this fold (Isa. 54:5, John 10:16). Jesus' bride is from every tribe, tongue and nation. He died and lives for all of mankind (John 3:16, Rev. 7:9, 10). Not just a specific person, not just a certain "religion", not just a certain "culture"; Jesus is indeed the Head of the Church and Saviour of the whole world. Revelation 22:17 says, "And the Spirit and the Bride say, Come. And let him that heareth say, Come. And let him that is athirst come. And whosever will, let him take the water of life freely.". This is an invitation for you and I to accept the Holy Spirit of God into our life, body, mind and soul, the living waters of Jesus Christ of Nazareth, and God, the Father, to wash away our sins and give us eternal life in Jesus Christ of Nazareth's Holy name. If you have not done this, do not delay, you will not regret accepting the life giving waters of Jesus Christ of Nazareth. Know that it is by His Holy and righteous blood shed on the cross for the forgiveness of our sins that we are healed, it is said that water even flowed out of Him on the cross, after being pierced by a Roman soldiers spear on His side to confirm His death (John 19:34). This is the like of the life giving, living waters, through His Holy Spirit even fulfilling the Old Testament prophetic Scriptures and Jesus' own words (Zech. 12:10, John 7:38). By the death of the eternal Passover Lamb of our Salvation, Jesus Christ of Nazareth, He was buried and He arose the third day to give us the hope and promise of life everlasting in His Holy name. Praise the Lord God Almighty, and Jesus Christ of Nazareth, His only begotten Son. Alleluia and praise the LORD. Amen and Amen.

Those whom may be struggling with "betrayal" issues, from a previous marriage or their present marriage, or even spiritually, from family, religious affiliation and/or the world around you, the Holy Bible speaks of a "he" and a "she", when referencing God (Jer. 23:6, 33:16). If "he" or "she", is coming to marry us, then that puts a "new" perspective, for the male and female part of mankind, that God Almighty has given us a wife or husband, undefiled and pure that loves us and will love us forever, no matter what has happened in this life, with our spouse, our family members before us, or in the world around us (Song 8:7, Rom. 8:38, 39). Proverbs 31:10-31 speaks of a virtuous wife from a human perspective, "Who can find a virtuous woman? for her price *is* far above rubies. The heart of her husband doth safely trust in her, so that he shall have no need of spoil. She will do him good and not evil all the days of her life. She seeketh wool, and flax, and worketh willingly with her hands. She is like the merchants' ships; she bringeth her food from afar. She riseth also while it is yet night, and giveth meat to her household, and a portion to her maidens. She considereth a field, and buyeth it: with the fruit of her hands she planteth a vineyard. She girdeth her loins with strength, and strengtheneth her arms. She perceiveth that her merchandise *is* good: her candle goeth not out by night. She layeth her hands to the spindle, and her hands hold the distaff. She stretcheth out her hand to the poor; yea, she reacheth forth her hands to the needy. She is not afraid of the snow for her household: for all her household *are* clothed with scarlet. She maketh herself coverings of tapestry; her clothing *is* silk and purple. Her husband is known in the gates, when he sitteth among the elders of the land. She maketh fine linen, and selleth *it*; and delivereth girdles unto the merchant. Strength and honour *are* her clothing; and she shall rejoice in time to come. She openeth her mouth with wisdom; and in her tongue *is* the law of kindness. She looketh well to the ways of her household, and eateth not the bread of idleness. Her children arise up, and call her blessed; her husband *also*, and he praiseth her. Many daughters have done virtuously, but thou excellest them all. Favour *is* deceitful, and beauty *is* vain: *but* a woman *that* feareth the LORD, she shall be praised. Give her of the fruit of her hands; and let her own works praise her in the gates.". That being said, God is not a respecter of persons, so this can be associated with the husband as well (Acts 10:34, Gal. 3:28). But the point is that we need not worry about betrayal. This is why Christ died on the cross for us, for the forgiveness of all our sins; to heal us of all these wounds (Isa. 53:5, 1 Pet. 2:24). After He was buried and He arose the third day to give us hope and a promise of eternal life in His Holy name. Alleluia and praise the LORD. Amen and Amen.

Discussion: Possibilities

> "In the beginning was the Word, and the Word was with God, and the
> Word was God. The same was in the beginning with God."
> - John 1:1, 2

It may be hard for us to wrap our minds around the concept of Jesus being God, but Him still having a Father in heaven. But I think of it this way, we can be both a father and a son in this life, so why cannot Jesus be the same? He said, "I and *my* Father are one." (John 10:30). God desires us to be one with Him as well (John 17:20-23). This is unity; this is walking with God in obedience to Him (2 Cor. 6:16, Gal. 5:16, 25; Eph. 2:10, 5:2). Our ancestors were made in His image, in His likeness in the beginning, through His Holy Spirit (Gen. 1:26, 27). So should we not be like Him also when we are redeemed by the blood of Jesus Christ of Nazareth, God, the Father's, only begotten Son? As Jesus said, "…with God all things are possible." (Matt. 19:26). God spoke with someone else, before Adam was created during the creation week, so there was obviously someone with Him in the beginning (Gen. 1:26). Was this Jesus Christ of Nazareth, the Word of God, likely so yes (Gen. 1:26, John 1:1-3). Was He born into this world in the flesh yet? Of course not, but as He said of Himself, "…Before Abraham was, I am." (John 8:58). Jesus Christ of Nazareth is our Creator; He existed with God even before we existed here on earth (John 1:1-3). So what does God have intended for us in this life and in "the world to come" (Mark 10:30)? Only God knows for certain, but while reading through these discussion questions and considering your relationship with God, the Father, Almighty and His only begotten Son, Jesus Christ of Nazareth, hopefully the answers you are looking for will come to you. As the Holy Bible, says, God is calling us to be peace makers (Matt. 5:9). He is calling us to know the truth, Jesus Christ of Nazareth is the truth, and the truth will make us free, so there is no reason why the truth of all things cannot be revealed to you and I as well (John 8:32, 14:6, 14:26). There is also the love of Christ that passes knowledge and the peace of God that passes all understanding (Eph. 3:19, Phil. 4:7). So keep these truths in mind while meditating on and answering any of this chapter's discussion questions. And remember that Jesus came into this world, conceived by the Holy Spirit of God, born of the virgin, Mary, espoused to Joseph (Matt. 1:18-25). He was raised as a child of Israel, of the tribe of Judah, with brothers and sisters (Matt. 2:1, 13:55, 56; Mark 6:3, Luke 2:42-52, Rev. 5:5). And He died on the cross for the forgiveness of our sins, He was buried and He arose the third day to give us the hope and promise of eternal life in His Holy name. To God be the glory in the name of His only begotten Son, Jesus Christ of Nazareth. Alleluia and praise the LORD. Amen and Amen.

Discussion Questions

1. Find some verses that describe God's way of seeing and thinking (Hint: Isa. 55:8, 9).

   _____

   _____

   _____

2. The Holy Bible says, "...with God all things are possible." (Matt. 19:26). Find some other verses that are encouraging for you to persevere in your life, trials and challenges, and in time of peace.

   _____

   _____

   _____

3. How have events and experiences in your life opened up your mind to thinking about doing the impossible? Think of an example and meditate on how God used that experience to prepare you for His path for you in this life.

   _____

   _____

   _____

Chapter 4: Hell – Hell on earth

> "Verily I say unto you, Whatsoever ye shall bind on earth shall be bound in
> heaven: and whatsoever ye shall loose on earth shall be loosed in heaven."
> - Matthew 18:18

Introduction

Jesus has given us, the human race, tremendous power here on earth. He has given each of us the ability to control ourselves. That is He gave us free will to choose, life or death, blessings or curses, and with these choices, the ability to not only control our natural life, but our spiritual life as well. As Jesus said, "And fear not them which kill the body, but are not able to kill the soul: but rather fear him which is able to destroy both soul and body in hell." (Matt. 10:28). The point is that God is a Spirit first and foremost, He created the earth to be inhabited and has a greater plan for mankind as a whole, as has been discussed in previous chapters, but with these responsibilities there are also consequences for those who disobey His commands, especially if they do not repent. The remainder of this chapter will speak about these consequences on the human mind, body and soul and finally the final judgement on this present earth as a whole. But ultimately the good news is life everlasting for those whom do repent and obey God, putting their faith and trust in our Saviour, Jesus Christ of Nazareth for life here on earth and life everlasting. He gave His life giving blood for us on the cross for the forgiveness of our sins, He was buried and the third day He was resurrected, conquering death, and giving us the promise and hope of eternal life in His Holy name. Praise the LORD God Almighty and His only begotten Son, Jesus Christ of Nazareth. Alleluia and praise the LORD. Amen and Amen. Read on to learn more.

Mental and Physical pain

Deuteronomy 28 and Leviticus 26, describe both the blessings of following God's commandments or the curses for not following them. Amongst the list of curses for not following God's commands is a list of mental "illnesses" that would come upon the unbeliever or rebellious person for not obeying God (Deut. 28:19, 20, 28, 29, 61, 65-67). With this information in hand, it may become obvious to the reader why the world we live in today has any number of solutions for mental and physical illnesses, including medication, various mental and physical exercises, "lifestyle" choices, "religious" solutions etc. But ultimately, it is the Holy Bible and truly Jesus Christ of Nazareth that has the perfect solution, because the causes and symptoms of all mental illnesses are clearly described in the Holy Bible and Jesus Christ of Nazareth came to fulfill the law and save us from our sins, He came to remove the curse from us (Matt. 5:17). He took the curse of our sins on Himself on the cross, but was resurrected to conquer the curse of disobedience to the law, that is death (Gal. 3:10, 11; Rev. 22:3, 4). The apostle, Paul's, epistle to the Ephesians talks about those whom are dead in their transgressions, is this not like the walking dead, zombies (Eph. 2:1-5). The great news is that we are a new creation in Christ Jesus of Nazareth. His blood is the only atoning sacrifice we will ever need again, to heal us of all of our maladies. Have you accepted Jesus' sacrificial offering for ALL of your sins? The Levitical priesthood of the Old Testament and medical doctors today, as of the date of writing this book in 2018 A.D., seem to have some similar responsibilities, examining sickness, giving some sort of advice, and possible treatment, and/or remedy as well (Lev. 11, 14, 17; Ezek. 47:12, Prov. 31:6, 7). Nevertheless we must remember God is our healer in Christ Jesus of Nazareth's Holy name (Ps. 103:2, 3). Proverbs 17:22 says, "A merry heart doeth good *like* a medicine…" that is the joy of the Holy Spirit that cannot be stolen from a follower of Christ Jesus of Nazareth (John 15:11, 16:22; Gal. 5:22, 23). God provides food, herbs, wine and oil for our service and joy (Ps. 104:14, 15). There seem to be good and "bad" herbs of the earth, just like Adam and Eve ate from the tree of knowledge of good and evil, man has the knowledge of both good and evil, and that includes using things that are found naturally, to turn them into something evil (Jer. 24). Jesus did not drink the vinegar mixed with gall offered to Him just prior to His crucifixion, which may have had some pain dulling properties, He experienced the full pain of the betrayal and sins of man on Him at first, then just before He gave up the ghost He took some vinegar offered to Him (Matt. 27:34, 48; Mark 15:23, 36). I am not saying that we should not be using pain killers in this world, but what I am saying is that pain killers will not solve the spiritual problems we have. Only Jesus Christ of Nazareth can heal us of our sin, all of them. And the Holy Bible does make clear that pain and suffering can be a consequence of sin, but also can be used to show the works of God in healing (Matt. 9:2, John 9:1-7). Some might suggest that this is a hard thing to say, but the reality is we are born into a sinful world, because of the sin passed down from Adam and Eve, through their blood line (Gen. 3:1-19). It took the Holy Spirit conceived, Son of God, living a righteous life amongst us and dying on the cross for the forgiveness of our sins in order for us to be healed and forgiven. You can be made whole; you can and will be healed of your sin, pain and suffering if you believe on, trust in and accept Jesus Christ of Nazareth as your Saviour. His Holy blood spilt on the cross is an offering made for the forgiveness of our sin, that no other medication or professional advice can match (Luke 8:43, 44). He died on the cross for the forgiveness of our sins, He was buried and the third day He arose to give us the hope and promise of eternal life in His Holy name. Alleluia and praise the LORD. Amen and Amen.

Suicide can be a common thought of those going through difficult times. Adam and Eve chose to eat from the tree of knowledge of good and evil, which God said would bring about death (Gen. 2:16, 17; 3:1-19). Saul and Judas both mentioned in the Holy Bible committed the act successfully (1 Sam. 31:1-7, Matt. 27:3-5). And Jonah and Job had desires similar to that, Job desiring never to have been born (Job 3:3, Jonah 4:3). The fact of the matter is that we were born into a sinful world and we are sinful from birth (Ps. 51:5, John 7:7). In order for us to remove the curse of self-hatred and self-harming thoughts, that basically are rooted in the choice our ancestors, Adam and Eve, made so long ago, is to accept the atoning sacrifice of Jesus Christ of Nazareth. He died on the cross for the forgiveness of our sins, He was buried and He was raised up the third day. And He, through God's Holy Spirit, is the only One whom can remove those evil desires from our mind and life (Matt. 28:18, John 17:2). God does not desire us to harm ourselves and He does not desire us to be harmed, this world is challenging enough as it is. He desires us to be at peace, to have joy, hope, faith and love in abundance (John 10:10, 14:27). All of these are fruits of accepting and following God's Holy Spirit, in Jesus Christ of Nazareth (Gal. 5:22, 23). Have you accepted Jesus Christ of Nazareth's atoning sacrifice for the forgiveness of your sins yet? If not, it is not too late. Ask Him to come into your life today. An Old Testament example of depression is the plague of darkness over the land of Egypt (Ex. 10:21-23). God hardened Pharaoh's heart, and the people could not see each other it was so dark, the darkness could even be felt (Ex. 10:20, 21). However, there was a light in the houses of the Israelites, the Holy Spirit, Jesus Christ of Nazareth (Ex. 10:23). Psalm 105:28 says, "He sent darkness, and made it dark; and they rebelled not against his word.". This may even indicate that both the Israelites and Egyptians were obedient to God. Of course, we do not have much of a choice in this matter. If God the Omnipotent is going to make us do something He will do it. Psalm 78:49 says, "He cast upon them the fierceness of his anger, wrath, and indignation, and trouble, by sending evil angels *among them*. He made a way to his anger; he spared not their soul from death, but gave their life over to the pestilence.". If these verses indeed are both associated with the same plague of darkness, then that plague was a spiritual one first and foremost and could be a spirit of depression, namely. But no doubt the Egyptians were physically blinded in some way as well.

This can be seen when Paul cursed Elymas in the book of Acts (Acts 13:8-12). Paul, formerly Saul, was also blinded by Christ, for coming against Christ's New Testament Church, he then repented and was healed (Acts 9:1-22, 22:1-16, 26:1-18). This is the consequence of coming against God's people. That is blindness, this happened more than once in the Old Testament, two angels smote some men of Sodom with blindness and God, answering Elisha's prayer, smote an entire foreign army with blindness temporarily (Gen. 19:11, 2 Kings 6:18-20). Nevertheless, we must remember that ultimately this same darkness came upon Jesus Christ of Nazareth at the cross, and even before that during His trial, he was literally blindfolded (Matt. 27:45, Luke 22:53, 64). The sun was darkened at His death, and the whole land was dark at this time, just like it was for the Egyptians (Matt. 27:45, Luke 23:44, 45). This is the reality; that Jesus took on the wrath, anger and indignation of God on Himself on the cross (Isa. 53). This would explain why He asked, "...My God, my God why hast thou forsaken me?" (Matt. 27:46, Mark 15:34). He was blinded by all the sins of mankind on that cross, feeling utterly separated from His Father. Jesus died on the cross for the forgiveness of our sins, He was buried and the third day He was raised up to give us the hope and promise of eternal life in His Holy name. For this same reason, all the prophecies that are spoken of regarding the "great tribulation", and the day of the LORD's wrath, etc., in the Old Testament and New, if you and I are willing to receive it, were completely fulfilled in Jesus Christ of Nazareth giving up His life blood for us on the cross at Passover 31 A.D. (Lev. 17:11, John 6:53, Rev. 12:11). Although tribulation, and possibly "great tribulation" may still be to come, as of the date of writing this book, in 2018 A.D., if we cover ourselves with the blood offering of Jesus Christ of Nazareth, we will in no uncertain terms be protected from the evils that come upon this world, no matter what they are, physically, spiritually or otherwise. Alleluia and praise the LORD. Amen and Amen. And we have hope in that He was buried, and raised up the third day to give us the hope and promise of eternal life in His Holy name. Alleluia and praise the LORD. Amen and Amen. He said He has been given power over all things in heaven and in earth. And He will never leave us or forsake us (Matt. 28:18, 20; Heb. 13:5). And He has given us His Holy Spirit to keep that promise (John 14:16-18). Alleluia and praise the LORD. Amen and Amen.

It says in Paul's first epistle to the Corinthians, that God will not put us through trials greater than what He knows we can handle (1 Cor. 10:13). This includes every trial we have ever been through, are going through, or will go through. God does say that He chastises those He loves, so goes the saying "tough love", but remember, He does not hurt you Himself (Heb. 12:6). Jesus ultimately took the chastisement of our peace upon Him on the cross, and ultimately chastisement can mean simply "correction" (Ps. 94:10, Isa. 53:5). He allows us to make our own choices and when we do make sinful or wrong choices, there are consequences, just like if we break the law of man there are consequences, so too is it the same with God's law. This is the gift God gave us, that is, authority, responsibility, and freedom of choice (Jos. 24:15). As the Holy Bible says, "...For unto whomsoever much is given, of him shall be much required..." (Luke 12:48). For those who are reading this and believe they are alone in their situation I can promise you, you are not. I have experienced most if not all of these curses in some form or another in my life and believe it or not, so did some if not all of the "great" leaders of the Holy Bible. David being one of the rather notable one's; He said that He became a proverb to his family, and that is exactly what one of the curses is, that people would mock or talk about the destituteness of the cursed (Deut. 28:37, Ps. 69:11). Jesus was mocked by those whom crucified Him (Matt. 27:38-44, Luke 23:35, 39). And Jesus had done nothing in His life to deserve any of it, but He suffered all of it for us, and asked God to forgive the betrayers (Luke 23:34). He loves you and I and He died for us. He knows our failures and desires us to accept God's forgiveness through His sacrifice on the cross. Jesus ultimately, is the only true friend we will ever need. Everything and everyone else in this life or the next are blessings from God at best. As mentioned above Jesus said on the cross, "…My God, my God, why hast thou forsaken me?" (Matt. 27:46, Mark 15:34). One of the reasons He likely said this was that He and God, the Father, were fulfilling the prophecies regarding family division and betrayal (Matt. 10:21, Mark 13:12, Luke 12:51-53, 21:16). Jesus said, "If any *man* come to me, and hate not his father, and mother, and wife, and children, and brethren, and sisters, yea, and his own life also, he cannot be my disciple." (Luke 14:26). This is the key to these harder verses that Jesus spoke about family trials, because He died on the cross for those sins too, so that we can have peace and love in our families today, and forever more in the name of Jesus Christ of Nazareth. Our families can and will be protected and kept holy by the sacrifice and offering God, the Father, gave to us, by His only begotten Son, Jesus Christ of Nazareth, whom died on the cross for the forgiveness of our sin. He was buried and He was raised up the third day to give us all the hope and promise of eternal life in His Holy name. With or without Christ these prophecies may be fulfilled in our life, as this can be observed in the brokenness of the world, as of the date of writing this book in 2018 A.D.. But with Christ we can and will even be protected and saved from these trials. As even Jesus says, "… one jot or one tittle shall in no wise pass from the law, till all be fulfilled." (Matt. 5:18). That includes "…Honour thy father and thy mother." and a man shall "…leave father and mother, and shall cleave to his wife.", and raise up godly children, as God wills (Mal. 2:15, Matt. 19:5, 14; Luke 18:20, Eph. 6:2). Alleluia and praise the LORD. Amen and Amen.

Hell - Gehenna – Valley of Hinnom

Misunderstanding scripture is possible; the book of Revelation is a very descriptive book and if you misunderstand the Scripture it can be a very "intense" part of the Holy Bible, regardless of where you sit in your relationship with the Creator. That being said, let us look at Revelation 14:9-11, it says, "… If any man worship the beast and his image, and receive *his* mark in his forehead, or in his hand, The same shall drink of the wine of the wrath of God, which is poured out without mixture into the cup of his indignation; and he shall be tormented with fire and brimstone in the presence of the holy angels, and in the presence of the Lamb: And the smoke of their torment ascendeth up for ever and ever: and they have no rest day nor night, who worship the beast and his image, and whosoever receiveth the mark of his name.". These are, in part, all events that are yet to unfold here on earth, likely during the "great tribulation", and are also associated with the mental and physical illnesses that can come from disobeying God as mentioned in the first section of this chapter, but IT IS NOT everlasting hell. Remember this; the prophetic nature of this verse likely is only a short period of time during a prophesied three and a half years of great tribulation, time, times and half a time, before the onset of the "Messianic Age" (Dan. 7:25, 12:7; Rev. 12:14, 20:4). See appendix G for more detail on the "mark of the beast". Psalm 110:1 says, "The LORD said unto my Lord, Sit thou at my right hand, until I make thine enemies thy footstool.". Jesus ascended into heaven to sit at the right hand of the Father after His crucifixion and resurrection, revealing Himself to and fellowshipping with His disciples for approximately forty days before His ascension (Acts. 1:1-4). Acts 2:34-36 again repeats this, it says, "For David is not ascended into the heavens: but he saith himself, The Lord said unto my Lord, Sit thou on my right hand, Until I make thy foes thy footstool. Therefore let all the house of Israel know assuredly, that God hath made the same Jesus, whom ye have crucified, both Lord and Christ.". Psalm 44:3 says, "For they got not the land in possession by their own sword, neither did their own arm save them: but thy right hand, and thine arm, and the light of thy countenance, because thou hadst a favour unto them.". Psalm 48:10 says, "According to thy name, O God, so *is* thy praise unto the ends of the earth: thy right hand is full of righteousness.". Psalm 63:8 says, "My soul followeth hard after thee: thy right hand upholdeth me.". It is Jesus Christ of Nazareth and God, the Father, that uphold us by His Holy Spirit working, in, through and with us (Ex. 15:6, 12; Deut. 33:2, Ps. 80:17, 98:1, 108:6, 138:7; Prov. 3:16, Eccl. 10:2, Isa. 41:10, 48:13, 62:8). Alleluia and praise the LORD. Amen and Amen. It is by His life giving blood that we are saved and it is by His Holy Spirit that we live and breathe. Praise the LORD God Almighty and His only begotten Son, Jesus Christ of Nazareth. Revelation 3:19 says, "As many as I love, I rebuke and chasten: be zealous therefore, and repent.". This is what Jesus Christ and God, the Father, are calling us to do, repent and believe on the gospel of the kingdom of God, and on His only begotten Son, Jesus Christ of Nazareth. Alleluia and praise the LORD. Amen and Amen.

At least one root to the reference of hell in the New Testament is, Gehenna in Greek, and Valley of Hinnom in Hebrew, Strong's number 1067 (Matt. 5:22). Now let us speak about the "valley of Hinnom", Joshua 15:8 says, "And the border went up by the valley of the son of Hinnom unto the south side of the Jebusite; the same *is* Jerusalem: and the border went up to the top of the mountain that *lieth* before the valley of Hinnom westward, which *is* at the end of the valley of the giants northward…". Jeremiah 19:2 says, "…the valley of the son of Hinnom, which *is* by the entry of the east gate…". This is the east gate of the city of Old Jerusalem. Jeremiah 19:6 says, "Therefore, behold, the days come, saith the LORD, that this place shall no more be called Tophet, nor The valley of the son of Hinnom, but The valley of slaughter." (Jer. 7:32). This likely speaks of, in part, the "great tribulation", but has likely happened in history as well, as Jerusalem has been attacked on various occasions by foreign nations (2 Kings 24:10-18, 25:1-21; Matt. 24:21, Rev. 2:22, 7:14). Jeremiah 32:35 says, "And they built the high places of Baal, which *are* in the valley of the son of Hinnom, to cause their sons and their daughters to pass through *the fire* unto Molech; which I commanded them not, neither came it into my mind, that they should do this abomination, to cause Judah to sin.". This is where the idea of a literal burning in "hell" at least partly comes from other references are made in the New Testament also (Matt. 5:22, 18:9, Mark 9:47, Rev. 19:20, 20:10, 14, 15). Our ancestors, not just from the tribe of Judah, did this to their own children, because they turned from God and served foreign gods (2 Kings 23:10, 2 Ch. 28:3, 33:6; Jer. 7:31). This still happens today unfortunately, in many ways in our world, through abortions, human trafficking and other abominations of all kinds, as of the date of writing this book in 2018 A.D. (Gen. 6:5, Matt. 24:37). This is part of the reason why God's judgement must come upon, not just the descendants of the tribes of Israel, but all of mankind. God will bring all of these works into judgement, and His counsel will stand, for those whom repent to everlasting life in Jesus Christ of Nazareth's Holy name, and to those whom do not, they will be cast into the lake of fire, and outer darkness, where there will be "…weeping and gnashing of teeth." (Dan. 12:1-3, Matt. 24:51, 25:30; Rev. 20:15). Jeremiah 7:20 says, "Therefore thus saith the Lord GOD; Behold, mine anger and my fury shall be poured out upon this place, upon man, and upon beast, and upon the trees of the field, and upon the fruit of the ground; and it shall burn, and shall not be quenched.". Jeremiah 8:7 says, "Yea, the stork in the heaven knoweth her appointed times; and the turtle and the crane and the swallow observe the time of their coming; but my people know not the judgment of the LORD.". Jeremiah 10:11 says, "Thus shall ye say unto them, The gods that have not made the heavens and the earth, *even* they shall perish from the earth, and from under these heavens.". This sums up our desolation, in our rebellion from God and His commandments. Thank God He gave us Jesus Christ of Nazareth, His only begotten Son, to save us from His impending judgement on all whom are living and are dead (John 5:25-29, Rev. 20:12). Praise the Lord God Almighty, and His only begotten Son, Jesus Christ of Nazareth. Alleluia and praise the LORD. Amen and Amen.

Joel 3:12-16 says, "Let the heathen be wakened, and come up to the valley of Jehoshaphat: for there will I sit to judge all the heathen round about. Put ye in the sickle, for the harvest is ripe: come, get you down; for the press is full, the fats overflow; for their wickedness *is* great. Multitudes, multitudes in the valley of decision: for the day of the LORD *is* near in the valley of decision. The sun and the moon shall be darkened, and the stars shall withdraw their shining. The LORD also shall roar out of Zion, and utter his voice from Jerusalem; and the heavens and the earth shall shake: but the LORD *will be* the hope of his people, and the strength of the children of Israel.". Although this was no doubt fulfilled in Jesus Christ of Nazareth, His life, death on the cross for the forgiveness of our sins, burial and resurrection three days later for our hope and promise of eternal life in His Holy name. This is also likely referencing the "Day of the LORD", or year of recompense, during the three and a half year "Great Tribulation", that is likely yet to come here on earth, just prior to the "Messianic Age", also known as the thousand years of Christ's rule with His saints (Matt. 24:21, Rev. 20:4). But all verses like this in the Holy Bible also relate to the "final judgement" as well (Rev. 20:11-15). This is the duality and three fold nature of the Holy Bible. It is spiritual and literal in nature, and it speaks of history, it is relevant today, and it is prophetic in nature as well, speaking of things yet to come (Ps. 147:5). This truly makes the Holy Bible of God, the greatest book ever written here on earth, the Book of Life. Alleluia and praise the LORD. Amen and Amen. The importance of putting all of these passages into proper perspective is understanding, where we are today in the Biblical prophetic time line, there is likely yet to come, the "Great Tribulation", the "Messianic Age", and the final resurrection, judgement and redemption of our physical bodies, when the final judgement comes and Jesus comes to take us where he is as of the date of writing this book in 2018 A.D. (Matt. 24:21, John 14:1-4, Rev. 20:11-15, 21:1-5). The reality of our physical death and the decay of our body, especially those who choose or are forced to be cremated in this life, is that we have a God that has redeemed our spirit, body and soul in Jesus Christ of Nazareth's Holy name, by His shed blood on the cross for the forgiveness of our sins, He was buried and the third day He arose to give us the hope and promise of eternal life in His Holy name. As Jesus said, "And fear not them which kill the body, but are not able to kill the soul: but rather fear him which is able to destroy both soul and body in hell." (Matt. 10:28). And as Jesus said, God is a Spirit (John 4:24). So we ought not to put too much emphasis on the temporary physical world and life we have here on earth. We must "...seek ye first the kingdom of God, and his righteousness...", which is a spiritual one, first and foremost, and then all other things here on earth and into eternity will be given to us (Matt. 6:33, Mark 10:30, Luke 18:30). Ezekiel 37 although spiritual in nature, first and foremost, is a great place to consider how God sees the dead, and what He can do to resurrect them. Not to mention the creation of Adam and Eve from the dust and Adam's rib, respectively (Gen. 2:7, 21, 22; 3:19). The point is that God can create our bodies from the dust, so we need not worry about that. He considers us clay in at least a few verses in the Old Testament

(Isa. 45:9, 64:8; Jer. 18:6). It is His Spirit that gives us life, and in Jesus Christ of Nazareth, we have it forever. Alleluia and praise the LORD. Amen and Amen.

Earth's "end"

The Holy Bible speaks about the "end", but it also says that the earth will last forever (Matt. 28:20, Eph. 3:21). So the question may be which is it? The answer, may be best put, that it is likely the "end" of this world, and the beginning of a new one (Matt. 12:32, Mark 13:31). This is how things can come to an end, but also the earth can last forever (Rev. 20:11-21:5). That is the basic plan described throughout the Holy Bible, namely in detail in the later chapters of the Book of Revelation. In some places, it is called the "world to come", or the "...new heaven(s) and a/the new earth..." (Isa. 65:17, 66:22; Matt. 12:32, Mark 10:30, Luke 18:30, 2 Pet. 3:12, Rev. 21:1). Regardless, the point is that life will continue forever, in Jesus Christ of Nazareth, and God, the Father's, kingdom. Alleluia and praise the LORD. Jeremiah 4:23-28 says, "I beheld the earth, and, lo, *it was* without form, and void; and the heavens, and they *had* no light. I beheld the mountains, and, lo, they trembled, and all the hills moved lightly. I beheld, and, lo, *there was* no man, and all the birds of the heavens were fled. I beheld, and, lo, the fruitful place *was* a wilderness, and all the cities thereof were broken down at the presence of the LORD, *and* by his fierce anger. For thus hath the LORD said, The whole land shall be desolate; yet will I not make a full end. For this shall the earth mourn, and the heavens above be black; because I have spoken *it,* I have purposed *it,* and will not repent, neither will I turn back from it.". This is similar to the beginning; Genesis 1:2 says, "And the earth was without form, and void; and darkness *was* upon the face of the deep. And the spirit of God moved upon the face of the waters.", before God "renewed" the earth (Gen. 1:2, Ps. 104:30, Lam. 5:21). The question is; has God already prophesied the end of the present earth, as we know it, in multiple places in the Holy Bible? The simple answer would be yes. But the key is that the end is only physical and temporal in nature. Just like Daniel's friends went through the fiery furnace, so also does this earth have a fiery trial to go through, but those who believe in Jesus Christ of Nazareth will never die (Dan. 3, John 11:26). We have the resurrection promise in Jesus Christ of Nazareth's Holy name and the promise of a "New Heaven and a New Earth" wherein dwells righteousness (Rev. 21:1-5). Alleluia and praise the LORD. This is why it is important to understand that God is a Spirit and that we were created with both physical bodies, but more important we are also spirit (Zech. 12:1, John 4:24, 6:63). My point is that although this earth may have a prophesied "end", our lives will never end if we put our trust and faith in Jesus Christ of Nazareth. Alleluia and praise the LORD. Amen and Amen.

Romans 8:19-21 says, "For the earnest expectation of the creature waiteth for the manifestation of the sons of God. For the creature was made subject to vanity, not willingly, but by reason of him who hath subjected *the same* in hope, Because the creature itself also shall be delivered from the bondage of corruption into the glorious liberty of the children of God.". 2 Peter 3 describes this "change" well, as melting and loosing. 2 Peter 3:3-14 says, "Knowing this first, that there shall come in the last days scoffers, walking after their own lusts, And saying, Where is the promise of his coming? for since the fathers fell asleep, all things continue as *they were* from the beginning of the creation. For this they willingly are ignorant of, that by the word of God the heavens were of old, and the earth standing out of the water and in the water: Whereby the world that then was, being overflowed with water, perished: the heavens and the earth, which are now, by the same word are kept in store, reserved unto fire against the day of judgment and perdition of ungodly men. But, beloved, be not ignorant of this one thing, that one day *is* with the Lord as a thousand years, and a thousand years as one day. The Lord is not slack concerning his promise, as some men count slackness; but is longsuffering to us-ward, not willing that any should perish, but that all should come to repentance. But the day of the Lord will come as a thief in the night; in the which the heavens shall pass away with a great noise, and the elements shall melt with fervent heat, the earth also and the works that are therein shall be burned up. *Seeing* then *that* all these things shall be dissolved, what manner *of persons* ought ye to be in *all* holy conversation and godliness, Looking for and hasting unto the coming of the day of God, wherein the heavens being on fire shall be dissolved, and the elements shall melt with fervent heat? Nevertheless we, according to his promise, look for new heavens and a new earth, wherein dwelleth righteousness. Wherefore, beloved, seeing that ye look for such things, be diligent that ye may be found of him in peace, without spot, and blameless.". As well in this passage, Peter ignorantly or knowingly mentions the "Messianic Age", one thousand years of Christ's rule with His saints that will come after the "Great Tribulation", but before the "Great White throne" judgement at the "end" of earth's present history (Rev. 4, 11-15). Giving the earth rest; 2 Chronicles 36:21 says, "To fulfil the word of the LORD by the mouth of Jeremiah, until the land had enjoyed her sabbaths: *for* as long as she lay desolate she kept sabbath, to fulfil threescore and ten years.". This was regarding the southern tribes of Israel, Judah namely, going into captivity into Babylon in approximately 600 B.C., but this idea of land rest could have a greater fulfillment here on earth in a time to come. The idea of giving land rest every seventh year is as old as the law that came down from Sinai at least (Lev. 25:1-7). See appendix C for more detail on the idea of the "end" of this present earth. Nevertheless, to God be the glory in the truth of all these things, in the name of His only begotten Son, Jesus Christ of Nazareth. Whom died on the cross for the forgiveness of our sins, He was buried and the third day He arose to give us the hope and promise of eternal life in His Holy name. Alleluia and praise the LORD. Amen and Amen.

Also, when Jesus was speaking about sending fire on earth, He was also likely talking about the Holy Spirit (Mark 9:49, Luke 12:49). As the Holy Bible talks about in various places, God being a consuming fire, the human tongue being a fire, etc. (Deut. 4:24, Acts 2:1-4, Jam. 3:6). The point is that God, in Spirit form, is like a flame, is it any wonder why there are so many that worship God's creation, the sun, as a sort of life giving entity (Ezek. 8:16). Ultimately though God is a Spirit, first and foremost, and there is life in His only begotten Son, Jesus Christ of Nazareth's Holy name. Even David said, "My soul *waiteth* for the Lord more than they that watch for the morning: *I say, more than* they that watch for the morning." (Ps. 130:6). The idea is to trust in your Maker, God Almighty and Jesus Christ of Nazareth, rain or shine, day or night, no matter the circumstances that seem to be taking place around us (Ps. 4:5). The Holy Bible speaks of judging in righteousness, not by sight (John 7:24). The Holy Bible also says in Malachi, "For I *am* the LORD, I change not; therefore ye sons of Jacob are not consumed." (Mal. 3:6). The three Israelites miraculously surviving in the Babylonian king's furnace would be another example, along with one walking among them looking like the "Son of God" (Dan. 3). From a literal perspective, this "end" could be caused by a large asteroid hitting earth, or a so called "sun burst" or any other number of possibilities. See the reference appendix A for a news article on the subject. But we must remember the reality is in Jesus Christ of Nazareth, not in the commands or ideas of men, including my own. The Holy Bible ought to be the first reference to go to regarding the truth of human history and what is to come. And we have the Holy Spirit that reveals to us the truth, through God's very creation itself (John 14:26, Rom. 1:20). Keep this in mind when "discerning" life here on earth today, and things to come. Isaiah 51:6 says, "Lift up your eyes to the heavens, and look upon the earth beneath: for the heavens shall vanish away like smoke, and the earth shall wax old like a garment, and they that dwell therein shall die in like manner: but my salvation shall be for ever, and my righteousness shall not be abolished.". This verse is a good explanation of the continuity between the physical and spiritual realm. Although the earth may not continually inhabit "life" in the flesh, as we know it, the good news is that God's salvation plan extends beyond this physical earth. This is the good news, that not only are we made up of flesh and bone, but we also have a spirit and soul form and structure that actually holds our bodies together and gives us purpose. That is we are made up of spirit, body and soul (1 Thess. 5:23). As God said in the beginning, "And the LORD God formed man *of* the dust of the ground, and breathed into his nostrils the breath of life; and man became a living soul." (Gen. 2:7). This is the key it is God's Word, Jesus Christ of Nazareth and the Holy Spirit that give us life and makes our flesh live; otherwise we are of the dust (Gen. 3:19). Praise the LORD God Almighty and His only begotten Son, Jesus Christ of Nazareth. Alleluia and praise the LORD. Amen and Amen.

Conclusion

We are brute beasts without the Holy Spirit of God (2 Pet. 2:12-16, Jude 1:4-10). Our carnal, that is fleshly, mind is enmity, that is hostile, to God (Rom. 8:7). Nebuchadnezzar is a perfect example of this, when He was changed to be beast like for seven years for not giving God the glory (Dan. 4). We need to remember God created us. We had no shame or knowledge of evil in the beginning, but by temptation we became learned in every evil thing (Gen. 1:27-31, 2:16, 17; 3, 6:5, 8:21). Our natural state was with God before disobedience, but now it is against God, because of the rebellion in the Garden of Eden (Gen. 3). In order to come back to the "natural" state of a right and healthy relationship with God we need to accept Him as the Creator, the Eternal, the All Knowing, and perfect (John 1:1-3, Rev. 4:11). He loves and desires us to have a relationship with Him and this desire was proven in the life, death and resurrection of Jesus Christ of Nazareth, His only begotten Son and our Saviour. Alleluia and praise the LORD. In the Old Testament, Isaiah speaks of the foreshadowing of Jesus' atoning offering for the forgiveness of our sins, it says, "Ho, every one that thirsteth, come ye to the waters, and he that hath no money; come ye, buy, and eat; yea, come, buy wine and milk without money and without price." (Isa. 52:3, 55:1; Matt. 11:28, John 4:10-14, 7:38). He was speaking of the offering that God gives us of eternal life in the name of His only begotten Son, Jesus Christ of Nazareth. God is the ultimate provider of all things (1 Ch. 29:14, John 1:1-3, Rev. 4:11). If we accept His offer then we receive the blessings that come with it. Deuteronomy 28:47 explains why the curses come for those who receive them, it says, "Because thou servedst not the Lord thy God with joyfulness, and with gladness of heart, for the abundance of all *things*...". How simple it is to follow God, be joyful and glad for the abundance of all things. Alleluia and praise the LORD. This is the giving way, this is being content in all circumstance, even when the world around you is prospering and you do not feel you are (1 Tim.6: 6-8, Heb. 13:5). This is love, giving ourselves up to Jesus Christ of Nazareth, God, the Father, Almighty and the Holy Spirit, like Christ gave up His life on the cross for us so that we can all ultimately live in His Holy name by His Holy Spirit. Because Jesus Christ of Nazareth died on the cross at Passover 31 A.D. for the forgiveness of our sins, He was buried and the third day He arose to give us the hope and promise of eternal life in His Holy name. Alleluia and praise the LORD. Amen and Amen.

Unbelief is the issue regarding wrestling with an unsound mind, carnal mind (Matt. 17:20, Heb. 3:12). Jesus is the author and finisher of our faith, of our belief (Heb. 12:2). The apostle, Paul, said,

"For whether we be beside ourselves, *it is* to God: or whether we be sober, *it is* for your cause." (2 Cor. 5:13). Even Jesus Christ of Nazareth was accused of being beside Himself by His own friends (Mark 3:21). One man's son, whom was a lunatic, could not be healed by the disciples because of their unbelief and faithlessness (Matt. 17:15-17). Jesus healed him and said if the disciples had faith of a mustard seed they could move mountains (Matt. 17:20). But He also said, that fasting and prayer was required to cast out this kind of devil (Matt. 17:21). After the legion of devils was cast out of a man dwelling among the tombs, he was in his "right mind" (Luke 8:30-35). God does not give us a spirit of fear, but of power, love and a sound mind (2 Tim. 1:7). And the fruit of the Holy Spirit is "… love, joy, peace, longsuffering, gentleness, goodness, faith, Meekness, temperance…" (Gal. 5:23). The apostle, Peter, says the end of our faith is the salvation of our souls (1 Pet. 1:9). Alleluia and praise the LORD. Repentance, accepting forgiveness, asking for the Holy Spirit to come into our mind, body and soul, and obeying God, the Father, Almighty in Jesus Christ of Nazareth's Holy name is the key to living a prosperous, healthy and peaceful life here on earth and receiving everlasting life in eternity. The Holy Bible speaks of curses being turned into blessings (Deut. 23:5, Neh. 13:2). And even at the end of Deuteronomy 28:68 it says, that "…ye shall be sold…, and no man shall buy *you.*". Although this may suggest that the purchase is final, this to me indicates the reality of the situation, which is ultimately, no matter how many curses we receive and for how long throughout life, we are ultimately God's creation, and His children through adoption in the name of Jesus Christ of Nazareth (John 1:1-3, 1 Cor. 6:20, 7:23; Rev. 4:11). The Holy Bible book, the Song of Solomon says, "Many waters cannot quench love, neither can the floods drown it: if a man would give all the substance of his house for love, it would utterly be contemned." (Song 8:7). The fact of the matter is ultimately, as children of God, we are His, He sent Jesus Christ of Nazareth to earth to die for the forgiveness of our sins, and He was resurrected to give us the promise of eternal life in Jesus Christ of Nazareth's Holy name. The Holy Bible says, "What? know ye not that your body is the temple of the Holy Ghost *which is* in you, which ye have of God, and ye are not your own? For ye are bought with a price: therefore glorify God in your body, and in your spirit, which are God's." (1 Cor. 6:19, 20). As children of God and followers of His only begotten Son, Jesus Christ of Nazareth, we are His servants and no one else's. The true God is life and life everlasting; He is our Father, provider, comforter and Saviour. There is no other name under heaven by which we can be saved, but by Jesus Christ of Nazareth's Holy name (Acts 4:12). Alleluia and praise the LORD. Amen and Amen.

Looking at the earth and its history as a whole, we can start from the beginning, and then unto the flood, with Noah's Ark as a kind of seed of the covenant of life (Gen. 1-10). That seed was watered with the floods and then it broke forth to grow when the floods subsided (Gen. 8:15-22). This seed has and continues to grow physically, by the growth of mankind and God's creation. The firstfruits of this seed are Jesus Christ of Nazareth, and His saints chosen throughout the ages, with the "Great Tribulation" and the onset of the "Messianic Age" being the culmination of the spring harvest of firstfruits (Rom. 8:23, 1 Cor. 15:20, 23; Jam. 1:18, Rev. 14:4). Then we have the summer of one thousand years of Christ's rule with His saints, after this the fall harvest with the "last great day", which is the "end" of the world (Matt. 13:39, 49, 50; 24:3, 28:20; John 6:39, 40, 44, 54; 7:37; Rev. 20:4, 11-15). Throughout the entire time we have been tried by fire, but the final fire will burn up the chaff of the harvest and the precious fruit will remain, as promised by God, we will not be consumed (Mal. 3:6, Matt. 3:11, 12; Rev. 3:18). We have the promise of Shadrach, Meshach and Abednego surviving the fiery furnace of Nebuchadnezzar, and we have the best promise of eternal life in Jesus Christ of Nazareth's Holy name, no matter what happens to us here on earth (Isa. 43:2, Dan. 3, Matt. 28:20). As the Holy Bible says, "…fear not them which kill the body, but are not able to kill the soul: but rather fear him which is able to destroy both soul and body in hell." (Matt. 10:28). Accepting the precious blood of Jesus Christ of Nazareth for the forgiveness of our sins protects us from the judgements and wrath of God (Rom. 5:9). Of course we are all going to "die", once here on earth, because of the fall from the beginning and the consequences of sin (Heb. 9:27, 28). But it is our soul that will live, and God will give us a new body and spirit, in Jesus Christ of Nazareth's Holy name, if we put our trust in Him and follow Him forever more. Praise the Lord, God Almighty, and His only begotten Son, Jesus Immanuel Christ of Nazareth. He was conceived by the Holy Spirit, in the virgin, Mary, espoused to Joseph (Matt. 1:18). He was born and raised as a child of Israel, of the tribe of Judah, with brothers and sisters (Matt. 2:1, 13:55, 56; Mark 6:3, Luke 2:42-52, Rev. 5:5). He ministered, healed, forgave, loved, and did miracles of provision. And finally He died on the cross for the forgiveness of our sins at Passover 31 A.D., He was buried and the third day He arose to give us the hope and promise of eternal life in His Holy name. Alleluia and praise the LORD. Amen and Amen.

Discussion: Forgiveness

"…Whatsoever ye shall bind on earth shall be bound in heaven: and
whatsoever ye shall loose on earth shall be loosed in heaven."
- Matthew 18:18

Forgiveness is the key to moving forward in our relationship with God and others. As Jesus said, "…whatsoever ye shall loose on earth shall be loosed in heaven." (Matt. 18:18). He also said, "And when ye stand praying, forgive, if ye have ought against any: that your Father also which is in heaven may forgive you your trespasses." (Mark 11:25). If we allow the blood of Jesus Christ of Nazareth to flow over us, cleansing us, forgiving us of our sins, and helping us to forgive ourselves as well as others, this will give us the freedom we are looking for in this life and forever more. When we no longer hold the grudges, the condemnation, the anger or the judgements that are at best by our own human standards and our understanding of how we believe God judges, then we are freed from the tyranny of God's wrath (John 3:36). As Jesus said, "Judge not, and ye shall not be judged: condemn not, and ye shall not be condemned: forgive, and ye shall be forgiven: Give, and it shall be given unto you; good measure, pressed down, and shaken together, and running over, shall men give into your bosom. For with the same measure that ye mete withal it shall be measured to you again." (Luke 6:37, 38). I realize for some this may be a hard "pill" to swallow, but if you as a believer spend more time thinking about the cross of Christ and meditating on what He did for you, you may find that the other stuff becomes less and less important. I have studied the Scriptures, both in the New and Old Testament, regarding Jesus' life, crucifixion and resurrection, and I have come to the conclusion, that it is only by the blood of Jesus Christ of Nazareth on the cross that I can forgive anyone, even myself. I am not saved by my own efforts, desires, prayers, or otherwise, it was by Jesus Christ of Nazareth's act on the cross that I am saved. When you realize this one simple truth for yourself as well, you may find your freedom that you have been looking for all your life. Here it is, ready for the taking, all for the glory of God, the Father, Almighty and His only begotten Son, Jesus Christ of Nazareth. Alleluia and praise the LORD. When reading through this chapter's discussion questions, consider how Christ died for you on the cross, He was buried and He arose the third day to give us the hope and promise of eternal life in His Holy name. And consider what this means for your relationship with Him and others here on earth, and forever more in His everlasting name. Alleluia and praise the LORD. Amen and Amen.

Discussion Questions

1. The apostle, Paul, admonishes in the New Testament to redeem the time for the days are evil, what does this mean for you?

    _____

    _____

    _____

2. Sometimes life challenges can bring us to a spiritual place that is dark to say the least. Jeremiah wrote an entire book of the Old Testament about it called Lamentations. What are some things you can do, when you are experiencing your "…walk through the valley of the shadow of death…" (Ps. 23:4)?

    _____

    _____

    _____

3. Why are we subject to bondage?

    _____

    _____

    _____

Chapter 5: Hell – Hell in the ground

"Behold, I shew you a mystery; We shall not all sleep, but we shall all be changed,
In a moment, in the twinkling of an eye, at the last trump: for the trumpet shall
sound, and the dead shall be raised incorruptible, and we shall be changed."
- 1 Corinthians 15:51, 52

Introduction

The concept of hell was aggrandized in the works of Dante, an Italian poet, whom wrote Dante's inferno. And according to at least one translation, was actually written as a sort of mockery of religious interpretations of hell at the time, hence the name, "The Divine Comedy". Much of the ideas of hell, such as purgatory and the "under world" may very well stem from that author's work. Nevertheless, there is a literal hell mentioned in the Holy Bible, and it is the point of this chapter of this book to discuss the topic in greater detail in order to clear up some of the misconceptions that the media, possible religious deception and other references may have brought into the reader's mind in understanding the truth about where we go when we die. The ultimate truth is that for those whom repent of sin and turn to Jesus Christ of Nazareth, we will "never die" (John 11:26). As some of the New Testament authors and even Jesus suggested, physical death is only a state of being, as if you were asleep (Matt. 9:24, Mark 5:39, Luke 8:52, John 11:11-14, Acts 7:60). If we repent, put our trust in and follow Jesus Christ of Nazareth in this life, after we die, we will be resurrected on the last day to life everlasting (John 5:29, 12:48). Alleluia and praise the LORD. Amen and Amen. Nevertheless, in this chapter I will discuss the idea of the physical, literal hell, read on to learn more.

Hell or the grave

Another word for hell in Greek is, hades, meaning the grave, the unseen, the pit or the ground; Strong's number 86 (Matt. 11:23, 16:18; Luke 16:23, Acts 2:27). Psalm 49:14 says, "Like sheep they are laid in the grave; death shall feed on them; and the upright shall have dominion over them in the morning; and their beauty shall consume in the grave from their dwelling.". Psalm 9:6 says, "O thou enemy, destructions are come to a perpetual end: and thou hast destroyed cities; their memorial is perished with them.". Psalm 9:17 "The wicked shall be turned into hell, *and* all the nations that forget God.". This verse really simplifies what is going to happen to the "wicked", they will be turned to dust, quite literally; which is what the Holy Bible says in multiple places (Gen. 3:19, Job 17:16, 20:11, 21:26, 34:15). Psalm 10:12-18 says, "Arise, O LORD; O God, lift up thine hand: forget not the humble. Wherefore doth the wicked contemn God? he hath said in his heart, Thou wilt not require *it*. Thou hast seen *it;* for thou beholdest mischief and spite, to requite *it* with thy hand: the poor committeth himself unto thee; thou art the helper of the fatherless. Break thou the arm of the wicked and the evil *man:* seek out his wickedness *till* thou find none. The LORD *is* King for ever and ever: the heathen are perished out of his land. LORD, thou hast heard the desire of the humble: thou wilt prepare their heart, thou wilt cause thine ear to hear: To judge the fatherless and the oppressed, that the man of the earth may no more oppress.". The good news in all of this is, as is said in these psalms, is that there is an end to death and destruction, and hell and sin. And in Christ Jesus of Nazareth we have life everlasting. Solomon had great wisdom, and said, "All go unto one place; all are of the dust, and all turn to dust again. Who knoweth the spirit of man that goeth upward, and the spirit of the beast that goeth downward to the earth?" (Eccl. 3:20, 21). The answer is, Jesus Christ knows, Jesus Christ of Nazareth said He himself is greater than Solomon, which means He also knows better of life and death than King Solomon (Matt. 12:42, Luke 11:31). Jesus said of Himself, "And whosoever liveth and believeth in me shall never die. Believest thou this?" (John 11:26). Do you believe in Jesus Christ of Nazareth, and His promise of eternal life to all whom obey and follow Him? Repent and believe the gospel of the kingdom of God, and God, the Father's, only begotten Son, Jesus Christ of Nazareth. Alleluia and praise the LORD. Amen and Amen.

Isaiah speaks of "Lucifer", whose fall was caused because of his desire to exalt himself. It says, "How art thou fallen from heaven, O Lucifer, son of the morning! *how* art thou cut down to the ground, which didst weaken the nations! For thou hast said in thine heart, I will ascend into heaven, I will exalt my throne above the stars of God: I will sit also upon the mount of the congregation, in the sides of the north: I will ascend above the heights of the clouds; I will be like the most High. Yet thou shalt be brought down to hell, to the sides of the pit." (Isa. 14:12-15). If this is a reference to Satan and his "fallen" angels, then it must be very clear what his and his followers' later end will be (Rev. 12:3, 4, 7-9; 20:10). That is just like any human life will receive, that is, death as a consequence of sin (Rom. 6:23, Mark 1:24, Luke 4:34, Heb. 2:14). The good news is we have eternal life in Jesus Christ of Nazareth's Holy name; He died on the cross for the forgiveness of our sins, He was buried and the third day He arose to give us the hope and promise of eternal life in His Holy name. Alleluia and praise the LORD. He has full authority over all things, life and death, because He conquered death on the cross, and was raised for our hope of eternal life in His Holy name. God speaks in the Holy Bible that He will break our covenant with death (Isa. 28:18). This covenant was made in the beginning by Adam and Eve, by disobeying God and eating from the tree of knowledge of good and evil, which God promised would bring about death (Gen. 3). And God did not lie, it was the serpent that lied from the beginning and said it would not bring forth death, but it did (Gen. 3:1-5). And the "fallen" world we live in today is the consequence of that disobedience to God, eating from the tree of knowledge of good and evil, listening to that old serpent, the dragon, the devil and Satan (Rev. 12:9, 20:2). But again, it is by Jesus Christ of Nazareth, the only begotten Son of God, whom came into this world and taught the truth about all things, and opened our eyes to eternal life in His Holy name, He has saved us from this covenant with death. Repent and believe the gospel of Jesus Christ of Nazareth and the everlasting kingdom of God Almighty. Do you desire to be healed of this covenant with death, with the pit, with the grave? Just place your trust in Jesus Christ of Nazareth and you will be healed. It is His Holy Spirit that gave and gives us life, and life everlasting, as God's Spirit inhabits eternity (Isa. 57:15). Put your trust in Him and you will not regret it. Praise the LORD God Almighty and His only begotten Son, Jesus Christ of Nazareth, Saviour of the whole world, and Redeemer of all mankind. Alleluia and praise the LORD. Amen and Amen.

Asleep

Not even David, a man after God's own heart is in heaven today, according to the apostle, Peter (1 Sam. 13:14, Acts 2:29-35, 13:22). He is currently asleep, as are all other deceased awaiting one of God's resurrections (1 Cor. 15.6, 20). Psalm 16:9 says, "Therefore my heart is glad, and my glory rejoiceth: my flesh also shall rest in hope.". It would seem our bodies go to the ground and our "spirits" go back to God (Eccl. 12:7, Matt. 27:50, Luke 23:46). John 5:24-27 says, "Verily, verily, I say unto you, He that heareth my word, and believeth on him that sent me, hath everlasting life, and shall not come into condemnation; but is passed from death unto life. Verily, verily, I say unto you, The hour is coming, and now is, when the dead shall hear the voice of the Son of God: and they that hear shall live. For as the Father hath life in himself; so hath he given to the Son to have life in himself; And hath given him authority to execute judgment also, because he is the Son of man.". The prophet Samuel from the Old Testament is a good example of this state of sleep in physical death. He was "awoken" from sleep by a person whom dealt with familiar spirits, on the order of King Saul, whom disguised himself to consult with the woman, because the practice of consulting with familiar spirits was banned in the land by Saul (1 Sam. 28:3-14). Samuel was manifested in some form or another and was angry with Saul for waking him up (1 Sam. 28:15). Of course as mentioned in the introduction, Jesus says if we believe in Him we will never die (John 11:26). Even some of the saints awoke out of their graves and were shown to many in the city immediately after Jesus gave up the ghost on the cross (Matt. 27:50-53). And Jesus' Spirit went directly into God's hands after giving up the ghost on the cross (Luke 23:46). Another proof of life after death would be the transfiguration, and the manifestation of Moses and Elijah, whom spoke with Jesus of His crucifixion that was approaching at Passover in 31 A.D. (Luke 9:28-31). My point in all of this is that, although there may still be a general resurrection and a resurrection of the elect to come, God is "I AM", so we can no doubt experience a resurrected life, a new, forgiven, and healed life today (Ex. 3:14, John 8:58). Alleluia and praise the LORD. Lazarus is a perfect example of this, He was dead and then raised from the dead by Jesus Christ of Nazareth and lived amongst the disciples again (John 11:11). Isaiah 27:13 says, "And it shall come to pass in that day, *that* the great trumpet shall be blown, and they shall come which were ready to perish in the land of Assyria, and the outcasts in the land of Egypt, and shall worship the LORD in the holy mount at Jerusalem.". This verse is relevant today, as of the date of writing this book in 2018 A.D., and if or when the "Messianic Age" comes, and has been relevant in the past regarding the ingathering of the children of Israel to serve God in Jerusalem, but it has a greater fulfillment in Jesus Christ of Nazareth, whom came to save the lost sheep of Israel, as well as the gentiles (Matt. 10:6, 15:24; John 4:23, 10:16). Alleluia and praise the LORD. Amen and Amen.

The Holy Bible, namely the book of Revelation seems to suggest a first and a second resurrection (Rev. 20:4, 5, 11-15). The first resurrection marks the end of the "great tribulation", and the beginning of the so called "Messianic Age" of one thousand years of Christ's rule with His elect (Rev. 20:4). The second resurrection likely is associated with the general resurrection of all of mankind at the end of the "Messianic Age", when the heavens and the earth are dissolved, and God judges all men according to their works, just prior to the "new heavens and new earth" (2 Pet. 3:7-13, Rev. 20:11-15). I do not desire the reader to be confused about the writing in this book, the majority of it is written with the topic in mind of the final resurrection, "the last great day" (John 6:39, 40, 44, 54; 7:37). But understanding God's full plan for mankind throughout history and yet to come here on earth and in eternity leads me to make a brief mention of the likelihood of the "Great Tribulation" and the one thousand year rule of Christ with His saints, the "Messianic Age", prior to the final judgment of all mankind (Matt. 24:21, Rev. 2:22, 7:14, 20:4, 11-15). I have written two other books on these topics that expand on them, but to keep it simple, the Holy Bible talks about a three and a half year "great tribulation", prior to a one thousand year period of Christ's rule with His saints, with the likelihood of another physical temple being built for worship, mentioned in Ezekiel 40-48. That all being said, obviously we as humans, at least on this side of the flood, are not likely going to live for upwards of one thousand years (Gen. 6:3, Ps. 90:10). But when we pass, the resurrection and final judgement will likely be in a "twinkling of an eye" (1 Cor. 15:51-58). Moses speaks of this in Psalm 90, it says, "For a thousand years in thy sight *are but* as yesterday when it is past, and *as* a watch in the night." (Ps. 90:4). The point is if you are interested in researching these other topics, you can look into your own Holy Bible, or if you are interested look for my other books on the topics, as well as other books on the topic available in this world. But keep in mind in all of this, Jesus Christ of Nazareth and His promises to you in this life and in eternity forever. He says of Himself, "...I am with you alway, *even* unto the end of the world. Amen." and "...I will never leave thee, nor forsake thee." (Matt. 28:20, Heb. 13:5). This is the promise we all have in our Saviour and God Almighty, in the name of Jesus Christ of Nazareth, whom died on the cross for the forgiveness of our sins, He was buried and the third day He arose to give us the hope and promise of eternal life in His Holy name. Alleluia and praise the LORD. Amen and Amen.

Change

As spoken of in chapter four regarding the apostle, Peter's, reference to the change that is to come here on earth. He said, "But the day of the Lord will come as a thief in the night; in the which the heavens shall pass away with a great noise, and the elements shall melt with fervent heat, the earth also and the works that are therein shall be burned up. *Seeing* then *that* all these things shall be dissolved, what manner *of persons* ought ye to be in *all* holy conversation and godliness, Looking for and hasting unto the coming of the day of God, wherein the heavens being on fire shall be dissolved, and the elements shall melt with fervent heat? Nevertheless we, according to his promise, look for new heavens and a new earth, wherein dwelleth righteousness." (2 Pet. 3:10-13). That being said, the Holy Bible does say, "Woe unto you that desire the day of the LORD!" (Amos 5:18). As Jesus said, "Take therefore no thought for the morrow: for the morrow shall take thought for the things of itself. Sufficient unto the day *is* the evil thereof." (Matt. 6:34). Ecclesiastes 1:4 says, "*One* generation passeth away, and *another* generation cometh: but the earth abideth for ever.". Ecclesiastes 1:9-11 says, "The thing that hath been it is *that* which shall be; and that which is done *is* that which shall be done: and *there is* no new *thing* under the sun. Is there *any* thing whereof it may be said, See, this *is* new? It hath been already of old time, which was before us. *There is* no remembrance of former *things;* neither shall there be *any* remembrance of *things* that are to come with *those* that shall come after.". Psalm 96:10 says, "Say among the heathen *that* the LORD reigneth: the world also shall be established that it shall not be moved: he shall judge the people righteously.". Psalm 104:5 says of God, "*Who* laid the foundations of the earth, *that* it should not be removed forever.". Psalm 119:90 says, "Thy faithfulness *is* unto all generations: thou hast established the earth, and it abideth.". The point here is that although the earth may go through a "change", a purging, or a "renewing", referred to as the "New Heavens and New Earth", according to the scriptures the "world" will abide forever (Ps. 96:10). Our greatest hope and understanding of this is in Jesus Christ of Nazareth and Him crucified. Just as He died for our sins, was buried and was raised up the third day. I would suggest so too will the earth and heavens go through a process of purging, and "death" of sorts, until they are "resurrected", as the "New Heavens and New Earth" (2 Pet. 3:7-13, Rev. 20:9-11, 21:1-5). Of course, this is an interpretation of the matter, so place your trust in God, the Father, Almighty and Jesus Christ of Nazareth for the truth of all of this. Praise the LORD God Almighty and His only begotten Son, Jesus Christ of Nazareth. Alleluia and praise the LORD. Amen and Amen.

Some scholars and "scientists" say that the earth is billions of years old, although the thought on how old has changed over time. However, this idea may go against an approximately 6000 year old earth according to the Biblical account, as of the date of writing this book in 2018 A.D. There are obviously two sides to the interpretation, either it is literal or there is room for interpretation (2 Pet. 1:20). Either the seven day creation was just that, or it was representative of some other larger timeline, although to make it simple I truly believe that it is literal. It is possible that the earth itself "without form and void", had been around for some length of time before the first day of creating it with form and substance, and it is possible that it had been in some previous cataclysmic event similar to what is spoken about at the end of Biblical history for this present earth we live on today. But to think about all of that any deeper to me would be vain. Because that is the past, and the earth and all the indications of life that are in it, fossils and any other signs of life are not likely older than approximately 6000 years as of the date of writing this book in 2018 A.D., according to Biblical records. Nevertheless as the Holy Bible says, "…with God all things are possible." (Matt. 19:26). Another example of this is, the same Hebrew word translated, "fill" at the beginning, is used as "replenish" to describe the commandment of God to Noah after the flood, that is, "replenish the earth" (Gen. 1:22, 28; Gen. 9:1). The question then is possibly open ended, the earth may have been inhabited before our present Biblical account, by a former earth and its inhabitants that was destroyed by an asteroid or some other cataclysmic event, or the beginning of all beginnings may have very well started with Adam and Eve approximately six thousand years ago from the date of writing this book in 2018 A.D.. Most important is to understand that due to Adam and Eve's transgression, we are all appointed once to die and then the judgement (Gen. 3, Heb. 9:27). So to spend too much time on history of possibly millions of years ago and not focus on the main message which is, Salvation in Jesus Christ of Nazareth, would be unfruitful to say the least. The important thing to remember is there was a beginning for this earth and the inhabitants that live on earth today (Gen. 1-2:3). We came from our earthly ancestors Adam and Eve and there is an "end" so to speak to this earth in its present form according to the Holy Bible (2 Pet. 3:7-13, Rev. 20:9-15). There will be a judgment day, and there will be a new heaven, a new earth and a new Jerusalem (Rev. 21:1-5). God is in the creation and restoration business (Matt. 12:13, 17:11; Mark 8:25, John 1:1-3, Gal. 6:1, Rev. 4:11). This is the beauty of Jesus' message of salvation in His Holy name and eternal life; it never ends (Isa. 9:7, Matt. 6:33). Alleluia and praise the LORD. Amen and Amen.

Psalm 33:9 says, "For he spake, and it was *done;* he commanded, and it stood fast.". This is in regards to the creation of the world that we live in. Isaiah 48:3 says, "I have declared the former things from the beginning; and they went forth out of my mouth, and I shewed them; I did *them* suddenly, and they came to pass.". God's creation week in Genesis 1, according to these two verses ought to be taken literally. Isaiah 51:6 says, "Lift up your eyes to the heavens, and look upon the earth beneath: for the heavens shall vanish away like smoke, and the earth shall wax old like a garment, and they that dwell therein shall die in like manner: but my salvation shall be for ever, and my righteousness shall not be abolished.". This speaks of things to come, but also the greatest truth, which is that God's kingdom, His salvation is forever (Matt. 6:13, Luke 1:33, John 6:51, 58; Rev. 14:6). What God has done with this earth and what He will do in the future is all His business and only partly ours, as our lives are temporary here (Gen. 3:19, Dan. 2:20-22). Our main focus should be to follow Him and help fulfill God's plan for earth and those whom inhabit it, so that when our time comes to give up the ghost and for Jesus to receive us, that we are prepared (John 14:1-3). Although God is unchanging, it would seem that we will be changed, according to at least a few references in the Holy Bible (Ps. 102:25-27; Prov. 24:21, 22; Mal. 3:6, 1 Cor. 15:51, 52; 2 Cor. 3:18, Phil. 3:20, 21; Heb. 1:10-12). Although He did not desire us to "change", "fall" or disobey Him in the beginning, we did, and have continued to throughout the history of earth according to the Holy Bible (Gen. 3, 6:5, 8:21; Isa. 24:5, Jer. 2:11, Dan.

4:16). So the reality is we need to "change", repent and believe in Jesus Christ of Nazareth to be saved, in order to become children of God, as Adam and Eve were created in the beginning. According to Solomon, we cannot and will not know all that God is doing from beginning to end, because He has put the world in our heart (Eccl. 3:11). But for those who love Him and obey Him, He will reveal His mysteries to us (Matt. 13:11, Luke 8:10). Follow God and Jesus Christ of Nazareth and His mysteries will be revealed to you. And last, God is a God of order, and He gives us a spirit of a sound mind, not fear (1 Cor. 14:40, 2 Tim. 1:7). Accepting God's Holy Spirit brings peace of mind. If your thoughts are not bringing you peace, then they are not likely of God, so just ask God to help you let them go. He desires for each of us to live in His peace, with Him, and God willing, with all of mankind in the name of His only begotten Son, Jesus Christ of Nazareth. He died on the cross for the forgiveness of our sins, He was buried and the third day He arose to give us the hope and promise of eternal life in His Holy name. Alleluia and praise the LORD. Amen and Amen.

Conclusion

Understanding that there is a literal hell and the truth of it is great, but more importantly is to remember that Jesus Christ of Nazareth did not come to condemn mankind, but to save us (John 3:17). This is the key to understanding the concept of hell. It is seemingly a temporary state of being for those whom believe in Jesus Christ of Nazareth and have given their life to Him. As the Holy Bible says, "O death, where *is* thy sting? O grave, where *is* thy victory? The sting of death *is* sin; and the strength of sin *is* the law. But thanks *be* to God, which giveth us the victory through our Lord Jesus Christ." (1 Cor. 15:55-57). For those who believe in and follow Jesus Christ of Nazareth, death cannot contain us, if we have accepted God's Holy Spirit we have become children of God and God's Holy Spirit cannot be destroyed. Our corruptible bodies may perish, but our spiritual bodies will live on forever, and if God so wills it, He will give us another fleshly body to live in, in eternity. This is the power and mystery of God, that those who trust in and obey Him will never die. Jesus proved this at His resurrection. Jesus conquered death. He conquered the destroyer and there is no power in heaven or earth that can reverse Jesus Christ of Nazareth's work at the cross of cavalry (Luke 23:33). Psalm 68:20 says, "*He that is* our God *is* the God of salvation; and unto GOD the Lord *belong* the issues from death.". All power in heaven and in earth has been given to Jesus Christ of Nazareth, and He has the keys of hell and of death (Matt. 28:18, Rev. 1:18). God is a bright light and light travels in a straight line until reflected or interrupted (John 1:4, 5, 7, 9; 3:19-21, 8:12, 9:5, 12:35, 36, 46; 1 Tim. 6:13-16). The point is, thinking about the past and assuming ideas that are not written in the Holy Bible is unfruitful. This earth and all that are in it are headed in a certain direction and ultimately the past will not be repeated on a grand scale likely, in so much that the "New Heavens and New Earth", will have no record of this present heaven and earth. Our memories of this life will perish, as the Holy Bible says, and we will be given a new body, with a renewed spirit and soul (2 Cor. 4:16, Eph. 4:21-24, Col. 3:10, 11). This is the entire point of repentance and being forgiven, it is to come back to God, the giver of life, not dwelling on the sins and corruption of the past. And we can do this by accepting Jesus Christ of Nazareth as our Lord and Saviour to heal us and forgive us. He died on the cross for the forgiveness of our sins, He was buried and the third day He arose to give us the hope and promise of eternal life in His Holy name. Alleluia and praise the LORD. Amen and Amen.

In about the fifth century B.C., Daniel was a prophet of God of the tribe of Judah and Belshazzar, Son and successor of king Nebuchadnezzar was king of Babylon, and Belshazzar experienced a miraculous visitation by God, whose hand wrote on the wall of the palace a message to him that needed interpretation (Dan. 5:5-12, 24-28). Daniel 5:11 and 12 say, "There is a man in thy kingdom, in whom *is* the spirit of the holy gods; and in the days of thy father light and understanding and wisdom, like the wisdom of the gods, was found in him; whom the king Nebuchadnezzar thy father, the king, *I say*, thy father, made master of the magicians, astrologers, Chaldeans, *and* soothsayers; Forasmuch as an excellent spirit, and knowledge, and understanding, interpreting of dreams, and shewing of hard sentences, and dissolving of doubts, were found in the same Daniel, whom the king named Belteshazzar: now let Daniel be called, and he will shew the interpretation.". The reality in all of these interpretations by myself or anyone else is that, if a person is led by the Holy Spirit, we can be gifted to reveal mysteries that God has revealed to us. But the great and wonderful reality is that God is not a respecter of persons and He reveals His truth to all of us, if we obey Him (Acts 10:34). I have heard that we ought to let the Holy Bible interpret itself and truly this is the easiest way to move forward in your relationship with God, the Father, Almighty in His only begotten Son, Jesus Christ of Nazareth's Holy name, through His Holy Spirit and with others . The Holy Bible without a shadow of a doubt is indeed the inspired "Word of God". If you are in doubt, ask God to provide for you in your wavering spirit, and ask Him to provide you with the spirit of Truth, His Holy Spirit, to reveal to you all things (John 14:26). Allow Him to dwell in you, through the acceptance of the free gift of the Holy Spirit given to us (Eph. 2:8, 9). This is the Spirit of life, and we can receive this Spirit by repenting and believing on the name of Jesus Christ of Nazareth, the only begotten Son of God. He died on the cross for the forgiveness of our sins, He was buried and the third day He arose to give us the hope and promise of eternal life in His Holy name. Alleluia and praise the LORD. He is the giver of life, revealer of truth and Saviour of the whole world. Trust in Him and you will be redeemed from this corrupt world and the fallen nature of man that lies within it, forever more. Alleluia and praise the LORD. Amen and Amen. In chapter six I will discuss the last portion of the topic of hell, speaking of the "lake of fire" amongst other similar ideas, read on to learn more. To God be the glory in the truth of all these interpretations. Alleluia and praise the LORD. Amen and Amen.

Discussion: Purity

> "Marriage *is* honorable in all, and the bed undefiled: but
> whoremongers and adulterers God will judge."
> - Hebrews 13:4

Jesus Christ of Nazareth is "Faithful" and abiding in Christ gives us His "faithfulness" (Rev. 19:11). The apostle, Paul, said it is not a sin to be married (1 Cor. 7:28). Of course, this ought to be common sense, as marriage is spoken of often in the Holy Bible of God as a commandment of God (Gen. 2:24, Mal. 2:15, Matt. 19:4-6). But as the Holy Bible of God says, people would pervert the gospel message, as well as do evil things, against God's commands and knowledge, etc. (Dan. 11:35, 2 Tim. 3:1-5). God commanded man to "…leave his father and his mother, and shall cleave unto his wife: and they shall be one flesh.", from the beginning starting with Adam and Eve (Gen. 2:24). Throughout the Holy Bible, God's commands are used to uphold and protect the marriage institution as a sacred and Holy union. Jesus Christ of Nazareth confirms this during His ministry saying, "…What therefore God hath joined together, let not man put asunder." (Matt. 19:6). He does speak of eunuchs being either made so of themselves, of man, or some of God's choosing (Matt. 19:12). But on the whole, the Holy Bible makes clear that an "undefiled" marriage is a worthy goal to attain in this life, by and through God's Holy Spirit in Jesus Christ of Nazareth's Holy name, the only begotten Son of God, and God, the Father, Almighty and, as God wills it, forever more in Christ Jesus of Nazareth's Holy name (Heb. 13:4). Husband and wife are said to be "heirs together" (1 Pet. 3:7). Is it any wonder the adversary attempts to steal our reward, he is jealous of something he cannot attain by himself (John 10:10). This would be the reason for bodily perversions of all kinds. That said, our bodies are created as temples of the living God (2 Cor. 6:16). We ought to learn first to treat our own body with good health, in the soul, mind and physical body, before God will trust us with another human being. This is why our early childhood, and "teenage" years are important in developing our relationship with God, the Father, Almighty, and His only begotten Son, Jesus Christ of Nazareth through the Holy Spirit of God, and mankind, as this sets the stage for our grown-up years. Nevertheless, Jesus Christ of Nazareth died on the cross to forgive us our sins, not to condemn us, He was buried and the third day He arose to give us the hope and promise of eternal life in His Holy name. So no matter where you may be at in life; married, divorced, unmarried, etc., you can always be forgiven in Christ Jesus of Nazareth's Holy name, first and foremost, and God willing He will open doors for you to move forward with a spouse, as He wills. Jeremiah says in Lamentations, "For the LORD will not cast off for ever: But though he cause grief, yet will he have compassion according to the multitude of his mercies. For he doth not afflict willingly nor grieve the children of men. To crush under his feet all the prisoners of the earth. To turn aside the right of a man before the face of the most High, To subvert a man in his cause, the LORD approveth not." (Lam. 3:31-36). God desires us to fulfill His purposes for us in this life, and He gives us the desires of our hearts (Ps. 37:4). So keep this in mind when considering the questions in this chapter's discussion section and where you stand in your relationship with your Creator and others here on earth, all for the glory of God, the Father, Almighty and His only begotten Son, Jesus Christ of Nazareth. Alleluia and praise the LORD. Thanks be to our God, and His only begotten Son, Jesus Christ of Nazareth, for all things. Amen and Amen.

Discussion Questions

1. What does God say about our bodies being His temple?

   _____

   _____

   _____

2. How are we cleansed?

   _____

   _____

   _____

3. How is our purity maintained?

   _____

   _____

   _____

Chapter 6: Hell – Lake of fire

"They are dead, they shall not live; *they are* deceased, they shall not rise: therefore
hast thou visited and destroyed them, and made all their memory to perish."
- Isaiah 26:14

Introduction

Certainly the topic of the judgement of the wicked is not a pleasant one to say the least. However, in order for God to be a just and perfect God, His word must be true, so He must punish those who do not obey Him or desire to follow Him. God is eternal, good, peaceful, restful, abundant, merciful, forgiving, glorious, joyful, kind, etc. (Gal. 5:22, 23). He does not change (Mal. 3:6). How could a God with these qualities allow for anything less? He cannot and will not. So for the remainder of this chapter I will discuss the topic of the lake of fire, eternal punishment and death in general. However, ultimately I will speak about the wonderful news for those whom repent of their evil ways and follow the Maker of heaven and earth. Glory be to God, in the name of Jesus Christ of Nazareth, God's only begotten Son, Redeemer and Saviour of the whole world. Alleluia and praise the LORD. Amen and Amen.

Final "battle"

Psalm 11:6 says, "Upon the wicked he shall rain snares, fire and brimstone, and an horrible tempest: *this shall be* the portion of their cup.". Psalm 55:18-23 says, "He hath delivered my soul in peace from the battle *that was* against me: for there were many with me. God shall hear, and afflict them, even he that abideth of old. Selah. Because they have no changes, therefore they fear not God. He hath put forth his hands against such as be at peace with him: he hath broken his covenant. *The words* of his mouth were smoother than butter, but war *was* in his heart: his words were softer than oil, yet *were* they drawn swords. Cast thy burden upon the LORD, and he shall sustain thee: he shall never suffer the righteous to be moved.". Jesus said He came to bring a sword on the earth, not peace (Matt. 10:34). The reality is God has some unfinished business with rebellious mankind. It has been, is and will continue to be fulfilled through Biblical prophecy in the news, and the world we live in today and in events to come. But more importantly, the reality is that we have been redeemed from judgement, anger, war and God's wrath by Jesus Christ of Nazareth. All of the wrath, anger, confusion and curses that come from disobedience to God's commands and laws, were taken upon Jesus Christ of Nazareth on the cross for us (Deut. 28:15-68, Matt. 28:18, Col. 1:20). We are redeemed sinners, washed clean by the blood of Jesus Christ of Nazareth, whom gave His life for us on the cross, if we accept Him as our Saviour (Col. 1:20, Heb. 9:12-14). Have you? If so, praise the Lord. This gift of redemption and eternal life in Jesus Christ of Nazareth is a free gift, and we receive it by faith, which is also a gift from God (Eph. 2:8, 9). If you desire eternal life, ask God's Holy Spirit to come into your life to dwell with you, in you and through you forever. God's Holy Spirit is the Spirit of life (Rom. 8:2). God is a Spirit (John 4:24). Like Jesus Christ of Nazareth, we will also have the opportunity to be resurrected and receive eternal life after our bodies give up the ghost in this life (1 Cor. 15:51, 52). Praise the Lord God Almighty. Alleluia and praise the LORD. Amen and Amen.

Revelation 20:8 and 9 speak of a final "battle" of Gog and Magog against the camp of the saints and "fire" coming down from heaven to consume them (Nah. 1:9, Isa. 29:1-7, Rev. 20:8, 9). Gog is not a listed descendant of Japheth; Magog is (Gen. 10:2). The only Gog mentioned in the Holy Bible is a descendant of Reuben, one of the sons of Israel (1 Chr. 5:4). This relationship between Gog and Magog could be due to the fact that Reuben, likely mostly modern France, was one of the first colonizers of the "new world" and isles of the world, along with the other European empires, associated with the "lost tribes of Israel", and the "native" population amongst them which likely were descendants of Magog, a son of Japheth (Gen. 10:2, 1 Chr. 5:4). This is how Gog and Magog are likely related in both Ezekiel 38, 39 and Revelation 20. This is of course an interpretation, but hopefully an accurate one, God willing. More information on the descendants of the tribes of this earth can be read about in another book I wrote "The Origin of Mankind", but the Holy Bible simply states the only tribes they could be and whom they could descend from naturally, that is Reuben of Israel, of Isaac, of Abraham, of Shem and Magog of Japheth, from after the flood, both sons of Noah (Gen. 10:2, 11, 17:19, 25:26, 29:32; 1 Chr. 5:4). Some have suggested that this verse is to be taken from a spiritual perspective however, not literally, but I would say the literal interpretation, would likely be similar to the truth anyhow. That being said, God knows the truth in all of this for certain. To God be the glory in the truth of these matters, in the name of His only begotten Son, Jesus Christ of Nazareth. Alleluia and praise the LORD. This "battle" is not to be mistaken with Ezekiel's vision of war in chapters 38 and 39 of his book. The battles may be similar in nature, but there is most certainly one just prior to the "Messianic age", which I wrote about in my book "Time, times and a dividing of time – what did John really see?" and is likely part of the time known in the Holy Bible as the "Great Tribulation" as of the date of writing this book in 2018 A.D. (Matt. 24:21, Rev. 2:22, 7:14). The final "battle" of Gog and Magog is when Satan is loosed for a little season at the end of the "Messianic age" (Rev. 20:7). This is the time just prior to the final judgement of all of mankind, with all those listed in the Lamb's book of life receiving eternal life. The end result is the "new heavens and new earth" and the "new Jerusalem" for all whom have repented and believe in the life giving name of Jesus Christ of Nazareth (Rev. 21:1-5). All of which has been spoken of in this book and most clearly in the book of Revelation chapters 20, 21 and 22, as well as Isaiah 65, etc., in the Holy Bible of God. Alleluia and praise the LORD. Amen and Amen.

I have spoken in previous chapters about the apostle, Peter's, second epistle that included the heavens and earth melting with fervent heat (2 Pet. 3:7-13). We could consider the lake of fire to be like the sun, the Holy Spirit, or even the inner super-heated core of the earth, reference appendices B and C for some more details of the sun's possible involvement in all of these prophecies (Rev. 19:20, 20:10, 20:14, 15). Simply put, here on earth, the "lake of fire" could be like the lava of a volcano. It is hard to say, what exactly God is describing, but it is sufficient to say, that we do not desire to be there in the long run. Albeit an active volcano would be a perfect example of a lake of fire, and likely is what God is describing. As volcanoes have been depicted in movies as a place to do "sacrifices" to "appease" the "gods" and may have been used literally for the same, but the reality is in Jesus Christ of Nazareth. Alleluia and praise the LORD. This is where faith in Jesus Christ of Nazareth comes in, with the hope, and His promise of eternal life in His Holy name. We cannot "work" our way into heaven, but our "works" and "words" will be judged someday (Matt. 12:36, 37; John 6:29, Rev. 2:23, 20:12, 13). We need to ultimately follow Jesus and believe on Him (John 1:12, 13; 6:29, 7:39; 9:35, 36). The gift of eternal life is exactly that, a gift (Eph. 2:8, 9). The Holy Bible says not to fear the one who kills the body, but to "fear" the one who kills both body and soul in "hell" (Matt. 10:28). I have heard that this is a "reverent" fear, fearing God with wonderment at His awesome ability. The New Testament says, "...workout your own salvation with fear and trembling." (Phil. 2:12). And the Holy Bible says, "The fear of the LORD *is* the beginning of wisdom..." (Ps. 111:10). The point is that we are to listen to Him, obey Him and follow Him first and foremost. This is what God desires, a loving relationship with His creation (Matt. 22:37). He loves us and that is why He gave His only begotten Son, Jesus Christ of Nazareth to die for us on the cross for the forgiveness of our sins, He was buried and the third day He arose to give us the hope and promise of eternal life in His Holy name. Trust in Jesus Christ of Nazareth and His promises for you and you will have eternal life in His Holy name. Alleluia and praise the LORD. Amen and Amen.

One point of view of the lake of fire could be the Holy Spirit. The Holy Spirit, God, the ministering "angels", our tongues, even Jesus, are all referenced in the likeness of "fire" in the Holy Bible (Deut. 4:24, Ps. 104:4, Jam. 3:5, 6; Rev. 1:14, 10:1). So the lake of fire could be representative of the "wicked" being burned up by the Holy Spirit, which God talks about regarding the wicked, and in parables the tares and chaff being "consumed", the example of Sodom and Gomorrah are a perfect example of this (Gen. 18, 19; Matt. 3:12, 10:15, 13:30; Luke 3:17, 17:28-30; Rom. 9:29, 2 Pet. 2:6-10, Jude 1:7). We are either consumed by "evil" or "good" in this life. And things can change, the wicked can repent and the righteous can fall away (Ezek. 18:21-24). This is why we need to be diligent in our relationship with God first and foremost and with the rest of His creation (Heb. 11:6, 12:14-16; 1 Pet. 1:10, 11; 2 Pet. 3:14). This is referred to as a race of sort by the apostle, Paul, love is longsuffering, patient, eternal, God is love (Rom. 9:16, 1 Cor. 9:24-27, Gal. 2:2, 5:7; Phil. 2:16, Heb. 12:1, 2; 1 John 4:8). And if we are to be "like" God someday we need to develop the same character as Him, this includes, "suffering" or enduring unto the end (Matt. 10:22). Alleluia and praise the LORD. The proof in this is Jesus enduring on the cross for us. He said, "...My God, my God, why hast thou forsaken me?" (Matt. 27:46, Mark 15:34). David said the same when he was enduring his enemies (Ps. 22:1). The point is that our relationship with God does not stop and even to our final breath we need to be having that conversation with Him. We can either submit to His Holy Spirit and be consumed in it now or be consumed by it at the day of judgement. No matter the case, at the name of Jesus Christ of Nazareth, eventually, every knee should bow (Ps. 22:29, 72:9; Isa. 45:23, Rom. 14:7-12, Phil. 2:10, 11). Patience is a key in developing our relationship with Him in this life (Luke 21:19, 2 Pet. 1:6, Rev. 14:12). And more importantly a conversation with Him to start, praying to God and asking Him to forgive us our sins, accepting the blood of Jesus Christ of Nazareth into our life, to wash away all of our sins and start a new life in His Holy name. Alleluia and praise the LORD. Amen and Amen.

Eternal Hell or perishing forever...

Revelation 21:8 makes clear what this "lake of fire" actually is, the "second death.". There must not be a place where the wicked are suffering eternally in a blazing fire, they are simply put, dead, no thoughts, just gone forever, perished (Ps. 9:6, 17; Ps. 10:15, 16). Isaiah 41:11 and 12 say, "Behold, all they that were incensed against thee shall be ashamed and confounded: they shall be as nothing; and they that strive with thee shall perish. Thou shalt seek them, and shalt not find them, *even* them that contended with thee: they that war against thee shall be as nothing, and as a thing of nought.". Ezekiel 28 seems to go into detail about the "King of tyre"; this of course was likely a real person, a descendant possibly of Japheth, one of the sons of Noah (Gen. 10:2). But this prophecy may actually be describing Satan as well. If this is the case we can know his end for certain. This may also describe fallen man in general, adorned with similar jewels as the tribes of Israel are represented by on the High Priests breastplate and in the "new Jerusalem" (Ex. 28:15-21, Ezek. 28:13, Rev. 21:19). The point is that Satan and his "fallen" angels are very much described as fleshly in the end, and can likely perish just like any fleshly person can. If God gave His only begotten Son, Jesus Christ of Nazareth, as the Son of man, why would He view Satan any differently? God is not a respecter of persons. The account of Lucifer, the "light bearer", in some respects if not all, is the history of mankind, we were made in the "image of God", we fell from God's grace and truth in the Garden of Eden and have done wickedness ever since (Gen. 1:26, 27; 3, 6:5, 8:21; Isa. 14:12). Jesus came to save us and forgive us our sins. This is the true image bearer of God, Jesus Christ of Nazareth. I am not suggesting that there are not evil spirits, as well as good, but what I am saying is that in Jesus Christ of Nazareth is the truth. Jesus very clearer cast out devils from people, and had His time of trial with Satan in the wilderness (Matt. 4:1-11, 12:28; Mark 1:12, 13, 39; Luke 4:1-13, 11:20). So there may be evil spirits, but we do not need to fear them nor obey them. Because in Jesus Christ of Nazareth we have the truth, the way and the life of God, the Father, Almighty and everlasting life in His only begotten Son, Jesus Christ of Nazareth's Holy name. Praise the Lord God Almighty and His only begotten Son, Jesus Christ of Nazareth, Saviour of the whole world and Redeemer of all mankind. Alleluia and praise the LORD. Amen and Amen.

Isaiah 27:1 says, "In that day the LORD with his sore and great and strong sword shall punish leviathan the piercing serpent, even leviathan that crooked serpent; and he shall slay the dragon that *is* in the sea.". In another book, I have interpreted "leviathan" as the cumulative fallen creation, as God describes in the book of Job (Job 41). And this interpretation would go along with Satan being a man, fleshly, in the end, which can perish just like the rest of us. Nevertheless, the point is there is an end to evil. The Holy Bible admonishes that there is an end to sin (Dan. 9:24). It is our sin that separates us from God, David felt this separation, and even Jesus Christ of Nazareth felt this separation on the cross because He took our sins upon Himself (Isa. 59:2). They both said, "My God, my God, why hast thou forsaken me?" (Ps. 22:1, Matt. 27:46, Mark 15:34). For them the feeling of being forsaken by God was temporary, but in Jesus Christ of Nazareth we have eternal life. Regarding destruction or perishing, the likely worst case scenario will be that we will no longer exist. 2 Thessalonians 1:9 states that for those who disobey, they will be "...punished with everlasting destruction...". When something is destroyed it no longer exists. Psalm 37:20 says, "But the wicked shall perish, and the enemies of the LORD *shall be* as the fat of lambs: they shall consume; into smoke shall they consume away.". Jeremiah 10:11 says, "Thus shall ye say unto them, The gods that have not made the heavens and the earth, *even* they shall perish from the earth, and from under these heavens.". Hebrews 2:14 says, speaking of Jesus Christ of Nazareth, "Forasmuch then as the children are partakers of flesh and blood, he also himself likewise took part of the same; that through death he might destroy him that had the power of death, that is, the devil...". 2 Peter 2:12 says, "But these, as natural brute beasts, made to be taken and destroyed, speak evil of the things that they understand not; and shall utterly perish in their own corruption;". Jude 1:4 says, "For there are certain men crept in unawares, who were before of old ordained to this condemnation, ungodly men, turning the grace of our God into lasciviousness, and denying the only Lord God, and our Lord Jesus Christ.". The entire Epistle of Jude would be a good section of the Holy Bible to read on the subject. Psalm 1:6 says, "For the LORD knoweth the way of the righteous: but the way of the ungodly shall perish.". Simply put we will be judged by our own words and actions (Matt. 12:37, Rev. 2:23, 20:12). But Glory be to God, that we have been redeemed from condemnation and sin by the Holy blood of Jesus Christ of Nazareth. Alleluia and praise the LORD. Amen and Amen.

God inhabits eternity (Isa. 57:15). And we have an everlasting covenant in Jesus Christ of Nazareth (Heb. 13:20, 21). God cannot allow sin into His habitation, it must be destroyed, and the memory thereof (Rev. 21:27). Nehemiah 1:5 says, "And said, I beseech thee, O LORD God of heaven, the great and terrible God, that keepeth covenant and mercy for them that love him and observe his commandments…". Nehemiah 4:14 says, "And I looked, and rose up, and said unto the nobles, and to the rulers, and to the rest of the people, Be not ye afraid of them: remember the LORD, *which is* great and terrible, and fight for your brethren, your sons, and your daughters, your wives, and your houses.". Psalm 99:3 says, "Let them praise thy great and terrible name; *for* it *is* holy.". Joel 2:31 says, the "… great and terrible day of the LORD…". God is great to those whom are going to be raised to salvation forever and terrible to those whom will perish in the "lake of fire" forever. 2 Peter 3:9 says, "The Lord is not slack concerning his promise, as some men count slackness; but is longsuffering to us-ward, not willing that any should perish, but that all should come to repentance.". God gives us the freewill to repent; God gives us a certain responsibility over our life and death, and whether or not we accept the gift of eternal life in the name of Jesus Christ of Nazareth, through repentance, the forgiveness of our sin and obedience to Him. God's goodness brings us to repentance (Rom. 2:4). Matthew 18:14 says, "Even so it is not the will of your Father which is in heaven, that one of these little ones should perish.". John 10:28 says, "And I give unto them eternal life; and they shall never perish, neither shall any *man* pluck them out of my hand.". This is a promise to those whom put all their life in the hands of God, the Father, Almighty in the name of His only begotten Son, Jesus Christ of Nazareth. Praise the Lord God Almighty and His only begotten Son, Jesus Christ of Nazareth. Alleluia and praise the LORD. Amen and Amen.

Lake of Fire

Is not the lake of fire the "Holy Spirit"? If God is a Spirit and He has the ability to kill both body and soul in hell, then it only makes sense that the lake of fire is God's Holy Spirit. The Holy Bible says that "…God *is* a consuming fire…." (Deut. 4:24, Heb. 12:29). But He also says, that those who believe in Him will not be consumed, because of His mercy (Lam. 3:22, Mal. 3:6). This promise is made clear when Shadrach, Meshach and Abednego survived the fiery furnace of king Nebuchadnezzar, along with one whom looked like the "Son of God" (Dan. 3). This is why Jesus came to earth to save us from eternal death, and the curse that was put on mankind from the beginning, after eating from the tree of knowledge of good and evil (Gen. 3). Jesus came to give us life and life more abundantly (John 10:10). 1 Peter 3:10-14 says, "For he that will love life, and see good days, let him refrain his tongue from evil, and his lips that they speak no guile: Let him eschew evil, and do good; let him seek peace, and ensue it. For the eyes of the Lord *are* over the righteous, and his ears *are open* unto their prayers: but the face of the Lord *is* against them that do evil. And who *is* he that will harm you, if ye be followers of that which is good? But and if ye suffer for righteousness' sake, happy *are ye:* and be not afraid of their terror, neither be troubled…". Who will be doing the judging? Romans 2:14 says, "For when the Gentiles, which have not the law, do by nature the things contained in the law, these, having not the law, are a law unto themselves…". We will be judged by our words and works (Matt. 12:37, Rev. 2:23, 20:12). 1 John 3:15 says, "Whosoever hateth his brother is a murderer: and ye know that no murderer hath eternal life abiding in him.". Do we really need to judge or condemn? NOT really AT ALL. Isaiah 26:19 speaks of the resurrection of the dead, "Thy dead *men* shall live, *together with* my dead body shall they arise. Awake and sing, ye that dwell in dust: for thy dew *is as* the dew of herbs, and the earth shall cast out the dead.". This is speaking of the second resurrection and final judgment. Matthew 5:22 says, "But I say unto you, That whosoever is angry with his brother without a cause shall be in danger of the judgment: and whosoever shall say to his brother, Raca, shall be in danger of the council: but whosoever shall say, Thou fool, shall be in danger of hell fire.". Understanding that we are made up of body, soul and spirit, and these are all in agreement is important (1 Thess. 5:23, 1 John 5:8). This is why it is possible that we can die twice (Jude 1:12). We die once in the body, and if we have not accepted Jesus Christ of Nazareth in this life as our Saviour, or otherwise judged unworthy by our works, our souls will perish in the "lake of fire", that is the second death (Rev. 20:12-15). Again 2 Peter 3:9 says, "The Lord is not slack concerning his promise, as some men count slackness; but is longsuffering to us-ward, not willing that any should perish, but that all should come to repentance.". Alleluia and praise the LORD. Amen and Amen.

For the final judgement, the fruit of the "wicked" are destined to wither and perish. Jude 1:6 says, "And the angels which kept not their first estate, but left their own habitation, he hath reserved in everlasting chains under darkness unto the judgment of the great day.". 2 Peter 2:4 says, "For if God spared not the angels that sinned, but cast *them* down to hell, and delivered *them* into chains of darkness, to be reserved unto judgement;". This is the last "hell", mentioned in the New Testament Greek, tartaroo, which is said to be the deepest abyss of hades, Strong's number 5020, which could also be referring to the bottomless pit mentioned in the book of Revelation (Rev. 9:11, 11:7, 17:8, 20:1, 3). But Jesus has the key to the bottomless pit (Matt. 28:18, Rev. 1:18, 20:1). Jesus cast out devils that said, "…art thou come hither to torment us before the time?" (Matt. 8:29). Even the devils knew Jesus was coming to judge. Psalm 21:7-12 says, "For the king trusteth in the LORD, and through the mercy of the most High he shall not be moved. Thine hand shall find out all thine enemies: thy right hand shall find out those that hate thee. Thou shalt make them as a fiery oven in the time of thine anger: the LORD shall swallow them up in his wrath, and the fire shall devour them. Their fruit shalt thou destroy from the earth, and their seed from among the children of men. For they intended evil against thee: they imagined a mischievous device, *which* they are not able *to perform*. Therefore shalt thou make them turn their back, *when* thou shalt make ready *thine arrows* upon thy strings against the face of them.". Isaiah 40:24 says, "Yea, they shall not be planted; yea, they shall not be sown: yea, their stock shall not take root in the earth: and he shall also blow upon them, and they shall wither, and the whirlwind shall take them away as stubble.". The book of Daniel hints at it (Dan. 12:1, 2). Revelation 20, 21, and 22 certainly detail it. The epistles of Peter speak about it, Paul spoke of it, John spoke of it in his epistles, Jesus spoke of it in the gospels, and so did the Old Testament prophets and others; that is the judgement. Psalm 7:9 says, "Oh let the wickedness of the wicked come to an end; but establish the just: for the righteous God trieth the hearts and reins.". Psalm 62:12 says, "Also unto thee, O Lord, *belongeth* mercy: for thou renderest to every man according to his work.". Eternal life is our choice. Revelation 3:20 says, "Behold, I stand at the door, and knock: if any man hear my voice, and open the door, I will come in to him, and will sup with him, and he with me.". Ezekiel 18:32 says, "For I have no pleasure in the death of him that dieth, saith the Lord God: wherefore turn *yourselves,* and live ye.". Alleluia and praise the LORD. Amen and Amen.

This is the call to repentance that has been taking place since Adam and Eve fell in the Garden of Eden (Gen. 3). The call that John the Baptist preached preparing the way for Jesus Christ of Nazareth whom continued the message with signs, miracles and wonders following (Matt. 3:2, 11, 12; 4:17). Not only did He continue the message, but He died on the cross, the Son of God, to take our sins upon Him to forgive us our sin. If you believe it, He has taken on your sins on the cross, He was buried and three days later arose to give you the hope and promise of eternal life in His Holy name. You have been forgiven of your sins. Do you believe? If so, repent and believe the gospel, be baptized in the Holy Spirit and follow Jesus Christ of Nazareth unto the end. Then He will give you eternal life. He healed a man with a withered hand, but He also cursed a fig tree that did not have fruit (Matt. 12:10-13, 21:19; Mark 3:1-5, Luke 6:6-10). He also spoke of those whom do not abide in Him, whom would wither and be cast into fire and burned (John 15:6, Jude 1:12). If we put our trust in Jesus Christ of Nazareth, we will bare much fruit, this is a promise He has given us. But our fruit, our works will be tried, and the works that are not of God will be burned up (1 Cor. 3:13-15). That is God's way of purifying His creation, and maintaining the purity, righteousness and justness of His everlasting Kingdom. Praise the LORD God Almighty, and His only begotten Son, Jesus Christ of Nazareth. Jesus came to heal, not to condemn, if you place your life in His hands He will lift you up and strengthen you, I promise you this. Praise Him and worship Him. Do not take my word for it, let Jesus Christ of Nazareth into your life, and see for yourself His goodness and life everlasting in His Holy name. Alleluia and praise the LORD. We have a better hope. Ephesians 3:17-19 says, "That Christ may dwell in your hearts by faith; that ye, being rooted and grounded in love, May be able to comprehend with all saints what *is* the breadth, and length, and depth, and height; And to know the love of Christ, which passeth knowledge, that ye might be filled with all the fulness of God.". The width, length, depth and height of this love can be seen in the "new Jerusalem" as interpreted in chapter three; it gives the great details with which God has planned out our lives here on earth today and in the world to come (Rev. 21:16). 1 Corinthians 7:31 says, "And they that use this world, as not abusing *it:* for the fashion of this world passeth away.". 1 John 2:17 says, "And the world passeth away, and the lust thereof: but he that doeth the will of God abideth for ever.". Matthew 24:34 and 35 say, "Verily I say unto you, This generation shall not pass, till all these things be fulfilled. Heaven and earth shall pass away, but my words shall not pass away.". In Christ we become a "new creature", our former things, old self, sin, etc., pass away (2 Cor. 5:17). God says of Himself, "...I the LORD, the first, and with the last; I *am* he." (Isa. 41:4). Whoever is the last person here on earth, God will be with them. He makes a promise of this, in Jesus Christ of Nazareth's Holy name. Jesus says, "...I am with you alway, *even* unto the end of the world. Amen." (Matt. 28:20). Praise the Lord God Almighty and His only begotten Son, Jesus Christ of Nazareth. Alleluia and praise the LORD. Amen and Amen.

Conclusion

The book of Jude does a great job of pulling out some realities of the world we live in today, as of the date of writing this book in 2018 A.D. I had spoken on the subject some in other books, especially the book I wrote, "Time, Times and a dividing of Times – What did John really see?". But the subject is about "oil", "pollution" and vehicular "technology" in general (Isa. 9:5). Jude 1:6 and 7 say, "And the angels which kept not their first estate, but left their own habitation, he hath reserved in everlasting chains under darkness unto the judgment of the great day. Even as Sodom and Gomorrha, and the cities about them in like manner, giving themselves over to fornication, and going after strange flesh, are set forth for an example, suffering the vengeance of eternal fire.". 2 Peter 2:4 says, "For if God spared not the angels that sinned, but cast *them* down to hell, and delivered *them* into chains of darkness, to be reserved unto judgement;". The great day is the day of our judgement by God, the Father, Almighty before the "new heavens and new earth" with the "new Jerusalem" (Rev. 20:11-15, 21:1-5). I see these chains in a modern day sense as the chains of a vehicle timing "belt"; it is covered in an engine compartment under a hood of the vehicle, "under darkness" (Jude 1:6). I would also suggest that those vehicles with "bigger" engines are more related with this, as the number of the beast is six hundred threescore and six, and the larger the engine, the greater the horse power, six cylinder engines, etc. (Rev. 13:18). Jude also says that they are, "…spots in your feasts of charity…" (2 Pet. 3:12, Jude 1:12). This could be due to literal pollution of oil in the ground near and in crop fields or the like. And they are "Raging waves of the sea, foaming out their own shame…" (Jude 1:13). That would describe the pollution that comes out of exhaust pipes of bigger vehicles. That being said, Jude says they are, "…trees whose fruit withereth, without fruit, twice dead, plucked up by the roots;" (Jude 1:12). The point is that "bigger" is not always better, vehicle technology is a gift from God, and man no doubt has abused it like everything else we have managed to pervert (Isa. 47:10, Jer. 3:21). But God desires us to repent of our sins and follow Him, in the name of Jesus Christ of Nazareth. This may also be an admonishment to support locally grown agriculture, trade, travel, and general conservation efforts of God's creation here on earth (Gen. 1:26, Jer. 29:5, 6; John 4:23). Of course we cannot do it without God's help, first and foremost, and it is by the example of Jesus Christ of Nazareth that we have our example. He rode into Jerusalem on a donkey's colt (John 12:12-15). He was not driving a seasoned, broken in veteran thoroughbred horse or anything like that. Jesus Christ of Nazareth is our example of a true, pure, undefiled human being. If we are to receive eternal life, we must follow His example. Alleluia and praise the Lord. Amen and Amen.

Jesus spoke of cutting off branches of the vine that do not bear fruit, and purging the ones that do bear fruit (John 15:2). The apostle, Paul, used a similar comparison regarding branches of the olive tree being broken off and wild branches being grafted in (Rom. 11:16-24). The Old Testament prophets spoke of the wicked turning from their ways, repenting, that is, which is what Jesus asks us to do (Isa. 55:6-9, Ezek. 3:18-21, Matt. 9:13). No matter, there is a need for a renewing of all things, including the creation of the "new heavens and new earth" with the "new Jerusalem" (2 Pet. 3:7-13, Rev. 21:1-5). As followers of Christ we have a certain responsibility to reflect Christ's character in this fallen world. We are the salt of the earth and are called to be a light to the world in the name of Jesus Christ of Nazareth (Matt. 5:13, 14; John 8:12). 2 Corinthians 2:15 and 16 describes in interesting detail what we are to God for those who are perishing and to those who are to receive eternal life, that is a "sweet savour of Christ". John goes into detail about our love, he says, "If we love one another, God dwelleth in us, and his love is perfected in us." (1 John 4:12). He also says, "Herein is our love made perfect, that we may have boldness in the day of judgement…" (1 John 4:17). We are also called to have "confidence" in that day and to not be "ashamed" (1 John 2:28). Philippians 1:6 says, "Being confident of this very thing, that He which hath begun a good work in you will perform *it* until the day of Jesus Christ". The point is, as a Christ follower, those whom have submitted our life to Jesus Christ of Nazareth, there is no condemnation, we have become adopted, children of God (Rom. 8:15). In Christ we have liberty, we have freedom, and we have life and life more abundantly (John 10:10). Alleluia and praise the LORD. John 11:40 says, "Jesus saith unto her, Said I not unto thee, that, if thou wouldest believe, thou shouldest see the glory of God?". He was speaking of the resurrection of Lazarus' body and life from the tomb after four days lying dead (John 11:14, 17). Speaking of Jesus Christ of Nazareth Himself, John 12:23 says, "And Jesus answered them, saying, The hour is come, that the Son of man should be glorified.". The Glory of God is in Jesus Christ of Nazareth's life during His thirty three and a half years before His death on the cross for the forgiveness of our sins, it is in His death on the cross for the forgiveness of our sins, and it is in His resurrected life to give us the hope and promise of eternal life in His Holy name (John 13:31, 32). Alleluia and praise the LORD. Eternal life or the second death, it is your choice ultimately. Believe on the name of the only begotten Son of God, Jesus Christ of Nazareth, and follow Him unto eternal life and you will be saved. Praise the Lord God Almighty and His only begotten Son, Jesus Christ of Nazareth. Alleluia and praise the LORD. Amen and Amen.

Discussion: Marriage

"…I will have mercy, and not sacrifice…"
- Matthew 9:13

One way to look at the "end" of the world is as a "burnt offering" to God (Gen. 8:20, 22:2; Isa. 28:22). But we must remember what the Scriptures say about our offerings to Him. He desires "…mercy, and not sacrifice…" (Hos. 6:6, Matt. 9:13). He says that all that are in the fields and forests are His (Ps. 50:10-12). There is nothing that we can give God that He does not already have. As the Holy Bible says, "…of thine own have we given thee." (1 Chr. 29:14). The point is God created this world to be inhabited, and He created it so that we can enjoy it (Isa. 45:18, John 10:10). The Holy Bible says, "…grieve not the holy Spirit of God…" (Eph. 4:30). As Jesus said of Himself, "…I am come that they might have life, and that they might have *it* more abundantly." (John 10:10). Jesus Christ of Nazareth is life; He is the way to become a child of God (John 14:6). He is life and life more abundantly (John 10:10). Praise the LORD God Almighty, and His only begotten Son, Jesus Christ of Nazareth. Alleluia and Praise the LORD. A spouse is a gift from God (Matt. 19:6, Rev. 19:7). For those whom have difficulty relating a relationship with God, to a marriage supper, Jesus used other parables to describe the Kingdom of God (Matt. 13, Luke 13:20, 21). The point is that God's kingdom has everything to do with marriage, but it can be related to in other ways as well. No matter what we choose to do here on earth in this life, we ought to put God first, and then He will direct our path for us (Prov. 3:6). To God be the glory in the name of His only begotten Son, Jesus Christ of Nazareth. Alleluia and praise the LORD. Amen and Amen.

Discussion Questions

1. What is the value of true love?

   _____

   _____

   _____

2. What does it mean for two to become one flesh?

   _____

   _____

   _____

3. Where does our faith and hope come from?

   _____

   _____

   _____

Chapter 7: Conclusions – What now?

"For yet a little while, and he that shall come will come, and will not tarry."
- Hebrews 10:37

Introduction

Of all the people, preachers, books, movies, etc. that have attempted to explain life after death, I believe that we have probably only scratched the surface. I know if I let my mind drift I can come up with some pretty crazy and creative ideas about what life may be like after death. That does not mean they are all correct. Revelation 21 speaks of the City of New Jerusalem, where "…there shall in no wise enter into it any thing that defileth, neither *whatsoever* worketh abomination, or *maketh* a lie: but they which are written in the Lamb's book of life." (Rev. 21:27). It is a city that has light all the time (Rev. 21:25). It is adorned with gold, jasper and other jewels (Rev. 21:18-21). It is a city that is shaped like no city I have ever heard of, unless you consider a cube shaped building a city (Rev. 21:16). Nevertheless, the point is, there is and will always be a place that is pure and is perfect and nothing will ever change that. We can enter that place through the knowledge of Jesus Christ of Nazareth, God's only begotten Son, and God, the Father by God's Holy Spirit. All we need to do is accept Him. How we go, when we go, who else goes, what we will be doing, etc., are all questions we may have and from time to time desire to dwell on, but the simplicity of the gospel message of the Kingdom of God and the knowledge of God's salvation message in His only begotten Son, Jesus Christ of Nazareth, is really what we need to focus on until we do reach our heavenly, eternal destination. Let us plant our feet firmly on the ground and stand steadfast in the knowledge of Jesus Christ of Nazareth, God's only begotten Son, and God, the Father, through fellowship with God's Holy Spirit, so that no one can take our crown of life (Rom. 5:1, 2; 14:4, 10; Rev. 3:11, 20:12). Alleluia and praise the LORD. In the end, I know that I do not have all of the answers, about every step we need to take here on earth and what exactly the "next life", heaven, etc., will be like. I have heard the sayings, "Let God be God" or "Let go and let God". And that is exactly what I intend to do. With that being said, let us all work out our "…own salvation with fear and trembling." (Phil. 2:12). Until that great day of the full revelation of God, the Father, and knowledge of His only begotten Son, Jesus Christ of Nazareth with God's Holy Spirit and the new heavens and new earth come, when the Bridegroom and His bride are fully united and where every tear will be wiped away and all things will be made new (Rev. 21:1-5). To simplify it the Old Testament says that, God is our reward, and in keeping His commandments is great reward (Gen. 15:1, Ps. 19:7-11). And we can always go back to John 3:16, "For God so loved the world, that he gave his only begotten Son, that whosoever believeth in him should not perish, but have everlasting life.". And last Romans 10:9 says, "That if thou shalt confess with thy mouth the Lord Jesus, and shalt believe in thine heart that God hath raised him from the dead, thou shalt be saved.". How much more simpler could it be? That all being said, let us "Fight the good fight of faith…" so that on that final day when we stand in front of our Maker we can hope He will say, "… Well done, *thou* good and faithful servant…" (Matt. 25:21, 1 Tim. 6:12). To God be the glory in the name of His only begotten Son, Jesus Christ of Nazareth. Alleluia and praise the LORD. Amen and Amen. The remainder of this chapter has a general summary for each of the previous chapters and a final conclusion for the book, read on for the summaries and final conclusion.

Chapter One Summary

A pen of iron and a rock, ink and paper, the printing press, typewriters and computers with printers; how similar are they all. Although the subject may not seem to be completely related to chapter one, the idea is that "...*there is* no new *thing* under the sun.", as the author of Ecclesiastes would say (Eccl. 1:9). The point here is that everything that has been done, will be done again, albeit things seem a little different, comparing a rock tablet and chisel or "pen of iron", to a computer word processor and printer. But really what is the difference between the two, they are both used to accomplish the same goal, write down information for someone to retrieve and read or view. This same simple principal can and will be applied to life here on earth as a whole (Ps. 90:9, Rev. 20:12). The one thing we can count on is that we have a new and everlasting life in Jesus Christ of Nazareth's Holy name. This is the "New" covenant God has made with us in the name of His only begotten Son, Jesus Christ of Nazareth. God made a covenant with mankind in the beginning; Genesis 1:28 and 29 says, "And God blessed them, and God said unto them, Be fruitful, and multiply, and replenish the earth, and subdue it: and have dominion over the fish of the sea, and over the fowl of the air, and over every living thing that moveth upon the earth. And God said, Behold, I have given you every herb bearing seed, which *is* upon the face of all the earth, and every tree, in the which *is* the fruit of a tree yielding seed; to you it shall be for meat.". And Genesis 2:16 and 17 say, "...Of every tree of the garden thou mayest freely eat: But of the tree of the knowledge of good and evil, thou shalt not eat of it: for in the day that thou eatest thereof thou shalt surely die.". But our ancestors failed to keep heed of God's warning about the tree of knowledge of good and evil and mankind has suffered for it (Gen. 3). God gave our ancestors the blood covenant in the wilderness of Sinai, along with the law, but again the children of Israel went astray (Exodus, Judges, 1 Kings, 2 Kings). But it was and is the prophesied coming of the Messiah, Jesus Christ of Nazareth, the Saviour of Israel, and the whole world that has given us the hope for a future that is everlasting life in His Holy name. It is by the precious blood of the Lamb of God, Jesus Christ of Nazareth, that we are saved from our sins, and are given that promise of eternal life in His Holy name. It is a gift, not by works, so that no man should boast (Eph. 2:8, 9). He died on the cross for the forgiveness of our sins, He was buried and the third day He arose to give us all the hope and promise of eternal life in His Holy name. Alleluia and praise the LORD God Almighty through His only begotten Son, Jesus Christ of Nazareth. Alleluia and praise the LORD. Amen and Amen.

Chapter Two Summary

Water, earth, fire, wind, beast, man, and the Spirit of God, the example of Elijah running from God comes to mind (1 Kings 19:1-18). This world is filled with ideas of how we came into being and where we may be going. But I would admonish the reader to place their trust in their Creator, Jesus Christ of Nazareth, God's only begotten Son, and God, the Father, Almighty through God's Holy Spirit for the truth of it all. After a storm, earthquake and fire, a still small voice came to Elijah and spoke with him (1 Kings 19:11, 12). This was the Spirit of God, the only Spirit we ever need to listen to. If you wait patiently, and be still, you can hear His still small voice (Ps. 46:10). And you can invite His still small voice into your life; body, mind and soul, forever through Jesus Christ of Nazareth, whose blood was shed for you and I on the cross, for the forgiveness of our sins. It is by His still small voice, the Holy Spirit, that we live and breathe (John 20:22, 23). It is by His still small voice that God gave life to Adam and Eve in the beginning (Gen. 2:7). And it is by His still small voice that God created the heavens and the earth (Gen. 1, 2:1-3). Obey Him and you will receive life everlasting in the name of

God's only begotten Son, Jesus Christ of Nazareth. Jesus says to us, "Let not your heart be troubled…" and He says He has "…overcome the world." (John 14:1, 16:33). It is by Him we live and breathe, and can do all things (John 14:6, Phil. 4:13). Remember this simple truth and you will be more than a conqueror in Christ Jesus of Nazareth (Rom. 8:37). Alleluia and praise the LORD. Amen and Amen.

Chapter Three Summary

Luke 12:32 says, "Fear not little flock; for it is your Father's good pleasure to give you the kingdom.". Jesus said of God, the Father, and Himself, "And this is life eternal, that they might know thee the only true God, and Jesus Christ, whom thou hast sent." (John 17:3). And the Holy Bible says God inhabits eternity (Isa. 57:15). Also the Holy Bible says if we are in sin we do not know God (1 John 3:6). But in Jesus Christ of Nazareth we have known God and we can hear His commands by His Holy Spirit, including in the physical Word of God, the Holy Bible of God (John 5:39, 14:26; Rom. 2:14, 15). Because God inhabits eternity, throughout time and space, and we are fleshly fallen human beings, we "live" in two different places seemingly, the fleshly worldly realm and the spiritual heavenly realm. This is the daily cross we must take up in this life, longsuffering and enduring the world around us in patience, in earnest hope of the promises for the world to come (Mark 10:30, Luke 9:23). But the good news is that God came into this broken world through His only begotten Son, Jesus Christ of Nazareth, so that we can know the Father through His only begotten Son, Jesus Christ of Nazareth. Alleluia and praise the LORD. This is the free gift of God, eternal life in His only begotten Son, Jesus Christ of Nazareth's Holy name. He was a sinless man, taking all of our sin upon Him, He died on the cross for the forgiveness of our sins, He was buried and the third day He arose to give us the hope and promise of everlasting life in His Holy name. Praise the Lord God Almighty and His only begotten Son, Jesus Christ of Nazareth. Alleluia and praise the LORD. It is by accepting Jesus Christ of Nazareth, and being baptized by His Holy Spirit that we can experience God, and eternal life in His Holy name. It is God's Holy Spirit that breathed life into Adam and Eve in the beginning, and it is by this same Spirit, that we will be raised up at the last day, to be taken where Jesus is, so that God may become "all in all" (Gen. 2.7, John 14:3, 1 Cor. 15:28). Alleluia and praise the LORD. Amen and Amen.

Chapter Four Summary

In chapter four I spoke about spiritual "hell" and Jesus' ability to heal us from our torment, both physically and spiritually. Jeremiah said in his lamentations that remembering trials, humbles us and gives us hope (Lam. 3:18-21). Jesus admonishes us to "…neither be ye of doubtful mind." (Luke 12:29). And He said, "…Till heaven and earth pass away, one jot or one tittle shall in no wise pass from the law, till all be fulfilled." (Matt. 5:18). Jesus came to set the captives free, both spiritual captives and/ or physical captives. One of the first public speeches He gave, during His Biblically recorded ministry was in a synagogue where He had been brought up in Nazareth on the Sabbath and as was custom He read; that day He read from the book of Isaiah given to Him (Luke 4:16, 17). He read saying, "The Spirit of the Lord *is* upon me, because he hath anointed me to preach the gospel to the poor; he hath sent me to heal the brokenhearted, to preach deliverance to the captives, and recovering of sight to the blind, to set at liberty them that are bruised, To preach the acceptable year of the Lord." (Isa. 61:1, 2; Luke 4:18, 19). Next the Holy Bible says, "And he closed the book, and he gave *it* again to the minister, and sat down. And the eyes of all them that were in the synagogue were fastened on him. And he began to say unto them, This day is this scripture fulfilled in your ears." (Luke 4:20, 21). Jesus confirmed the fulfillment of this Scripture in His ministry; He said, "For even the Son of man came not to be ministered unto, but to minister, and to give his life a ransom for many." (Mark 10:45). He did indeed heal the brokenhearted, He raised the dead and forgave sinners, He recovered the sight of the blind, He preached the gospel to the poor, and loosed people from captivity spiritually and physically, even after His resurrection and ascension to the right hand of the Father, namely Peter, one of the twelve appointed founding apostles of the New Testament Church was taken out of prison by the angel of the Lord, Paul and Silas also were set free from captivity (Matt. 4:23, 9:1-8; Mark 5:1-20, John 9, 11:1-45; Acts 12, 16). My point here is that Jesus came to make us free, the truth, Jesus Christ of Nazareth, will and does make us free from ALL bonds, addictions, enslavements, etc. (John 8:32). Jesus died on the cross for the forgiveness of all of our sins, He was buried and the third day He arose to give us the hope and promise of eternal life in His Holy name. Alleluia and praise the LORD. Amen and Amen.

Chapter Five Summary

1 Thessalonians 4:14-18 says, "For if we believe that Jesus died and rose again, even so them also which sleep in Jesus will God bring with him. For this we say unto you by the word of the Lord, that we which are alive *and* remain unto the coming of the Lord shall not prevent them which are asleep. For the Lord himself shall descend from heaven with a shout, with the voice of the archangel, and with the trump of God: and the dead in Christ shall rise first: Then we which are alive *and* remain shall be caught up together with them in the clouds, to meet the Lord in the air: and so shall we ever be with the Lord. Wherefore comfort one another with these words.". This is a great summary of all that has been spoken of in the various chapters of this book for someone whom is looking for a simpler explanation of what comes after this life. Whether Paul knew what he was saying or not, we must remember that our reality is in Jesus Christ of Nazareth, whom died on the cross for the forgiveness of our sins, He was buried and the third day He arose to give us the hope and promise of eternal life in His Holy name, forever. Alleluia and praise the LORD. Amen and Amen.

Chapter Six Summary

Jesus said of Himself, "I am the way, the truth, and the life: no man cometh unto the Father, but by me. If ye had known me, ye should have known my Father also: and from henceforth ye know him, and have seen him." (John 14:6, 7). The apostle, Paul, said, "Therefore judge nothing before the time, until the Lord come, who both will bring to light the hidden things of darkness, and will make manifest the counsels of the hearts: and then shall every man have praise of God." (1 Cor. 4:5). In the "bigger picture" of much of the writing of this book, this should be an important take away, to "Judge not, that ye be not judged." (Matt. 7:1). Jesus said, "For God sent not his Son into the world to condemn the world; but that the world through him might be saved." (John 3:17). So with all of that being said, of any judgements I have made in the writing of this book or interpretations I have made outside of Holy Scripture, let the truth of all of these interpretations be tried by the truth of Jesus Christ of Nazareth and what He says of Himself, "…I am the way, the truth, and the life: no man cometh unto the Father, but by me." (John 14:6). Praise the LORD God Almighty, and His only begotten Son, Jesus Christ of Nazareth. Alleluia and Praise the LORD. Amen and Amen.

Conclusion

God looks forward to our completion, perfection, our "end", His glory in us, in this life, and in eternity (Ps. 116:15). The point is that He is preparing us and molding us like clay, and is refining us in a furnace like gold, to make us in His image, in His likeness (Job 10:9, 13:12, 33:6; Isa. 29:16, 45:9, 48:10, 64:8; Jer. 18:6, Zech. 13:9). He is preparing us for a "new" life, "eternal" life in Jesus Christ of Nazareth's Holy name, our Lord, our Lord and Saviour. The apostle, Paul, says, that we are a "new" creature in Christ (2 Cor. 5:17). We can begin to experience this eternal life in Jesus Christ of Nazareth today. Jesus said that the kingdom of God does not come by observation, but that it is within us (Luke 17:20, 21). Nevertheless, as mentioned in 1 Thessalonians 4:16, 17 and 18; God inspired the apostle, Paul, to admonish us to comfort each other with the promises that the dead will rise again and those who remain will be "caught" up into the clouds to be with the Lord forever. The point is that someday we will all be given our "heavenly" reward, as many as receive Jesus Christ of Nazareth as their Lord and Saviour, that is eternal life in Christ Jesus of Nazareth's Holy name, and we will be with Jesus Christ of Nazareth, God's only begotten Son, and God, the Father, through His Holy Spirit forever. This is the power of the Holy Spirit of God in the Body of Christ, the One whom comes for the bride and the bride is prepared for by God (John 14:2, 2 Tim. 2:21, Rev. 21:2). This book in general speaks of growth of God's family, rest for God, the earth and mankind and purging us and this world of sin. That all being said, the Holy Bible does admonish not to desire the "hastening" of the "end", or the "Day of the Lord" (Amos 5:18). This is because God created this earth to be inhabited today (Isa. 45:18). He desires us to live a life for Him today. Regardless of the "Great Tribulation" or the "end" of this present earth's history, we need to focus on living for God and others today. As Jesus said, "Take therefore no thought for the morrow: for the morrow shall take thought for the things of itself. Sufficient unto the day *is* the evil thereof." (Matt. 6:34). He desires us to have a relationship with Him now, in order to "prepare" us for eternal life, and to live a life worth living in love towards one another here on earth today. In Jesus Christ of Nazareth we have life, and life everlasting. There is no other name under heaven by which we can be saved (Acts 4:12). Praise the LORD God Almighty and His only begotten Son, Jesus Christ of Nazareth. Alleluia and praise the Lord. Amen and Amen.

The book of Revelation maybe the final "official" message God has given to mankind. The book of Revelation, if interpreted correctly maps out the completion of God's plan here on earth currently (Rev. 20). And even talks about the things to come, after this earth's passing away, in the "world to come" (Rev. 21, 22). God's plan is eternal and He desires us to be a part of it. Will you? One psalmist even said, "Precious in the sight of the LORD *is* the death of his saints." (Ps. 116:15). Revelation 1:7 says, "Behold, he cometh with clouds; and every eye shall see him, and they *also* which pierced him: and all kindreds of the earth shall wail because of him. Even so, Amen.". The reality is that this current world and the memories of people and experiences in it are not going to last forever likely. God is creating for us a new heaven and new earth, all of the memories of pain, suffering, trials, and evils of all kinds that we may have or will experience in this life will perish and our souls in Jesus Christ of Nazareth will be redeemed by His Holy and righteous blood unto everlasting life, if we follow Him, obey Him and give our lives up for Him. This is the promise He makes for all of His faithful believers. Are you ready to make that commitment for Christ? He is waiting for you. And I can promise you, if you accept Him into your heart, mind and soul, you will never be the same again. He is our life, our Redeemer, our ultimate Saviour and friend. There is no other name under heaven by which we can be saved (Acts 4:12). God desires us to repent, and believe in the name of His only begotten Son, Jesus

Christ of Nazareth and His works (John 10:38). God calls us to redeem the time (Eph. 5:16, Col. 4:5). He makes a promise in Joel 2:25-27 it says, "And I will restore to you the years that the locust hath eaten, the cankerworm, and the caterpiller, and the palmerworm, my great army which I sent among you. And ye shall eat in plenty, and be satisfied, and praise the name of the LORD your God, that hath dealt wondrously with you: and my people shall never be ashamed. And ye shall know that I *am* in the midst of Israel, and *that* I *am* the LORD your God, and none else: and my people shall never be ashamed.". God promises to preserve the poor, the stranger, the simple, the faithful and the saints (Ex. 22:21, 23:9; Lev. 19:33, 34; 24:22; 25:35, 36; Deut. 10:18, 19; 24:14, 15, 17, 18; 27:19; Ps. 41:1, 2; 116:6, 146:9). The point of all of this is salvation in the name of Jesus Christ of Nazareth, whom was crucified and died on the cross for the forgiveness of our sins, He was buried and the third day He arose to give us the hope and promise of eternal life in His Holy name. Alleluia and praise the LORD. Amen and Amen.

Matthew 25:31-46 says, "When the Son of man shall come in his glory, and all the holy angels with him, then shall he sit upon the throne of his glory: And before him shall be gathered all nations: and he shall separate them one from another, as a shepherd divideth *his* sheep from the goats: And he shall set the sheep on his right hand, but the goats on the left. Then shall the King say unto them on his right hand, Come, ye blessed of my Father, inherit the kingdom prepared for you from the foundation of the world: For I was an hungred, and ye gave me meat: I was thirsty, and ye gave me drink: I was a stranger, and ye took me in: Naked, and ye clothed me: I was sick, and ye visited me: I was in prison, and ye came unto me. Then shall the righteous answer him, saying, Lord, when saw we thee an hungred, and fed *thee?* or thirsty, and gave *thee* drink? When saw we thee a stranger, and took *thee* in? or naked, and clothed *thee?* Or when saw we thee sick, or in prison, and came unto thee? And the King shall answer and say unto them, Verily I say unto you, Inasmuch as ye have done *it* unto one of the least of these my brethren, ye have done *it* unto me. Then shall he say also unto them on the left hand, Depart from me, ye cursed, into everlasting fire, prepared for the devil and his angels: For I was an hungred, and ye gave me no meat: I was thirsty, and ye gave me no drink: I was a stranger, and ye took me not in: naked, and ye clothed me not: sick, and in prison, and ye visited me not. Then shall they also answer him, saying, Lord, when saw we thee an hungred, or athirst, or a stranger, or naked, or sick, or in prison, and did not minister unto thee? Then shall he answer them, saying, Verily I say unto you, Inasmuch as ye did *it* not to one of the least of these, ye did *it* not to me. And these shall go away into everlasting punishment: but the righteous into life eternal.". This is a long quotation, but it pretty much sums up the judgement, in Christ Jesus of Nazareth, we have eternal life. Although it is not by works that we are saved, it is by grace, and mercy and faith, which is a free gift from God (Eph. 2:8, 9). Jesus says, "Ye shall know them by their fruits." (Matt. 7:16). So if you are questioning where you or anyone else stands with our Maker, look at the fruit of your life, the fruit of the Holy Spirit is "…love, joy, peace, longsuffering, gentleness, goodness, faith, Meekness, temperance: against such there is no law." (Gal. 5:22, 23). Does your life reflect these fruits? If not, repent and believe in the gospel and follow Jesus Christ of Nazareth. He says our works have been prepared for us a head of time (Eph. 2:10). So open the Holy Bible, and let the Holy Spirit lead you by His merciful and gracefully guiding hand. You will not regret it, I promise. God loves you. Alleluia and praise the LORD. Amen and Amen.

Discussion: Conclusion

"And I saw a new heaven and a new earth: for the first heaven and the
first earth were passed away; and there was no more sea."
- Revelation 21:1

This verse is probably the simplest verse for considering life here on earth, and what is to come. It says the "first" heaven and "first" earth, this should be a good indication that, as far as we here on earth are concerned, there was no "earth" or "heaven" before this one. This could be argued till the cows come home, but as the Holy Bible says, "The LORD preserveth the simple..." (Ps. 116:6). So it is much easier to take this verse for what it says, nothing more or nothing less. Revelation 21:4 says, "And God shall wipe away all tears from their eyes; and there shall be no more death, neither sorrow, nor crying, neither shall there be any more pain: for the former things are passed away.". This should be a great and simple promise for the "world to come", but not only that, God desires us to experience His kingdom today, here on earth now (Mark 10:30, Luke 17:20, 21). All that is required is that we accept His free gift of eternal life in the name of His only begotten Son, Jesus Christ of Nazareth. The conversion process, the "renewing" or "regeneration" of our soul, mind and body can and will be done today, in the name of Jesus Christ of Nazareth. He healed the sick, the blind, the dumb, and forgave sinners during His earthly ministry, and has been doing the same through His Holy Spirit, since then by His precious blood spilt on the cross for the forgiveness of our sins. Do you realize this? Then give God, the Father, Almighty the glory in the name of His only begotten Son, Jesus Christ of Nazareth. He died on the cross for the forgiveness of our sins, He was buried and the third day He arose to give us the hope and promise of eternal life in His Holy name. Alleluia and praise the LORD. When reading through this chapter's discussion questions, consider what has been done for you, in the name of Jesus Christ of Nazareth, and how you ought to move forward in His Holy name, as He wills you. Alleluia and praise the LORD. Amen and Amen.

Discussion Questions

1. Psalm 102:25-28 does a great job of explaining simply how the earth was established and what His plans are for it into the "future". Read the Psalm and meditate on how this truth affects your life here on earth and possibly your descendants after you.

    _____

    _____

    _____

2. What does it mean to you, to be a "new creature" or "new man", in Jesus Christ of Nazareth's Holy name?

    _____

    _____

    _____

3. What part do you have to play in the new things God is doing here on earth and into eternity?

    _____

    _____

    _____

Afterword

Some of the big questions in life may be, "Is there life after death?" and "Where do we go when we die?". These questions do not usually come to the forefront of our conscience until we are faced with some sort of life altering experience that brings these concerns to our minds. But the answers to these questions may be the most important one's we ever learn in this life. This book has spoken about, God willing, the truth of the answers of these questions, and has gone into greater detail about some of what the Holy Bible says and what some of the common misconception of the afterlife may be. It is hoped that the reader in the end receives a certain amount of peace about the topic and a healthy foundation in the knowledge of Jesus Christ of Nazareth in order to move forward in your own journey through this life and into eternity with God and others, God willing.

Ecclesiastes 12:7 says, "Then shall the dust return to the earth as it was: and the spirit shall return unto God who gave it.". This is the easiest explanation of death and eternal life. However, we still have a soul that is unaccounted for in this verse. This is where faith in Jesus Christ of Nazareth and the idea of Adam and Eve becoming "living souls" comes to be important (Gen. 2:7). If we believe in Jesus Christ of Nazareth and the resurrection of not only the spirit, but the body and soul, as well, then this is the complete package, that so many are looking for, that "eternal" fountain of youth, the deep desire in us to not die, to not age and to not feel pain. This is what Jesus Christ of Nazareth promises through His Holy and righteous name (Rev. 21:7). In John 17:3, Jesus speaks of God, the Father, and Himself, Jesus Christ of Nazareth, the only begotten Son of God, He says, "And this is life eternal, that they might know thee the only true God, and Jesus Christ, whom thou hast sent.". Do you know the only true God and Jesus Christ of Nazareth, God's only begotten Son, whom God, the Father, sent to us? What are you waiting for? Ask Him to come into your life and show you His way, the truth of eternal life.

Those who choose Jesus Christ of Nazareth in this life, including you and I, and choose to take up our cross daily unto the end, will receive the reward of eternal life in Jesus Christ of Nazareth's Holy name. Alleluia and praise the LORD. The Holy Bible says, "That if thou shalt confess with thy mouth the Lord Jesus, and shalt believe in thine heart that God hath raised him from the dead, thou shalt be saved." (Rom. 10:9). So what are you waiting for? If you believe, confess and you will be saved. Pray to God in earnest prayer, and He will come into your mind, heart and commune with your soul.

Do you believe? Then ask. As the Holy Bible says, "Ask, and it shall be given you; seek, and ye shall find; knock, and it shall be opened unto you: For every one that asketh receiveth; and he that seeketh findeth; and to him that knocketh it shall be opened." (Matt. 7:7, 8). Praise the LORD God of heaven and earth, in the name of His only begotten Son, Jesus Christ of Nazareth's Holy name. Alleluia and praise the LORD. Amen and Amen.

APPENDICES

Appendix A

References
Books

1. Concordia Commentary – Revelation, by Louis A. Brighton, 1999, Concordia Publishing House
   - "Garden of Eden" pg. 623-633
   - A description of the similarity of Revelation 22 to a new Garden of Eden.
2. The Fall Feasts of Israel, by Mitch and Zhava Glaser, 1987, Moody Press Chicago
   - "Garden of Eden" pg. 62

Websites

1. http://www.cbn.com/spirituallife/inspirationalteaching/Metaxas_Moon_Communion.aspx
2. http://www.bbc.com/news/science-environment-34684761
3. http://dedication.www3.50megs.com/457.html

Media

1. https://www.youtube.com/watch?v=9BEULHeAHWo, reading of Genesis 1:1-10, by Bill Anders, Jim Lovell and Frank Borman, starting about 29:10 minutes into the video, retrieved 02/04/2018

Note: The author does not guarantee the availability of all references, especially websites, as organizations from time to time change names, addresses and discontinue services. Nor does the author guarantee the accuracy of the references. As the Holy Bible says, "Prove all things; hold fast that which is good." (1 Th. 5:21). That being said, God willing, you will be brought to the proof and references you are seeking. As Jesus said, "…seek, and ye shall find…" (Matt. 7:7).

Appendix B

Being born again, Christ's "second coming" and other religious ideas
Introduction

Why this appendix? It was written to tackle some of the questions that can arise when asking about receiving Christ Jesus of Nazareth as our Lord and Saviour, being "born again" of the Holy Spirit, receiving everlasting life, other religious perspectives, and the like. Although I will not go into detail about many things, as most of my other writings have touched on various subjects regarding the religions of this world, and other "worldly" ideas that often have some root of truth in the Holy Bible of God. I will say that God, through Christ Jesus of Nazareth has made life and eternal life in Him simple. He says of Himself, "Come unto me, all *ye* that labour and are heavy laden, and I will give you rest. Take my yoke upon you, and learn of me; for I am meek and lowly in heart: and ye shall find rest unto your souls. For my yoke *is* easy, and my burden is light." (Matt. 11:28-30). Jesus Christ of Nazareth's burden is light!!! Alleluia and praise the LORD. Amen and Amen. He said of God, the Father, and Himself, "And this is life eternal, that they might know thee the only true God, and Jesus Christ, whom thou hast sent." (John 17:3). Our eternal life is in the knowledge that there exists, God, the Father, in heaven, and His only begotten Son, Jesus Christ of Nazareth with His Holy Ghost (Matt. 28:19) . Alleluia and praise the LORD. Amen and Amen. And He has given us all, of His Holy Spirit, so that we can be taught, lead, shown, and comforted by Him for all things, in this life, and in the world to come, life everlasting (John 14:26, 16:13; 1 John 4:13). Alleluia and praise the LORD. Amen and Amen. Nevertheless, read on to learn a little more about being "born again" of the Holy Spirit of God, and life, and life everlasting in the Holy name of His only begotten Son, Jesus Christ of Nazareth. Alleluia and praise the LORD. Amen and Amen.

Spirit, Water and blood, Eternal life

Unless you are born again, you cannot see the kingdom of God (John 3:3). This requires the baptism of the Holy Spirit (John 1:29-37, John 3:5). Ultimately, it is God's Holy Spirit that gives us life (Rev. 11:11). As Jesus said, God is a Spirit (John 4:24)! Water baptism is an outward display and testimony of accepting God's Holy Spirit, as water is a sign of life (Mark 9:41, John 3:5). And God uses this sign throughout the Holy Bible to describe life, "living waters", etc. (Jer. 2:13, 17:13; Zech. 14:8). These are the living waters that came out of Jesus Christ of Nazareth, the living Word of God, and literally water spilled out of Him for us on the cross (John 4:10-14, 7:37-39, 19:34). Blood of course is also a sign of life as well, in actuality; it is what keeps our bodies alive in a fleshly sense (Gen. 4:10, 9:4; Deut. 12:23). Jesus' shedding His blood for us on the cross is not just a sign, related to the blood sacrifices of the Old Testament laws, but is the new covenant in the blood of a righteous and perfect man, Jesus Christ of Nazareth (Ex. 12:1-14, Matt. 26:26-28). This sacrifice is all we need to accept, to cleanse us of our sins, and receive eternal life in Jesus Christ of Nazareth's Holy name. Alleluia and praise the LORD. Amen and Amen. The apostle, Paul, said, "…flesh and blood cannot inherit the kingdom of God…" (1 Cor. 15:50). Isaiah 46:3 and 4 confirm when we will be "born again", it says, "Hearken unto me, O house of Jacob, and all the remnant of the house of Israel, which are borne *by me* from the belly, which are carried from the womb: and *even* to *your* old age I *am* he; and *even* to hoar hairs will I carry *you:* I have made, and I will bear; even I will carry, and will deliver *you*.". According to this description, it would seem we are in the "womb" of God throughout our entire life here on earth. This points to when we are truly going to be born into the kingdom of God, that is, once we shed this corruptible fleshly body, and receive our eternal glorified body in Jesus Christ of Nazareth's Holy name, now and at our final resurrection, at the "last day" (John 11:24-27)! Alleluia and praise the LORD. Amen and Amen. And John said in one of his epistles, "We know that whosoever is born of God sinneth not; but he that is begotten of God keepeth himself, and that wicked one toucheth him not." (1 John 5:18). Alleluia and praise the LORD. Amen and Amen. This ought to be the greatest news ever, that we, through Jesus Christ of Nazareth's Holy and righteous blood shed on the cross for the forgiveness of our sins, whom died and was buried and the third day arose, has given us the hope and promise of eternal life in His Holy name. And He has given us His Holy Spirit to be with us, through us, and in us to teach us of all things and things to come (John 16:13). Alleluia and praise the LORD. Amen and Amen.

Christ coming again

Jesus mentions His coming as being both like "coming" in clouds and as lightning (Matt. 24:27, 30). The Old Testament and New Testament speak in many places of God being present in a cloud, at the tabernacle in the wilderness, in the temple at Jerusalem and it happened in the New Testament at the transfiguration of Jesus, speaking with Elijah and Moses witnessed by Peter, John and James (Ex. 13:21, 16:10, 19:9, 16; 24:15, 16; 40:34-38, Lev. 16:2, Num. 9:15, 1 Kings 8:10, 11; Luke 9:34, 35). It is also spoken of the "cloud of witnesses" that we are all surrounded by, that is, fellow believers that are witnessing each other's change growing in our relationship with God in Christ and with our fellowman (Heb. 12:1, 2). The Holy Ghost can also be considered to be like a cloud, and a dove, which descends upon those who receive Him in Jesus Christ of Nazareth's Holy name, by Jesus' shed blood on the cross, dying on the cross for the forgiveness of our sins, He was buried and arose from the grave three days later to give us the hope and promise of eternal life in His Holy name (Luke 1:35, 3:22). Alleluia and praise the LORD. Amen and Amen. As will be suggested in the next two paragraphs, Jesus' second coming is likely a process, Peter suggested He "came" in His transfiguration, showing His brightness and glory in the Spirit of the kingdom of God (2 Pet. 1:16, 17). Jesus spoke about a "great tribulation" before His "coming" again (Matt. 24:21). But in this it would seem that people would remain on earth after His coming again (Matt. 24:22). This part of His coming likely inaugurates the "Messianic age" or 1000 years of Christ rule on earth with His saints (Rev. 20:6). And last, when Christ comes with God Almighty and His angels to finally judge this entire earth at the end of the so called "Messianic age", where all of the dead are raised and judged at the final judgement day of God Almighty (Matt. 13:36-43, 47-49; 16:27, 25:31-46). This is represented by a brightness, a fervent heat or in the book of Revelation, fire coming down from God out of heaven (2 Thess. 2:8, 2 Pet. 3:10, Rev. 20:9). This could be some sort of solar storm or sun burst in the natural realm, that consumes the living flesh from the earth or something similar, which is also likely related to the discipline of Gog and Magog at the "end" of this earth's current history, where the earth will be dissolved (2 Pet. 3:12, Rev. 20:8, 9). And then the general resurrection of the dead, the final judgement and the creation of the "New Heaven and the New Earth", with the "New Jerusalem" coming down from heaven as a bride for her husband (Rev. 20:11-15; 21:1, 2). This would be the similitude of a new creation week, with the Holy Spirit creating a "New Earth", after these heavens and this earth and its elements are dissolved (Gen. 1-2:3, Isa. 24:19, 34:4). Alleluia and praise the LORD. Amen and Amen. Nevertheless, we can have this same relationship with our Creator today, that is, a new life in Christ Jesus of Nazareth's Holy name today. By accepting His shed blood on the cross for the forgiveness of our sins, whom died on that cross for the forgiveness of our sins, He was buried and arose the third day to give us the hope and promise of eternal life in His Holy name. Alleluia and praise the LORD. Amen and Amen. As

Jesus Christ, Himself said, "...The kingdom of God cometh not with observation:...for, behold, the kingdom of God is within you." (Luke 17:20, 21). Alleluia and praise the LORD. Amen and Amen. This is done by accepting Him as our Lord and Saviour, whom has given us of His Holy Spirit to dwell in us, to teach us and to help us, and to comfort us (John 14:16-18, 26; 15:26, 27; 16:7-15). As Jesus said of Himself, "I will not leave you comfortless: I will come to you." (John 14:18). Alleluia and praise the LORD. Amen and Amen.

No doubt His coming is a process of time here on earth according to prophetic fulfillment of ALL the law and prophecies of the Holy Bible (Matt. 5:18, 24:35; Mark 13:31, Luke 21:33). 1 John 2:28 says, "And now, little children, abide in him; that, when he shall appear, we may have confidence, and not be ashamed before him at his coming.". The final result is some will be resurrected to eternal life and some may be resurrected to eternal damnation (Matt. 25:46, Mark 3:29, John 5:29). Ultimately in Revelation 1:7, it does say that "...he cometh with clouds; and every eye shall see him, and they *also* which pierced him: and all kindreds of the earth shall wail because of him.". So in the end we will all likely be well aware of Christ's coming again, whether it is in our own time and relationship with God in Christ or as a collective of mankind at some point in time in history. Jesus makes clearer the truth of His coming if the Scriptures are searched and the truth is revealed by the Holy Spirit of God in Christ Jesus of Nazareth's Holy name, as the testimony of Jesus Christ is the spirit of prophecy (John 16:13, Rev. 19:10). First in the gospel according to Matthew, Jesus said some amongst Him, at the time of His ministry in the first century A.D., would not taste death until they saw the Son of man coming in His kingdom (Matt. 16:28). Later in the gospel according to John, after Jesus was resurrected He said something very similar to Peter regarding John, He said, "If I will that he tarry till I come, what *is that* to thee? follow thou me." (John 21:22). And then the next verses go on to explain in greater detail what He meant. The point is that John seems to be, at least one, whom Jesus was going to reveal Himself to as He returns. Well, John was the apostle given the vision of Christ's coming again, the book of Revelation. So John, through vision, actually experienced Christ Jesus of Nazareth's full second coming. Those who are truly interested in understanding the second coming of Jesus Christ of Nazareth would be wise to read the Book of Revelation, with little exception, it describes fully the second coming of Jesus Christ of Nazareth. Alleluia and praise the LORD. Amen and Amen. As the Holy Bible says, "The LORD said unto my Lord, Sit thou at my right hand, until I make thine enemies thy footstool." (Ps. 110:1, Matt. 26:64, Mark 12:34-36, 14:62, 16:19; Luke 22:69). Jesus will remain at His Father's side until His enemies are made His footstool (Heb. 10:12, 13). This is very likely a process of time, as I have discussed in the book I wrote, "The Day Star and Us". Jesus gave us His Holy Spirit to dwell in us, through us, and amongst us until the end (Matt. 28:20, John 14:16-18). When we come together in Jesus Christ of Nazareth's Holy name, He is with us (Matt. 18:20). All of the Scriptures must be fulfilled in order for Christ to fully come again and take us to where He is (Matt. 5:18, John 14:3). This in all likelihood includes, a "Great Tribulation", the "Messianic Age" of 1000 years of Christ's rule with His saints; likely ruling from the spiritual realm and then the final judgement, which I have touched upon in this book, as of the date of writing this book in 2018 A.D. (Matt. 24, Rev. 20:6, 11-15). Regardless, the most important thing to remember is to maintain, start or renew our relationship with God, the Father, Almighty and His only begotten Son, Jesus Christ of Nazareth today, through the indwelling of His Holy Spirit. He is indeed with us until the end of the world, and forever more in Christ Jesus of Nazareth's Holy name, whom shed His blood and died on the cross for the forgiveness of our sins, He was buried and arose the third day to give us the hope and promise of eternal life in His Holy name (Matt. 28:20, John 14:16-18). Alleluia and praise the LORD. Amen and Amen. God bless and keep the faith.

Other religious ideas

The religion of Islam and the word "allah"; in Hebrew "alah" means curse, swear or oath etc., and also "alah" or "allah" means, oak, Strong's numbers 423, 424 and 427, respectively (Gen. 23:41, 35:4; Jos. 24:26). Jacob encouraged his children at the oak of Shechem, to put away the strange gods amongst them, and he hid them there (Gen. 35:2-4). Joshua admonished Israel near an oak at Shechem, to put away their strange gods, much like Jacob did a few centuries earlier, placing a "great stone" there for a witness between God and them (Jos. 24:23-26). And Jesus Christ of Nazareth is the true Rock and witness of God, with God Almighty, His Father, and ours through His Holy Spirit given to all whom believe (Matt. 7:24, 25; Rom. 9:33, 1 Cor. 10:4). Alleluia and praise the LORD. Amen and Amen. The words "al" and "lah" in Hebrew mean, not and not or nothing, Strong's number 409 and 3809, respectively (Dan. 2:24, 4:35). I am not trying to point out anything more than the meaning of this word and its root words in Hebrew. Of course, this is my interpretation of the matter. Interestingly God calls the nations of the world a drop of a bucket and also calls us less than nothing, He calls Jacob and His descendants worms and compares all the inhabitants of the earth to worms (Isa. 40:15, 17; 41:14, Job 25:6, Ps. 22:6, Mic. 7:17). So you can do with these ideas what you will. The reality is we are nothing without the true God in Jesus Christ of Nazareth's Holy name. Alleluia and praise the LORD. Amen and Amen. The True God, has his name, Elohim, El, Jah, Jehovah, Yahweh, the LORD, etc. (Gen. 1:1, 17:1; Ex. 15:2, 3). This is why the name Joel, Jah El, The LORD is God, and others like it are used for people's names in the Holy Bible, because they are used to describe God's character (Joel 1:1). Ishmael was a son of Abraham, along with Isaac, albeit from different mothers, around approximately 1800 B.C.. He seems to be the "father" of most Arabs and associated with the religion of Islam, through likely one of his descendants, Mohammad, approximately 600 A.D. (Gen. 16:16, 25:13-18). Ishmael's name means, God will hear, Strong's number 3458 (Gen. 16:11). And he was not the only person to be named Ishmael in the Holy Bible, some Israelites were named as such, as well (2 Kings 25:23, 25; 1 Chr. 8:38, 2 Chr. 19:11, 23:1; Ezra 10:22, Jer. 40:8, 14-16; 41). But the reality is in Christ Jesus of Nazareth, whom came into the world, born of the virgin, Mary, espoused to Joseph, conceived by the Holy Spirit of God, the Spirit of truth. He was raised as a child of Israel, by His parents, He had earthly brothers and sisters, i.e. family (Matt. 12:46; 13:55, 56; Mark 6:3, Luke 2:51). He loved them and us, and ultimately He showed His love for all of mankind by dying on the cross for the forgiveness of our sins, then He was buried and on the third day He arose giving us the hope and promise of eternal life in His Holy name. Alleluia and praise the LORD. Amen and Amen.

Evolution is another tricky concept, I am convinced that it is not really the truth, at least as modern evidence portrays it, as of the date of writing this book in 2018 A.D.. I am rather convinced of the Biblical account of creation, without a shadow of a doubt (Gen. 1-2:3). I do believe that the "theory" of evolution and all its evidences are a direct result of Adam and Eve's eating from the tree of knowledge of good and evil (Gen. 3:1-7). However, I will say something about it further. If we look at the Scriptures, the serpent was in the garden and was more subtle than all the beasts and he beguiled Eve (Gen. 3:1, 13). Eve then listened to the serpent, and Adam in turn listened to Eve and they both ate from the tree of knowledge of good and evil (Gen. 3:6). This deception that was in the serpent then went into mankind after that (Gen. 3:22, 23). Last, Jesus Christ of Nazareth cast a devil, a legion, out of a man and they went into the swine, they then in turn ran into the sea (Mark 5:1-13). This was prophetic I believe, because they said to Jesus, have you come to torment us before the time (Matt. 8:29). The time likely being the "Messianic Age" and then the final judgement after this at the "last day" (Rev. 20:1-3, 7-10). In the Messianic Age, Satan, is bound for one thousand years (Rev. 20:2). Some scripture, including the one where the swine ran into the sea may indicate that that is where Satan will be bound, in the sea, albeit the Holy Bible says he is chained with a great chain, in the bottomless pit (Rev. 20:1-3). Of course, people are also referenced as waters in the book of Revelation (Rev. 17:15). But never the less, maybe this is the entire idea of "evolution", mapped out in the Holy Bible of God. It may not be truly "evolution" as this world understands it, but the devolution of man, having eaten from the tree of knowledge of good and evil, being driven out of the Garden of Eden as a consequence (Gen. 3:6, 17-24). And then truly the restoration of our God likeness, by the blood of Jesus Christ of Nazareth, shed on the cross for the forgiveness of our sins, He was buried, and then He arose the third day to give us the hope and promise of eternal life in His Holy name (John 17:22-26). Alleluia and praise the LORD. Amen and Amen. And additionally, we do not have to worry about this so called "evolutionary" process repeating itself, because the book of Revelation says, there is no more sea in the "New Heaven and New Earth", which Jesus is preparing for those whom believe on Him and follow Him (John 14:3, Rev. 21:1). Alleluia and praise the LORD. Amen and Amen.

Last, I will not go into great detail on this, but I think the Scriptures make abundantly clear that Jesus Christ of Nazareth was before Abraham, and He is also the "first" (John 8:58, Rev. 1:17). The apostle, Paul, speaks of the first man Adam and the "last" Adam, Jesus, the first of the flesh and the last of the spirit (1 Cor. 15:45). Why am I saying all of this? I truly believe that Jesus received His born again body, the spiritual body, at His miraculous conception in His mother, Mary, espoused to Joseph, then His earthly birth in 4 B.C., His baptism by John the Baptist at the beginning of His ministry in 27 A.D., and then His death for the forgiveness of our sins, His burial at Passover, and His resurrection three days later during the feast of unleavened bread in 31 A.D. (John 3:3-7, Matt. 1:18-20, 25; 3:16, Luke 2:6, 7; John 13:1, 19:17, 18, 40, 42; 20:11-17). Jesus even seems to indicate during His ministry that He is a Father, by calling a woman, Daughter, spiritually speaking of course (Matt. 9:22). Is it not possible then that Jesus Christ of Nazareth is Adam, born again of the Spirit of God? We know the first Adam died because of his transgression of eating from the tree of knowledge of good and evil. He died as God said he would, along with his wife, Eve, although her death is not expressly mentioned in the Holy Bible (Gen. 5:5). But that may have been the only transgression Adam ever made and Jesus Christ of Nazareth died on the cross for those sins too! But Jesus Christ also arose the third day to give us all the hope and promise of eternal life in His Holy name. Alleluia and praise the LORD. Amen and Amen. Nevertheless, as the Scriptures say about these things and all others in the book of Revelation, "He that is unjust, let him be unjust still: and he which is filthy, let him be filthy still: and he that is righteous, let him be righteous still: and he that is holy, let him be holy still. And, behold, I come quickly; and my reward *is* with me, to give every man according as his work shall be. I am Alpha and Omega, the beginning and the end, the first and the last. Blessed *are* they that do his commandments, that they may have right to the tree of life, and may enter in through the gates into the city. For without *are* dogs, and sorcerers, and whoremongers, and murderers, and idolators, and whosoever loveth and maketh a lie. I Jesus have sent mine angel to testify unto you these things in the churches. I am the root and the offspring of David, *and* the bright and morning star." (Rev. 22:11-16). Alleluia and praise the LORD. Amen and Amen. Ultimately, we must remember regardless of the truth of all of these things, our reality is in Christ Jesus of Nazareth. He is the truth, and the truth will make us free (John 8:32, 14:6). Alleluia and praise the LORD. Amen and Amen. He died on the cross for the forgiveness of our sins, He was buried and the third day He arose from the grave, giving us the hope and promise of eternal life in His Holy name. Alleluia and praise the LORD. Amen and Amen.

Conclusion

Micah 4:5 says, "For all people will walk every one in the name of his god, and we will walk in the name of the LORD our God for ever and ever.". Revelation 21:5 says, "And he that sat upon the throne said, Behold, I make all things new. And he said unto me, Write: for these words are true and faithful.". The reality of being "born again" of the Holy Spirit, is that God, through Christ Jesus of Nazareth, has forgiven us of all our sins, by His only begotten Son's shed blood on the cross, His death, His burial and His resurrection three days later. Alleluia and praise the LORD. Amen and Amen. In Song of Solomon it says, "Many waters cannot quench love, neither can the floods drown it: if a man would give all the substance of his house for love, it would utterly be contemned." (Song 8:7). Psalm 93:4 says, "The LORD on high *is* mightier than the noise of many waters, *yea, than* the mighty waves of the sea.". This is the reality and hope we have in Jesus Christ of Nazareth, through His Holy Spirit given to us (Matt. 28:18). Although He is mighty indeed, He remains that still small voice that spoke to Elijah, after the wind, earthquake and fire (1 Kings 19:11-18). He is our comforter, and our healer, our Saviour and Redeemer, in the name of Jesus Christ of Nazareth, God's only begotten Son. Alleluia and praise the LORD. Jesus Christ of Nazareth is the only solution and the best solution. He has given us eternal life in His Holy name. He died on the cross for the forgiveness of our sins, He was buried and He arose the third day to give us the hope and promise of eternal life in His Holy name. Alleluia and praise the LORD. Amen and Amen.

Appendix C

Destruction of Earth – "Great Tribulation" and the "end"...
Introduction

God openly admits He is fully in control of all things and has created all things (John 1:1-3, Rev. 4:11). In Isaiah, it says of God, "...I have created the waster to destroy." (Isa. 54:16). And God speaks through the prophet Hosea, saying, "O Israel, thou hast destroyed thyself; but in me *is* thine help." (Hos. 13:9). Nevertheless, we have our hope in God's only begotten Son, Jesus Christ of Nazareth. Alleluia and praise the LORD. Amen and Amen. The apostle, John, says in one of his epistles, "... For this purpose the Son of God was manifested, that he might destroy the works of the devil." (1 John 3:8). Alleluia and praise the LORD. Amen and Amen. This, Son of God, is that Jesus Christ of Nazareth, whom overcame the world, and all power in heaven and in earth has been given to Him (Matt. 28:18). Alleluia and praise the LORD. Amen and Amen. This same Jesus Christ of Nazareth said of Himself, "...I will build my church; and the gates of hell shall not prevail against it." (Matt. 16:18). Alleluia and praise the LORD. Amen and Amen. In Isaiah it says, "The wolf and the lamb shall feed together, and the lion shall eat straw like the bullock: and dust *shall be* the serpent's meat. They shall not hurt nor destroy in all my holy mountain, saith the LORD." (Isa. 65:25). This is our reality in the name of Jesus Christ of Nazareth. Alleluia and praise the LORD. Amen and Amen. If you are willing to go a little further in this topic of discussion of destruction, and God's sovereignty over it, read on to learn more. And of course the Holy Bible of God is the best place to go to learn about any topic of discussion, including the topic of destruction, as the Holy Bible says, "*He that is our God is* the God of salvation; and unto GOD the Lord *belong* the issues from death." (Ps. 68:20). This is the reality we have in Jesus Christ of Nazareth, whom holds the keys to hell and death (Rev. 1:18). He overcame all of these things, He shed His righteous and Holy blood on the cross and died on the cross for the forgiveness of our sins, He was buried and He arose the third day to give us the hope and promise of eternal life in His Holy name. Alleluia and praise the LORD. Amen and Amen. Nevertheless, read on to learn more about this idea of the "destruction" of earth.

Great Tribulation and the likelihood of "nuclear" war

I have written another book on the subject of the "great tribulation", and spoke in it mostly of God's miraculous involvement in it through earthquakes, storms, etc., as well as man's part in it, I did not however mention anything of "nuclear" war. For good reason, as Jesus said, that "...except those days should be shortened, there should no flesh be saved: but for the elect's sake those days shall be shortened." (Matt. 24:22). So I thought for mankind's sake, that nuclear war should not even be an option. That being said, I have looked into the topic a bit further since, and will speak about the verses that could be interpreted as related to "nuclear" war, with a conclusion to the matter as far as I am concerned. There are only a handful of verses that I have found that would even come close to being related to nuclear war. They either are associated with "consuming away" or something to do with "iron teeth", that is, something made by man's hands as weapons (Ps. 39:11, 57:4; Prov. 30:14, Isa. 41:15, Dan. 7:7, Zech. 14:12). Psalm 57:4 says, "My soul *is* among lions: *and* I lie *even among* them that are set on fire, *even* the sons of men, whose teeth *are* spears and arrows, and their tongues a sharp sword.". Proverbs 30:14 says, "...generation, whose teeth *are as* swords, and their jaw teeth *as* knives, to devour the poor from off the earth, and the needy from *among* men.". This indicates that people and their mouths are associated with violence and destruction, which is spoken of in other places in the Holy Bible. James calls the tongue "...a fire...and setteth on fire the course of nature...", and he says our mouths give out blessings and cursings, etc. (Jam. 3:6, 9, 10). So we can see that our mouth is a powerful tool, that God has given us and created, as we can speak nothing, but by God, as He is the breath of life, woe to us if we speak otherwise (Ex. 4:11, Prov. 16:1, Isa. 57:19, Amos 4:13). Also, an aside, the Holy Bible says God hates the doctrine of the "Nicolaitanes" (Rev. 2:6, 15). I am not sure that it is a coincidence that the word "Nicolaitane" and "nuclear" are similar, but I will leave that up to you to decide. To God be the glory in the truth of all of this. Alleluia and praise the LORD. Amen and Amen. Praise the LORD God Almighty and His only begotten Son, Jesus Christ of Nazareth. He shed His righteous and Holy blood on the cross for the forgiveness of our sins. He died on that cross and was buried and the third day He arose to give us the hope and promise of eternal life in His Holy name. Alleluia and praise the LORD. Amen and Amen.

Next, we have Isaiah 41:15 and 16, which say, "Behold, I make thee a new sharp threshing instrument having teeth: thou shalt thresh the mountains, and beat *them* small, and shall make the hills as chaff. Thou shalt fan them, and the wind shall carry them away, and the whirlwind scatter them; and then shalt though rejoice in the LORD...". I see these verses as the best possible argument for "nuclear" weaponry involvement in the "great tribulation" spoken of in the Holy Bible (Matt. 24:21, Rev. 2:22, 7:14). With the possibility of them being used to crumble mountains, etc., but the reality is mountains and hills could also be referencing governments and idolatrous religion as well, as the Holy Bible does make these comparisons (Matt. 4:8, Rev. 17:9, 10; 21:10). And the "new sharp threshing instrument", could simply be talking about our "industrial" tractors, combines and the general manufacturing age of the 19th and 20th centuries in general (Ps. 72:16, Prov. 27:25, Isa. 17:13). This may be understood better by looking at Daniel 7:7. Daniel 7:7 says, "After this I saw in the night visions, and behold a fourth beast, dreadful and terrible, and strong exceedingly; and it had great iron teeth: it devoured and brake in pieces, and stamped the residue with the feet of it: and it *was* diverse from all the beasts that *were* before it; and it had ten horns.". This is likely speaking of the same "ten toes" of Nebuchadnezzar's statue dream, as well as the "ten horns" or "ten kings" related to the book of Revelation beast (Dan. 2:41-44, Rev. 12:3, 13:1; 17:3, 7, 12, 16). I know that these prophecies have been compared with the "Holy Roman Empire" of the past. And some scholars have suggested that a form of it will "arise" again in the "time of the end" prior to the "Messianic Age", and this may be true, as of the date of writing this book in 2018 A.D. (Rev. 17:8). But we must remember that Jesus Christ of Nazareth, the Lamb of God, has been, is, and will be victorious no matter what mankind desires to do here on earth (Dan. 2:44, 45; Rev. 17:14). Alleluia and praise the LORD. Amen and Amen. Nevertheless, there are more verses regarding "teeth" in the Holy Bible of God. Psalm 58:6 says, "Break their teeth, O God, in their mouth: break out the great teeth of the young lions, O LORD.". This could be speaking of nuclear weaponry as a fairly resent military weapon, compared to weaponry used for warfare throughout the ages (Dan. 11:38). Also, Psalm 112:10 says, "The wicked shall see *it,* and be grieved; he shall gnash with his teeth, and melt away: the desire of the wicked shall perish.". This could be related to the eating of unhealthy food, over consumption of alcohol or other medicines, etc., rather than nuclear weaponry, or the idea of using "nuclear weapons" perishing in the mouths of those whom desire them to be used. Also, nuclear power at least in part is used to drive some processes that create various processed food products and medicines, etc., in this world as of the date of writing this book in 2018 A.D.. Psalm 124:6 says, "Blessed *be* the LORD, who hath not given us *as* a prey to their teeth.". So this is our reality in Jesus Christ of Nazareth's Holy name. He shed His Holy and righteous blood on the cross for the forgiveness of our sins, He died on that cross, He was buried and the third day He arose to give us the hope and promise of eternal life in His Holy name. Alleluia and praise the LORD. Amen and Amen.

Last, Zechariah again speaks of something similar to what could happen during nuclear fallout, it says, "…this...plague…the LORD will smite…flesh shall consume away…eyes shall consume away…tongue shall consume away…" (Zech. 14:12). Again this could be nuclear fallout, but this could be related to natural death, with flesh eating diseases, cancers, etc., as well as eye diseases, cataracts, glaucoma, etc., and the same with the tongue, cancers and other diseases. This could even speak of the very "end" of earth's current history as spoken of in the previous appendix and in other places in this book and namely in the Holy Bible of God, regarding the suns energy, fire from heaven, consuming the earth (2 Pet. 3:7-12). Also, in the book of Acts, a governing official was literally consumed by worms while sitting in his seat, because the people worshipped him as God, and he did not give the true God, God, the Father, and Jesus Christ of Nazareth, God's only begotten Son, the glory (Acts 12:23). To God be the glory in the name of His only begotten Son, Jesus Christ of Nazareth. Alleluia and praise the LORD. Amen and Amen. Also, Psalm 37:20 says, "But the wicked shall perish, and the enemies of the LORD *shall be* as the fat of lambs: they shall consume; into smoke shall they consume away.". And Psalm 39:11 says, "…rebukes dost correct man for iniquity, thou makest his beauty to consume away like a moth…". So this could in general explain the overall natural aging process of a person, regardless of other external factors, as we have seventy or eighty years here on earth, and at best one hundred and twenty (Gen. 6:3, Ps. 90:10). Alleluia and praise the LORD. Amen and Amen. Regarding the truth of all of these ideas, let us look at the example of Elijah, a true prophet of God, and the false prophets of Baal (1 Kings 18:19). Elijah set up an altar to make an offering to the LORD and told the prophets of Baal to do the same (1 Kings 18:23-35). The idea was that, Elijah said, whichever offering is consumed by fire that comes down from heaven; that will indicate the true God, and who is serving Him (1 Kings 18:24). Well, fire came down from heaven and burned up Elijah's offering, and then he slew the false prophets of Baal (1 Kings 18:36-40). This may be the scenario we are in today. We have to wait on God, so that He shows us, whom He is and whom He is with (Ps. 27:14, 37:34; Prov. 20:22, Luke 12:36, 23:51; Acts 1:4). That being said, the reality is, "…all have sinned, and come short of the glory of God;" (Ps. 14:3, 53:3; Rom. 3:23). We all need to repent and believe the gospel of the kingdom of God, and believe in and on the name of His only begotten Son, Jesus Christ of Nazareth, regardless of "nuclear war", our natural death or otherwise (Matt. 3:2, 4:17; Mark 1:15, Luke 13:3, 5). That is, our reality is in Jesus Christ of Nazareth, whom died on the cross for the forgiveness of our sins, spilling His righteous and Holy blood, He was buried and on the third day He arose to give us the hope and promise of eternal life in His Holy name. To God be the glory. Alleluia and praise the LORD. Amen and Amen.

Is the earth ever going to come to an end?

According to Ecclesiastes 1:4, "*One* generation passeth away, and *another* generation cometh: but the earth abideth for ever.". Depending on a person's interpretation of the Holy Bible of God, however, it could go either way. The most important point to understand is that God's kingdom is spiritual first and foremost and it certainly will never be destroyed (John 4:24, 10:28; Eph. 3:21). This should take away any concern of whether or not the earth is going to be "destroyed" in some way, either by human hands, natural means, or by God Almighty with His mighty powers, today, tomorrow or any time in the future. Nevertheless, let us consider a few possibilities of how earth's destruction, so to speak, could come about. The first scenario, although there is not much difference to a human or any other creature alike, is that physical life on the planet may cease to exist for some time period (Gen. 1:2, Jer. 4:23). This would maintain the continuity of the Holy Bible, with God's calling for a "new heaven and new earth" and new Jerusalem (Isa. 65:17, 66:22; 2 Pet. 3:12, Rev. 21:1, 2). The Holy Bible does talk about the "end" of this current earth's history in more than one place, and Christ's return with judgement, and then a resurrection and eternal life and a "new heaven and new earth", and "new Jerusalem" for those whom are saved and everlasting punishment to those whom are not (Matt. 25:46, Rev. 20:11-15; 21:1, 2). The point is that likely at some point in the future of this earth and its inhabitants there will be some sort of destruction, by fire, and likely a starting anew (2 Pet. 3:7, Rev. 20:11, 21:1, 2). This is where faith in Jesus Christ of Nazareth becomes so important, because if we believe in Jesus Christ of Nazareth, God's kingdom is a spiritual one first and foremost, and the physical realm becomes less important in that case (John 4:24, 6:63). So even if our bodies, this earth and everything in it were destroyed, we can still receive eternal life in Jesus Christ of Nazareth's Holy name, because He can and will create a "new heaven and new earth" and "new Jerusalem" (Isa. 65:17, 66:22; 2 Pet. 3:12, Rev. 21:1, 2). Alleluia and praise the LORD. Amen and Amen. Ultimately, my words will not be able to accurately describe this point. But we must put our trust in Jesus Christ of Nazareth for the truth of all of this. Alleluia and praise the LORD. Amen and Amen. He shed His righteous and Holy blood on the cross for the forgiveness of our sins, He died on the cross, He was buried and the third day He arose to give us the hope and promise of eternal life in His Holy name. Alleluia and praise the LORD. Amen and Amen.

The second scenario, albeit not really any different than the first, is that the heavens, the earth and all of the earth's inhabitants are "dissolved" or destroyed, etc.. Psalm 75:3 says, "The earth and all the inhabitants thereof are dissolved: I bear up the pillars of it. Selah.". 1 John 2:17 says, "This world and everything in it is passing away". However as the apostle, Paul, says in 2 Corinthians 5:1, "For we know that if our earthly house of *this* tabernacle were dissolved, we have a building of God, an house not made with hands, eternal in the heavens.". This should put anyone's mind at ease of where our treasures should be stored (Matt. 6:19-21). 2 Peter 3:10-12 confirms this idea of earth's "change", it says, "But the day of the Lord will come as a thief in the night; in the which the heavens shall pass away with a great noise, and the elements shall melt with fervent heat, the earth also and the works that are therein shall be burned up. *Seeing* then *that* all these things shall be dissolved, what manner *of persons* ought ye to be in *all* holy conversation and godliness, Looking for and hasting unto the coming of the day of God, wherein the heavens being on fire shall be dissolved, and the elements shall melt with fervent heat?". That being said, the Holy Bible also says, "Woe unto you that desire the day of the LORD! to what end *is* it for you? the day of the LORD *is* darkness, and not light." (Amos. 5:18). So ultimately, we ought to watch and pray, and ask God, "…Our Father which art in heaven, Hallowed be thy name. Thy kingdom come, Thy will be done in earth, as *it is* in heaven." (Matt. 6:9, 10). But in the end, the result should be the same in that we are looking for a "new heaven and a new earth" and "new Jerusalem" (2 Pet. 3:13, Rev. 3:12, 21:1, 2). Putting the truth of God's kingdom and our relationship with it into proper perspective makes the question of whether or not the earth will be completely destroyed, as a less important issue. Although it is natural for us to care about our family, and our descendants after us, we need to place our trust first and foremost in Jesus Christ of Nazareth for the truth of these matters (Mark 12:29, 30). Trust that He is in control and that He will provide for us, body, soul and spirit, unto the end of our natural lives here on earth and for those whom come after us, until the "world to come", and eternal life (Mark 10:29, 30; Luke 18:29, 30). Alleluia and praise the LORD. Amen and Amen.

Last, regarding the issue of "nuclear weaponry" and God's involvement in the "end", there may be a hint during the wilderness journey of Israel, mentioned in the book of Exodus. Aside from God's miraculous involvement in the beginning of creation, He asked Moses and the Israelites to make an altar of earth or with stones not hewn by man's hands, and without steps, during their sojourn in the wilderness, after exiting Egypt (Ex. 20:24-26). This may be a clear sign that God has already prepared the "altar" of "sacrifice" ahead of time, for the "Great Tribulation", and the very "end" of earth's current history, as we know it (Matt. 24:21, Rev. 2:22, 7:12, 20:11). Alleluia and praise the LORD. Amen and Amen. This may be a sign that we can expect miracles like the crossing of the Red sea, and others similar to it again (Ex. 14). Alleluia and praise the LORD. Amen and Amen. As we already do and have. Our very existence is a miracle. Alleluia and praise the LORD God, the Father, Almighty, and His only begotten Son, Jesus Christ of Nazareth, for the truth in all of this. Alleluia and praise the LORD. All thanks and glory be to our God. Alleluia and praise the LORD. Amen and Amen.

New Heavens and New Earth

Malachi 4:1 says, "For, behold, the day cometh, that shall burn as an oven; and all the proud, yea, and all that do wickedly, shall be stubble: and the day that cometh shall burn them up, saith the LORD of hosts, that it shall leave them neither root nor branch.". Isaiah 30:26 says, "Moreover the light of the moon shall be as the light of the sun, and the light of the sun shall be sevenfold, as the light of seven days…". This describes a solar event of epic proportions. This is no doubt related to the fire coming down from heaven consuming the wicked in the book of Revelation and elsewhere in the Holy Bible at the very "end" of this earth's current history (Deut. 32:22, Mark 13:38-42, Rev. 20:9). And Matthew 13:49 and 50 say, "So shall it be at the end of the world: the angels shall come forth, and sever the wicked from among the just, an shall cast them into the furnace of fire: there shall be wailing and gnashing of teeth.". Psalm 104:4 says, "Who maketh his angels spirits; his ministers a flaming fire…". Isaiah 13:8 says, "…they shall be amazed one at another; their faces *shall be as* flames.". This of course was fulfilled in Jesus Christ of Nazareth at His transfiguration with Moses and Elijah (Matt. 17:2). Matthew 17:2 says of Jesus Christ of Nazareth, He "…was transfigured before them: and his face did shine as the sun, and his raiment was white as the light.". An Old Testament example of the consuming fire is the people consumed by fire in the wilderness for disobedience to God and Moses' authority and other examples like Sodom and Gomorrah (Gen. 18, 19; Num. 11:1-3, 16:35, 26:10). Some contemporary examples would be various military weapons technology like, napalm, nuclear, etc. and other natural events like meteorites, and thunder storms creating wild fires. But we have hope in the example of Daniel's three friends in the fiery furnace of Nebuchadnezzar, the king of Babylon (Dan. 3:19-30). They survived the trial, and Nebuchadnezzar saw, one with the likeness of the Son of God, walking with them in the midst of the furnace (Dan. 3:25). Jesus Christ of Nazareth is this Son of God (Matt. 14:33, John 1:34). God calls Himself a "consuming fire" (Deut. 4:24). And Jesus Christ of Nazareth is described similarly in various places in the Holy Bible, as He and the Father are One (Luke 12:49, John 10:30, Rev. 1:14, 2:18, 4:5, 10:1, 19:12). The point is we ought to place all our faith, hope and trust in the name of Jesus Christ of Nazareth, as He is the Faithful and True witness, the Alpha and Omega, the first and the last, the beginning and the end (Rev. 3:14, 22;13). Alleluia and praise the LORD. Amen and Amen.

Malachi 4:2 says, "But unto you that fear my name shall the Sun of righteousness arise with healing in his wings…". Matthew 13:43 says, "Then shall the righteous shine forth as the sun in the kingdom of their Father. Who hath ears to hear, let him hear.". Malachi 4:2 continues, "...and ye shall go forth, and grow up as calves of the stall.". This seems to describe the seven day creation week, including, a new creation of the sun, moon and stars on the fourth day and sixth day creation of beasts and man and rest on the seventh day, after the destruction of this present earth and its history (Gen. 1:1-2:3). Psalm 68:13 says, "Though ye have lien among the pots, *yet shall ye be as* the wings of a dove covered with silver, and her feathers with yellow gold.". This could very well describe us coming up from the dust, like Adam did, and receiving the Holy Spirit of God, in the breath of life like Adam did, and just like it descended on Jesus Christ of Nazareth at His baptism by John the Baptist in 27 A.D. (Gen. 2:7, Matt. 3:16, Mark 1:10, Luke 3:22, John 1:32). Alleluia and praise the LORD. Amen and Amen. The gold could very well be representative of the sun, and the silver representative of the clouds, from where God spoke of Jesus after His baptism and during His transfiguration with Elijah and Moses saying, "...This is my beloved Son, in whom I am well pleased...", "...hear Him..." (Matt. 3:17, 17:5; Mark 1:11, 9:7; Luke 3:22, 9:35; 2 Pet. 1:17). This also could be a very good indication of what Jesus meant by "...they shall see the Son of man coming in the clouds of heaven with power and great glory." (Matt. 24:30, 26:64; Mark 13:26, 14:62; Luke 21:27, Acts 1:9-11, Rev. 1:7, 10:1, 14:14-16). That is, the reality of Jesus Christ of Nazareth's second coming is spiritual first and foremost, as He has given us His Holy Spirit to dwell with us and in us, until the "end" of the world, and forever more, in His Holy name (Matt. 28:20, John 14:16-18). Alleluia and praise the LORD. Amen and Amen. Revelation 21:1-5 says, "And I saw a new heaven and a new earth: for the first heaven and the first earth were passed away; and there was no more sea. And I John saw the holy city, new Jerusalem, coming down from God out of heaven, prepared as a bride adorned for her husband. And I heard a great voice out of heaven saying, Behold, the tabernacle of God *is* with men, and he will dwell with them, and they shall be his people, and God himself shall be with them, *and be* their God. And God shall wipe away all tears from their eyes; and there shall be no more death, neither sorrow, nor crying, neither shall there be any more pain: for the former things are passed away. And he that sat upon the throne said, Behold, I make all things new. And he said unto me, Write: for these words are true and faithful.". This is the reality we have awaiting us in Christ Jesus of Nazareth. Alleluia and praise the LORD. Amen and Amen. He shed His righteous and Holy blood on the cross for the forgiveness of all of our sins. He died and was buried and the third day He arose to give us the hope and promise of eternal life in His Holy name. Alleluia and praise the LORD. Amen and Amen.

2 Peter 3:10 says, "But the day of the Lord will come as a thief in the night; in the which the heavens shall pass away with a great noise, and the elements shall melt with fervent heat, the earth also and the works that are therein shall be burned up.". This could very well describe the sun's energy consuming everything here on earth and breaking everything into its base elements, making it "...without form and void..." (Gen. 1:2, Jer. 4:23). Looking at chemistry and the one hundred plus elements in the periodic table, with the laws of Entropy and Enthalpy, these laws of chemistry would agree well with the degradation of the sun's energy and the elements of this universe in general. Nevertheless, the apostle, Paul, speaks of submitting with "...all gravity..." (1 Tim. 3:4). All the laws of the natural world are relevant to a Christ follower, that being said, the word chemistry may have some association with the worshipping of "Chemosh", a god of the Moabites of the Old Testament, which is an abomination to the true God (1 Kings 11:33, 2 Kings 23:13). And in particular the one Hebrew word for the sun is, shemesh, Strong's number 8121; so no doubt these are associated, as we can see in this world today these signs in some nations flags and other insignia, etc. (Gen. 15:12). And even though, the sun, moon and stars were created for a purpose, for signs and for seasons, days and years (Gen. 1:14-18).

God admonishes us not to worship the host of heaven, the things He created by His Word, by His Holy Spirit in Jesus Christ of Nazareth's Holy name (Deut. 4:15-19, 17:2-5). Alleluia and praise the LORD. Amen and Amen. We are to worship the true God in Spirit and in truth, whom is a Spirit, first and foremost (John 4:24). Alleluia and praise the LORD. Amen and Amen. So our reality ought to be in Christ Jesus of Nazareth, whom overcame all of these natural laws, He created them all after all (John 16:33, John 1:3, Rev. 4:11). He walked on water, turned water into wine; He revealed His glory at the transfiguration and at His resurrection (Matt. 14:25-32, 17:2; Mark 9:2, 3; Luke 9:29, 24:26; John 1:14, 2:1-11, 4:46; 1 Pet. 1:21). All power in heaven and in earth has been given to God's only begotten Son, Jesus Christ of Nazareth, who lives and reigns with God, the Father, and His Holy Spirit, forever and ever (Matt. 28:19). Alleluia and praise the LORD. Amen and Amen. He shed His Holy and righteous blood on the cross and died for the forgiveness of our sins. He was buried and the third day He arose giving us the hope and promise of eternal life in His Holy name. Alleluia and praise the LORD. Amen and Amen.

Conclusion

Nehemiah 9:6 says, speaking of God Almighty, "Thou, *even* thou, *art* LORD alone; thou hast made heaven, the heaven of heavens, with all their host, the earth, and all *things* that *are* therein, the seas, and all that *is* therein, and thou preservest them all; and the host of heaven worshippeth thee.". It is interesting that all of God's creation worships Him, of course, Jesus said something similar about these things, He said the stones would cry out and worship Him if people held their tongues (Luke 19:40). In Daniel 8:10 some prophecy speaks about a "little horn" and the host of heaven, it says, "And it waxed great, *even* to the host of heaven; and it cast down *some* of the host and of the stars to the ground, and stamped upon them.". This likely has something to do with false prophets, false Christs and wolves in sheep's clothing in general (Matt. 7:15, 24:11, 24; Mark 13:22). As I have found doing some research about signs in the heavens, there are multiple interpretations, for various prophecies in the Holy Bible, where the scholarly interpretations do not always agree one hundred percent with one another. That being said, the Holy Bible does say, "…here a little, and there a little…" (Isa. 28:10). And this prophecy seems to actually have been fulfilled, at least once, when Ahab, a king of Israel, was deceived by a lying spirit in the mouth of his prophets (2 Chr. 18:5, 10, 11). Micaiah, a true prophet of God, albeit accused of always prophesying evil against Ahab, explained what had happened in the spiritual realm for Ahab the king to be deceived (2 Chr. 18:7, 14-17). 2 Chronicles 18:18-22 says, "Again he said, Therefore hear the word of the LORD; I saw the LORD sitting upon his throne, and all the host of heaven standing on his right hand and *on* his left. And the LORD said, Who shall entice Ahab king of Israel, that he may go up and fall at Ramothgilead? And one spake saying after this manner, and another saying after that manner. Then there came out a spirit, and stood before the LORD, and said, I will entice him. And *the LORD* said unto him, Wherewith? And he said, I will go out, and be a lying spirit in the mouth of all his prophets. And *the LORD* said, Thou shalt entice *him,* and thou shalt also prevail: go out, and do *even so.* Now therefore, behold, the LORD hath put a lying spirit in the mouth of these thy prophets, and the LORD hath spoken evil against thee.". The point of all of this is to show that God indeed is sovereign over all of His creation, man, beast, nature and the spirit world (John 1:3, Rev. 4:11). Alleluia and praise the LORD. Amen and Amen.

Luke 14:26 says, "If any *man* come to me, and hate not his father, and mother, and wife, and children, and brethren, and sisters, yea, and his own life also, he cannot be my disciple.". John 12:25 says, "He that loveth his life shall lose it; and he that hateth his life in this world shall keep it unto life eternal.". The point is we are called to forsake all and follow Jesus Christ of Nazareth (Luke 14:33). The first commandment is summed up in that "…thou shalt love the Lord thy God with all thy heart, and with all thy soul, and with all thy mind, and with all thy strength: this *is* the first commandment." (Mark 12:30). That being said, He also said, "It is easier for a camel to go through the eye of a needle, than for a rich man to enter into the kingdom of God. And they were astonished out of measure, saying among themselves, Who then can be saved? And Jesus looking upon them saith, With men *it* is impossible, but not with God: for with God all things are possible. Then Peter began to say unto him, Lo, we have left all, and have followed thee. And Jesus answered and said, Verily I say unto you, There is no man that hath left house, or brethren, or sisters, or father, or mother, or wife, or children, or lands, for my sake, and the gospel's, But he shall receive an hundredfold now in this time, houses, and brethren, and sisters, and mothers, and children, and lands, with persecutions; and in the world to come eternal life. But many *that are* first shall be last; and the last first." (Mark 10:25-31). This is the promise we have in Christ, that even though we forsake all, He provides us life and life more abundantly (Matt. 19:27-30, John 10:10). Alleluia and praise the LORD. Amen and Amen. Peter had a wife, and there is no indication in the Holy Bible that He divorced her, that would have been against the commandments of God anyhow (Matt. 5:32, Mark 10:4-9, 1 Pet. 3:7). But He did need to let go of his position as a fisherman, and whatever other duties that included, in order to follow Jesus and become one of His disciples, albeit even after Jesus' resurrection the disciples were found fishing (Matt. 4:19, 20; John 21:1-14). Of course Jesus showed them all wonderful things regarding provision, turning water into wine, in multiplying fishes and loaves, tax money appearing in a fish's mouth, and other miracles (Matt. 14:17-21, 15:34-38, 17:27; Mark 6:38-44, 8:5-9; Luke 9:13-17, John 2:1-11, 6:9-13, 14:17-21). The point is that God is ultimately in control of all of these things, and that He is the ultimate provider of all things for all people. Alleluia and praise the LORD. Amen and Amen. And in Christ Jesus of Nazareth, we all have that perfect and abundant provision. He was miraculously conceived in and born of the virgin, Mary, espoused to Joseph (Matt. 1:20-25). Jesus did miracles during His earthly ministry, including healings and provision (Matt. 4:23, 14:17-21). And ultimately, He went to the cross and shed His Holy and righteous blood on the cross for the forgiveness of our sins. He died and He was buried and the third day He arose to give us the hope and promise of eternal life in His Holy name. Alleluia and praise the LORD. Amen and Amen.

Last, Jesus said that the Holy Spirit, the Comforter, would be sent to us in these "last days" (Joel 2:28, 29; Acts 2:17, 18). He said before His crucifixion, burial, resurrection and ascension to the right hand of the Father, "Nevertheless I tell you the truth; It is expedient for you that I go away: for if I go not away, the Comforter will not come unto you; but if I depart, I will send him unto you. And when he is come, he will reprove the world of sin, and of righteousness, and of judgment: Of sin, because they believe not on me; Of righteousness, because I go to my Father, and ye see me no more; Of judgment, because the prince of this world is judged. I have yet many things to say unto you, but ye cannot bear them now. Howbeit when he, the Spirit of truth, is come, he will guide you into all truth: for he shall not speak of himself; but whatsoever he shall hear, *that* shall he speak: and he will shew you things to come. He shall glorify me: for he shall receive of mine, and shall shew *it* unto you. All things that the Father hath are mine: therefore said I, that he shall take of mine, and shall shew *it* unto you. A little while, and ye shall not see me: and again, a little while, and ye shall see me, because I go to the Father." (John 16:7-16). So no matter my interpretation of these things, our reality must be in Jesus Christ of Nazareth, and what He has said and promises for those whom follow Him. That is,

He promises us life and life more abundantly, and eternal life in His Holy name (John 10:10). Alleluia and praise the LORD. Amen and Amen. He shed His Holy and righteous blood on the cross for the forgiveness of our sins, He died on that cross and was buried and the third day He arose to give us the hope and promise of eternal life in His Holy name. Alleluia and praise the LORD. Amen and Amen.

Appendix D

Work, Family, Child rearing, Emotions and Spiritual life
Introduction

Before I go into detail about family, and child rearing, I would like to address the issue that this world seems to be in today, as of 2018 A.D., regarding the brokenness in some cases of the "traditional" family unit. God said that we could receive curses for disobedience to His commandments, one of them is Deuteronomy 28:49-51, it says, "The LORD shall bring a nation against thee from far, from the end of the earth, *as swift* as the eagle flieth; a nation whose tongue thou shalt not understand; A nation of fierce countenance, which shall not regard the person of the old, nor shew favour to the young: And he shall eat the fruit of thy cattle, and the fruit of thy land, until thou be destroyed: which *also* shall not leave thee *either* corn, wine, or oil, *or* the increase of thy kine, or flocks of thy sheep, until he have destroyed thee.". This is amongst other curses God speaks of, which I spoke in some detail about in chapter four, that being said, Jesus came to give us life and life more abundantly (John 10:10). He came to forgive us our sins, and He also said to forsake all and to follow Him (Luke 14:33, Acts 5:31). So in this sense the curses mentioned in Deuteronomy would almost seem to be harmless in the end, no matter what we do, as long as we repent and follow Jesus Christ of Nazareth. He came to forgive us our sins, and give us eternal life in His Holy name. Alleluia and praise the LORD. The last verse of Deuteronomy 28:68 says, "And the LORD shall bring thee into Egypt again with ships, by the way whereof I spake unto thee, Thou shalt see it no more again: and there ye shall be sold unto your enemies for bondmen and bondwomen, and no man shall buy *you*.". It would seem then that we are not slaves to men, but we are bought with a price, that is by the blood of Jesus Christ of Nazareth, that leads us unto eternal life in His Holy name (Isa. 52:3, 55:1, 1 Cor. 6:20, 7:20). Alleluia and praise the LORD. Nevertheless, in this appendix I will go into greater detail about life with family, work and our spiritual experience in this life, and in the "world to come" eternal life. Alleluia and praise the LORD. Amen and Amen.

Work and Family

This section is an interpretation of Ezekiel, chapter one, in the Holy Bible, in the light of work and life with family and God Almighty. Ezekiel 1:4 says, a "...whirlwind came out of the north, a great cloud, and a fire infolding itself...". This may be technology from Northern countries of the world and the clouds could be clouds of smoke from manufacturing industry and the like. And the "...fire infolding itself..." could describe motors and engines, electric current running through coiled wires on electric motors, etc., used in manufacturing, etc., "...a brightness *was* about it..." could be lights used to light up facilities (Ezek. 1:4). And "...out of the midst thereof as the colour of amber, out of the midst of the fire." is the colour of incandescent light bulbs lite up (Ezek. 1:4). Ezekiel 1:5 says, "...out of the midst...the likeness of four living creatures...their appearance...the likeness of a man.". This may represent any manual labour that is required in manufacturing. Ezekiel 1:6 says, "...everyone had four faces, and everyone had four wings.", possibly referencing the measure of a man that is of the angel (Rev. 21:17). This also likely indicates there is more to a person than just their "job". Ezekiel 1:7 says, "...their feet *were* straight feet...the sole of their feet *was* like the sole of a calf's foot: and they sparkled like the colour of burnished brass.". This may represent the young, youthfulness of a "labourer", tenderness, etc.; Moses had all his strength and sight as a youth at his death at the age of one hundred and twenty (Deut. 34:7). Ezekiel 1:8 says, "...the hands of a man under their wings on their four sides; and they four had their four wings.". This is more confirmation of human likeness. Ezekiel 1:9 says, "Their wings *were* joined one to another; they turned not when they went; they went everyone straight forward.", likely representing "team" work and cooperation required in manufacturing and "group" work of any kind. Ezekiel 1:10 says, "…likeness of their faces, they four had the face of a man, and the face of a lion, on the right side…". This is more indication that these represent people. The lion may indicate individuality and dominion, also strength and ferocity if required. Continuing Ezekiel 1:10 says, "…they four had the face of an ox on the left side…". The ox likely represents labour, strength, yoke of daily work, but also sacrifice (Prov. 7:22, 14:4). And "…they four also had the face of an eagle…", likely representing freedom, man's desire to do what we please without restriction (Ezek. 1:10, Isa. 40:31). Ezekiel 1:11 says, "Thus *were* their faces: and their wings *were* stretched upward; two *wings* of every one *were* joined one to another, and two covered their body.". This may show honour and recognition, worship of our Creator, God in heaven and Jesus Christ of Nazareth. Alleluia and praise the LORD God Almighty. The wings joined confirm unity of labourers, labour organizations and possibly religious labour fraternities of all kinds, as of the date of writing this book in 2018 A.D.. The two covering the body again shows individuality and our ability to protect ourselves, cover ourselves, etc., independence in Christ, individuality in Christ Jesus of Nazareth's Holy name. Alleluia and praise the LORD. Amen and Amen.

Ezekiel 1:12 says, "…they went straight forward: wither the spirit was to go, they went; *and* they turned not when they went."; representing following God's Holy Spirit, unity, etc. (Ps. 133:1). Ezekiel 1:13 says, "…the likeness of the living creatures, their appearance *was* like burning coals of fire, *and* like the appearance of lamps: it went up and down among the living creatures; and the fire was bright, and out of the fire went lightening.". Burning coals and lamps could be compared to the gospel message, being kind to one another, including the parable of the virgins with the lamps and Jesus' disciples as a light of the world (Matt. 5:14-16, 6:22, 25:1-13; Luke 12:35, John 13:34). Fire and lightening could be the Holy Spirit and Jesus coming like lightening; the angel of the Lord was described to have a countenance like lightening at the empty tomb after Jesus' resurrection, likely a good sign and example of Jesus' "second coming", that is, He is here and lives forever more (Matt. 24:27, 28:1-4, Acts 2:1-4). Alleluia and praise the LORD. But Jesus also compared Satan to lightening (Luke 10:18). Burning coal, literally could be fuel used in manufacturing, welding, grinding, forging and electrical supply in general in manufacturing and the like. Ezekiel 1:14 says, "…the living creatures ran and returned as the appearance of a flash of lightning.". With vehicles going to and from work, they can seem fast like lightening, compared to thousands of years ago, especially with electronic communications. This could also be speaking of Jesus' second coming, the "…coming of the Son of man…" (Matt. 24:27). Or again Satan was described like lightening, that would describe man's fallen corrupt side as well (Luke 10:18, Rom. 3:23). This is why we need God, the Father, through Jesus Christ of Nazareth by His Holy Spirit; no matter what "job" or "jobs" we have been given to do in this life. Alleluia and praise the LORD God Omnipotent. In general, I think this may suggest there will always be room for the "Jack of all trades. Master of none.", "Get it done.", type attitude in this life. I could be wrong, as this is an interpretation, but the reality is in Jesus Christ of Nazareth, the Saviour of us all and Redeemer of all mankind. Alleluia and praise the LORD. Amen and Amen

Ezekiel 1:15 says, "…as I beheld the living creatures, behold one wheel upon the earth by the living creatures, with his four faces."; this may represent Adam and Eve (Gen. 2:24). Ezekiel 1:16 says, the "… appearance of the wheels and their work *was* like unto the colour of beryl: and they four had an likeness: and their appearance and their work *was* as it were a wheel in the middle of a wheel.".

This may represent the work to bear children, if the wheel is considered a woman, wife, and "living creature" as a man, husband. The wheel in a wheel may be child bearing, weaning and raising up the child to become like Christ Jesus of Nazareth. I have interpreted this in other writings as vehicles, bearings, rims, etc., but this likely is speaking of the wife's role in marriage as well. Alleluia and praise the Lord for the truth in all of this. Ezekiel 1:17 says, "When they went, they went upon their four sides: *and* they turned not when they went.". Again, there is the similarity to the living creature with four sides, also the straightness of the wheels direction, the woman, wife, spouse has a "job" or "jobs" just like the man, husband, spouse. Ezekiel 1:18 says, "As for their rings, they were so high that they were dreadful; and their rings *were* full of eyes round about them four.". This may represent engagement and wedding rings, usually three total but the engagement ring is for both. A cut and polished diamond also reflects in many directions, "eyes", that could include the eyes of the multiple family members, husband, wife and children, relatives and the like. Hebrews 13:4 says, that "Marriage *is* honourable in all, and the bed undefiled…". Alleluia and praise the LORD. Ezekiel 1:19 says, "And when the living creatures went, the wheels went by them: and when the living creatures were lifted up from the earth, the wheels were lifted up.", this likely represents the commandment for a man to "… cleave unto his wife…" (Gen. 2:24, Matt. 19:4-6). Husband and wife live life together as God meant and created it to be from the beginning (Gen. 2:24). Ezekiel 1:20 says, "Withersoever the spirit was to go, they went, thither *was their* spirit to go; and the wheels were lifted up over against them: for the spirit of the living creature *was* in the wheels.". Again, confirming "…they shall be one flesh." (Gen. 2:24, Matt. 19:4-6). Ezekiel 1:21 says, "When those went, *these* went; and when those stood, *these* stood; and when those were lifted up from the earth, the wheels were lifted up over against them: for the spirit of the living creature *was* in the wheels.". This can represent families traveling together, husband, wife and children, on vacations, leisure activities, and in other family oriented activities, including fellowship with the body of Christ, the Church of God (Deut. 12). Alleluia and praise the LORD. Amen and Amen.

Ezekiel 1:22 says, "And the likeness of the firmament upon the heads of the living creature *was* as the colour of the terrible crystal, stretched over their heads.". This could be a prism, or a diamond of the engagement ring that breaks white light into the rainbow colour, ROYGBIV; red, orange, yellow, green, blue, indigo, violet. Also this may be a sign of God's covenant that He will never flood the earth again (Gen. 9:12-15). And a sign of God's presence in the marriage covenant in general, in Christ Jesus of Nazareth's Holy name. Alleluia and praise the LORD. Ice, frost, etc.; this colour of the "terrible crystal" could represent the northerly climate on earth in general; of course the South Pole is cold as well (Job 37:9, 22). Jesus dwelt in the north of Israel, in Galilee, and so did at least some of His twelve disciples (Isa. 41:25, Matt. 2:22, 23; 4:12-22). And there is prophecy in the Holy Bible about the north countries, of course the north western European and North American, even some Russian and north eastern Europeans are likely generally descendants of the Tribes of Israel, including parts of South America and dispersed throughout the world as well (Isa. 49:12, Jer. 3:12, 18; Ezek. 38:6, 15; 39:2). The colour could represent, white, snow, etc.; the Nazarites were described as "…purer than snow… whiter than milk…", Jesus' appearance at the transfiguration was described similarly, so was the angel of the Lord at Jesus' tomb after His resurrection (Lam. 4:7, Mark 9:3, Matt. 28:1-4). In general this could speak of the ancients, elders, hoary haired (Lev. 19:32, Prov. 16:31, Dan. 7:9, Rev. 1:14, 4:4). God is the Ancient of Days (Dan. 7:9, Rev. 1:14). Jesus Christ of Nazareth and God are One (John 10:30). This could also be speaking of natural phenomena in the firmament of heaven, earth's atmosphere, weather, and the moon, sun and stars in the firmament of heaven also (Gen. 1:14-19, Job 38:29). But the terrible crystal is over the creatures head, so ultimately God is sovereign over all of His creation (John 1:1-3, Rev. 4:11). In the Book of Revelation there is a sea of glass, like crystal before the throne of God (Rev. 4:6). This may also point to television screens, computer screens, and also water, seas, oceans, lakes and living waters, rain. Four beasts are also mentioned in Revelation four similar to Ezekiel's vision in the midst and around the throne full of eyes before and behind (Rev. 4:6-8). The new Jerusalem, the Holy Jerusalem, descending out of heaven, the glory of God, is described to be like jasper, clear as crystal (Rev. 21:11). And the river coming out of the throne of God and the Lamb in the new Jerusalem, the Holy Jerusalem, is clear as crystal (Rev. 22:1). Ezekiel 1:23 says, "And under the firmament *were* their wings straight, the one toward the other: everyone had two, which covered on this side, and everyone had two, which covered on that side, their bodies.". At home, husband and wife have their whole body available to take care of each other and family. Also this represents rest and protection of our body in general, and taking care of our body in Christ (1 Cor. 6:15-20, Eph. 5:33). Alleluia and praise the LORD. Amen and Amen.

Ezekiel 1:24 says, "And when they went, I heard the noise of their wings, like the noise of great waters, as the voice of the Almighty, the voice of speech, as the noise of an host: when they stood, they let down their wings.". This represents God's presence in family, God's voice in the family unit; God speaks through our actions, deeds, words and thoughts (Ps. 102:24, Ezek. 10:5, 1 John 3:18). Ezekiel 1:25 says, "And there was a voice from the firmament that *was* over their heads, when they stood, *and* had let down their wings.". This represents God's protection and presence when we rest; this is a work of faith (Rom. 4). Ezekiel 1:26 says, "And above the firmament that *was* over their heads *was* the likeness of a throne, as the appearance of a sapphire stone: and upon the likeness of the throne *was* the likeness as the appearance of a man above upon it.". This represents God's dominion over the family unit; this is why Satan desires to break families apart, because they are God's kingdom. In Christ Jesus of Nazareth, the Son of man and Son of God, we can and have overcome the adversary. Alleluia and praise the LORD in the name of Jesus Christ of Nazareth. Alleluia and praise the LORD. Ezekiel 1:27 says, "And I saw as the colour of amber, as the appearance of fire round about within it, from the appearance of his loins even upward, and from the appearance of his loins even downward, I saw as it were the appearance of fire, and it had brightness round about.". The same God, in Christ, that is involved and is above the head of the family unit is also a part of the "living creature", work life (Ezek. 1:4, 13). Ezekiel 1:28 says, "As the appearance of the bow that is in the cloud in the day of rain, so *was* the appearance of the brightness round about. This *was* the appearance of the likeness of the glory of the LORD. And when I saw *it*, I fell upon my face, and I heard a voice of one that spake.". This is confirmation of God's presence. It is also confirmation of the rainbow as a token of God's covenant with us that He will never flood the earth again (Gen. 9:12-15). God is glorified by our bearing much fruit (John 15:8). This can be at work and at home with family. Jesus said, "The work of God is to believe in the one whom he sent.", that is, to believe in and on Jesus Christ of Nazareth (John 6:29). This is a work of faith (Rom. 4). There are four wheels and four faces; that may represent physical work, physical family, spiritual work and spiritual family, and these are all one, wheels, wheel, faces, face (John 17:22, 23). Alleluia and praise the LORD. Amen and Amen.

The root Hebrew word for "sapphire" can mean score, mark or scribe, Strong's number 5608; and may have something to do with God judging our works. It may also have to do with our life being written in the Lamb's book of life, etc. (Rev. 20:12). Jesus Christ of Nazareth is the author and finisher of our faith (Heb. 12:2). Exodus 24:10 says, "And they saw the God of Israel: and *there was* under his feet as it were a paved work of a sapphire stone, and as it were the body of heaven in *his* clearness.". King David wrote of God, "The LORD said unto my Lord, Sit thou at my right hand, until I make thine enemies thy footstool." (Ps. 110:1). Does not this vision in Exodus, and the vision of Ezekiel confirm that this is the case? God is indeed sovereign. Jesus Christ of Nazareth did overcome us all and is over all, and in all with God, the Father, and the Holy Spirit, as we accept Him as our Lord and Saviour. Alleluia and praise the LORD. Sapphire is one of the stones on the high priest's breastplate, again showing God's sovereignty over His children (Ex. 39:11). The anointed cherub in the Garden of Eden was covered with a sapphire stone amongst other precious gems; that may represent Adam and Eve (Ezek. 28:13). Sapphires are also found in the earth, and of course Jesus Christ of Nazareth actually walked on the earth during His earthly ministry, again, overcoming and confirming Scripture of making the earth His footstool (Job 28:6, Ps. 110:1, John 16:33). It is a foundational stone in the new Jerusalem wall of the city (Rev. 21:19). The first stone mentioned in the new Jerusalem foundation is jasper, and the last is amethyst (Rev. 21:19). In the book of Revelation, chapter four, the One whom sat upon the throne was like jasper and sardine stone and a rainbow was "…round about the throne, in sight like an emerald." (Rev. 4:3). This could be to do with the church in Sardis, "…be watchful and strengthen..." and again the rainbow is a confirmation of the covenant to not flood the earth again (Gen. 9:13-17, Rev. 3:2). The wall of the new Jerusalem is made of jasper (Rev. 21:18). The Revelation 4:3 description of the throne is similar to the Ezekiel 1 description, which shows that John's vision and Ezekiel's vision are related. Nevertheless, our truth and life are in Jesus Christ of Nazareth, whom came into the world, born of the virgin, Mary, espoused to Joseph and He was raised a child of Israel by Joseph and Mary (Matt. 1:18-25, Luke 2:42-52). He had brothers and sisters (Mark 6:3). And starting at about the age 30, He ministered for three and a half years, healing, teaching, forgiving and preaching the kingdom of God (Luke 3:23). And on Passover 31 A.D., He gave up His life on the cross for the forgiveness of our sins. He died and was buried and the third day He arose to give us the hope and promise of eternal life in His Holy name. Alleluia and praise the LORD. Amen and Amen.

Child rearing

This interpretation of child rearing is based on personal experience and observation from living with family, my own development and helping with the development of people around me throughout my thirty four years here on earth so far, as of 2018 A.D.. This will be very general and brief, but I will expand using Biblical examples for greater detail. Child development and age milestones mentioned in the Holy Bible; conception, birth with joy, eighth day physical circumcision, one month old vow to the Lord, after days of purification are complete presented to the Lord: thirty three days for a male and threescore days and six for a female new born (Gen. 17:10-12, Lev. 12; Luke 1:41-44, 2:21, 2:22-39; John 16:21). Year one to five teaching, nourishing, weaning, little to no "responsibility" for the child, or more generally from conception to age seven, teaching and nourishing, including physical and spiritual growth (Lev. 27:6, Luke 2:40). From age five to twenty, vow to the Lord, development under parental guidance and within societal structures (Lev. 27:5, Luke 2:40, 52). This can be further broken down from above for age seven to fifteen, flowering both spiritually and physically (Luke 2:40-52). Jesus was twelve and stayed behind speaking with the authorities at the temple, but then when His parents returned to find Him, He submitted Himself to them and their authority (Luke 2:42-52). And age fifteen to twenty a certain degree of responsibility and independence can be given, with the child continuing to flower both physically and spiritually (Luke 2:52). Jesus spoke to a man, whom from youth obeyed God's commandments (Mark 10:17-22). He had riches. This may be an indication of financial success to those whom obey God's commandments. God gives power to get riches (Deut. 8:18). In general from the time of conception until the age of twenty may be viewed as a time of learning for children. No matter, the truth is in Jesus Christ of Nazareth, and the reality is He is completely involved in every heart beat we have, and every breath we take in this life, and in the "world to come". He was born into this world, conceived of the Holy Ghost, born of the virgin, Mary, espoused to Joseph (Matt. 1:18-25). He was raised as a child of Israel, of the tribe of Judah, and had brothers and sisters (Mark 6:3, Luke 2:42-52, Rev. 5:5). He ministered, taught, forgave, healed, did miracles of provision and has saved us from our sins. He died on the cross at Passover 31 A.D., for the forgiveness of our sins. He was buried and the third day He arose to give us the hope and promise of eternal life in His Holy name. Alleluia and praise the LORD. Amen and Amen.

Age twenty to sixty, vow to the Lord by estimation (Lev. 27:3). At age twenty a child of Israel is numbered among the children of Israel, including for war, and an offering to the Lord is expected starting at this time; this likely reflects the financial responsibilities starting at age twenty, including offerings, tithing, paying taxes, etc. (Ex. 30:14, 38:26; Num. 1:3, 18). From age twenty to twenty five, a trade or vocation may be more specialized in training at this time, Jesus was a carpenter; and possibly a marriage proposal (Mark 6:3). From age twenty five to thirty; entering into service of the tabernacle of the Lord for the Levites started at age twenty five (Num. 8:24). This may also be associated with general job security beginning, starting a family and the like; of course these things can begin earlier as well, possibly closer to age twenty for some. Anna, a prophetess of the New Testament, seems to have started her marriage at age twenty seven, if the age of virginity starts at age twenty (Luke 2:36-38). From age thirty to fifty; at age thirty service of burden continues and service of work begins in the tabernacle for the Levites (Num. 4:3, 23, 30, 35, 39, 43, 47). Jesus was physically baptized by His second cousin, John the Baptist, a Levite, the son of Elisabeth and Zacharias, Elisabeth was Mary's cousin, and Jesus started His ministry at about the age of thirty (Luke 1:5, 36; 3:21-23). At age fifty a Levite finishes work in the tabernacle and begins "ministry", to keep the charge (Num. 8:25, 26). This is not exactly "retirement" age in this world, but it is close to it. This would include teaching, counselling, giving advice based on life experience, education, and the like. The "ruler" or elders, according to, the apostle, Paul, mentioned in his epistle to the Hebrews are responsible for watching over the younger, and are required to give account of their actions (Heb. 13:17). That being said, Jesus Christ of Nazareth was and is a minister of God, and as mentioned He started ministering at the age of thirty, and ultimately He is our example of how to live our life. But He also worked the works of God that were given to Him to do here on earth during His three and one half years of ministry, and He still works, as He is, "I AM", the first and the last, the beginning and the end (John 6:28-35, 8:57, 58; 9:4; Rev. 1:11, 22:13). At every age Christ Jesus of Nazareth is with us. God is no respecter of persons, so that also includes categorizing by age or life experience (Acts 10:34, 35). He calls us to become like little children (Matt. 18:3). What does this mean? To answer this think about what children are like, what your childhood was like? Simple? Limited memory and understanding? etc.? Paul the apostle spoke of the simplicity that is in Christ (2 Cor. 11:3). And the Holy Bible says, God preserves the simple (Ps. 116:6). So you can decide. But ultimately, we must remember that Jesus Christ of Nazareth came to forgive us our sins, He died on the cross for the forgiveness of our sins, He was buried and the third day He arose to give us the hope and promise of eternal life in His Holy name. Alleluia and praise the LORD. Amen and Amen.

Emotions

In this last section I will speak briefly about some emotions that we as human beings created in God's image can experience from time to time in this world. Starting with Wonder, Amazement and Awe; Jesus was sore amazed before His crucifixion, and marveled at faith and at unbelief (Matt. 8:10, Mark 6:6, 14:33, 34). Jesus is Wonderful, and we are each fearfully and wonderfully made (Ps. 139:14, Isa. 9:6). Next, Love, Hope and Faith; God is love (1 John 4:8). God loves us, and Jesus loves us, so much so, that He gave up His life to die on the cross for the forgiveness of our sins, He was buried, but He was also raised up the third day to give us the hope and promise of eternal life in His Holy name. Jesus commands us to love one another (John 13:34). He also speaks about what we can do with the faith of a mustard seed, that is move mountains and uproot trees and move them (Matt. 17:20, Luke 17:6). Nevertheless, Jesus Christ of Nazareth is the author and finisher of our faith (Heb. 12:2). Now, Joy, Happiness and Laughter; Jesus says that no man can take our joy (John 16:22). Alleluia and praise the LORD. Amen and Amen.

Now onto the seemingly "heavier" emotions; Sorrow, Grief and Sadness; Jesus wept when He found out His friend Lazarus was dead, but He also raised him up again (John 11:35, 38-45). Even a father cried with tears to Jesus, for his dumb and deaf spirit possessed child, whom Jesus healed by casting out the spirit (Mark 9:17-29). The Holy Bible says it is not grievous to keep God's commandments (1 John 5:3). Next, Fear, Torment and Vexation; Perfect love casts out fear (1 John 4:18). If we are going to fear, we ought to fear God only (Ps. 111:10, Matt. 10:28). God does not ultimately desire us to fear (Luke 12:32, 2 Tim. 1:7, Rev. 1:17). He gives us a spirit of a sound mind (2 Tim. 1:7). Now, Anger, Hatred and Evil; Jesus asks us to forsake all and follow Him (Luke 14:26, 27, 33). He does also say though, that even though we forsake all, we do not lose it (Mark 10:29, 30). We actually gain it and more by letting family, possessions, even our own life go for His sake (Luke 18:29, 30). And ultimately He gives us free will in all of this, and He is very gracious in this and all commands He gives us (Ps. 86:15). Jesus disrupted the temple money change tables, as He accused the money changers and those that sold in God's temple of turning God's temple into a den of thieves, when it ought to be a house of prayer, and He cursed a fig tree for not having fruit (Matt. 21:12, 13, 19, 20). We are called to pray, not act out our anger and hatred (Matt. 5:44, 45; Eph. 4:26). Jesus said to turn the other cheek and pray for our persecutors, our enemies, and to love those whom hate us (Matt. 5:39, 44, 45). He says to bless those whom curse us (Matt. 5:44). And if a man asks us to walk a mile with him, walk with him two (Matt. 5:41). Ultimately, God says of Himself, "...Vengeance is mine..." (Rom. 12:19). Jesus came to forgive, not to condemn, and He asks us to do the same (Matt. 6:14, 15; John 3:17). Alleluia and praise the LORD. Amen and Amen.

Last, we will talk about the emotions that can seem to pull us. Starting with Jealousy, Covetousness and Envy; The Holy Bible says that God is a jealous God; one of His names is indeed, Jealous (Ex. 34:14). He desires us to love Him, with all of our heart, soul, mind and strength (Matt. 22:37). And love our neighbour as our self (Matt. 22:39). Now, Lust, Wanting and Desire; In the Old Testament, the children of Israel were allowed to eat whatsoever their heart lusted after within their gates; but not the blood, tithes, the firstlings of the flocks, the vows, freewill offerings or the heave offerings (Deut. 12:15-20). I would suggest this was still likely within the Biblical commands and laws of what should and should not be eaten according to cleanness (Lev. 11). Nevertheless, in the Old and New Testament covetousness and lust are not generally looked upon as a good thing, especially when we are lusting after things or people whom are not ours to lust after (Ex. 20:17, Mark 4:18, 19). This is where Jesus says, "...whosoever looketh on a woman to lust after her hath committed adultery with her already in his heart." (Matt. 5:28). The Holy Bible does say, "...let patience have *her* perfect work, that ye may be perfect and entire, wanting nothing." (Jam. 1:4). But the Holy Bible ultimately says God satisfies our desires (Ps. 145:16). The apostle, James, says that our wars come from our lusts (Jam. 4:1). Ultimately, if we place our trust in Jesus Christ of Nazareth, He will lead us out of all temptation (1 Cor. 10:13, Heb. 2:18). He knows all the temptation that we could possibly endure, as He has endured it Himself, in His earthly body (Heb. 4:15). And ultimately He asks us to lay down all of our desires and give them to Him; because ultimately He is our Creator and He only provides us with all things (John 1:1-3, Rev. 4:11). The Holy Bible says the Word of God, Jesus Christ of Nazareth, created all things (John 1:1-3). That includes everything we see, think or do; have thought, seen or done; and will think, see or do (John 1:1-3, Rev. 4:11). God is sovereign over all things, and has given all things to His only begotten Son, Jesus Christ of Nazareth (John 13:3, 16:15; Rev. 3:21). Alleluia and praise the LORD. Finally, Peace, Contentment and Neutrality; Jesus gives us peace, not as the world gives us, but as God gives us through His Holy Spirit (John 14:27). And the apostle, Paul, asks us to be content with what we have (Heb. 13:5). Nevertheless, the reality is in Jesus Christ of Nazareth, whom died on the cross for the forgiveness of all of our sins. He was buried and the third day He arose to give us the hope and promise of eternal life in His Holy name. Alleluia and praise the LORD. Amen and Amen.

Conclusion

Psalm 78:52 says, God "...made his own people to go forth like sheep, and guided them in the wilderness like a flock.". Psalm 107:41 says, God "...maketh *him* families like a flock.". He also says that He shall, "...gently lead those that are with young." (Isa. 40:11). Jesus is the good shepherd (John 10:11, 14). He is the door to the sheep (John 10:9). And He is the Lamb of God, that has given up His life on the cross for the forgiveness of the sins of the whole world (John 1:29, 1 John 2:2). Alleluia and praise the LORD. However, we may think we have failed in this life, God can and will lift us up out of the mire, dust us off, and clean us up, because He loves us (Ps. 69:14, 113:7, 8). He will prepare a place for us, an eternal habitation, that neither moth nor rust can destroy (Matt. 6:19-21, John 14:1-3). He will give us life and life more abundantly here on earth, as He wills it, and in the "world to come" eternal life (Luke 18:30, John 10:10). Alleluia and praise the LORD. God desires us to teach our children, these same things, that is the Word of God and His promises (Deut. 7:9). The apostle, Paul, admonishes, "And, ye fathers, provoke not your children to wrath: but bring them up in the nurture and admonition of the Lord." (Eph. 6:4). Jesus asks us to become like little children (Matt. 18:3). God's praises are perfected in children (Ps. 8:2, Matt. 21:16). Jesus calls His disciples children, and John refers to the flock of God as "little children" (John 13:33, 1 John 2:1, 12, 13, 18, 28; 3:7, 18; 4:4, 5:21). Solomon, before asking for wisdom, said he was "...a little child: I know not *how* to go out or come in." (1 Kings 3:7). This is the simplicity that is in Christ Jesus of Nazareth, because it is ultimately God's Holy Spirit that keeps us, gives us our breath, and provides for us, through Jesus Christ of Nazareth, the Word of God (Matt. 28:18, John 1:1-3, 17:2; Rev. 4:11). He was made flesh, conceived by the Holy Spirit in the virgin, Mary, espoused to Joseph (Matt. 1:18-25). Born a child of Israel, of the tribe of Judah, and raised up with brothers and sisters in Nazareth of Galilee (Mark 6:3, Luke 2:42-52, Rev. 5:5). He started His earthly ministry at the age of about thirty, and for three and a half years taught about the New Covenant of God for the whole world in His Holy and righteous

113

blood, from about autumn 27 A.D. to Passover 31 A.D. (Luke 3:23, Heb. 12:24). At that time, He died on the cross for the forgiveness of our sins, spilling His Holy and righteous blood on the cross for the forgiveness of our sins. He was buried and the third day He arose, giving us the hope and promise of eternal life in His Holy name. Alleluia and praise the LORD. Amen and Amen.

Appendix E

Aliens, Strangers and Pilgrims
Introduction

This appendix speaks of various examples of aliens, including both the Biblical concept of the alien, as well as other creative interpretations of aliens that have been depicted in cartoons, movies, television shows and other media, as of the date of writing this book in 2018 A.D.. Before I go into any more detail I would like to speak about some experiences I have had in the last few years that may help put some of these ideas following into proper perspective. After being released from the military in 2010 A.D., I spent some time looking for work, studying, fasting and praying, in the city where I went to University. On the second occasion I rented a room in the attic space of a two storey house, yes it was rather small, and had one window with a small air conditioning unit in it. One night when I was sleeping an, what I thought at the time, evil spirit in a vision came up the stairs to the room and disturbed me in my sleep, so I woke up. Over seven years later, living with family again, I had a similar dream, but this time I was the one walking up stairs to visit a person sleeping in a bed in the top portion of a house. After this dream I started to question deeply, what I thought I understood about the "spirit" and "fleshly" world. Another experience more recently happened while I was driving a family member home from a doctor's appointment at the local hospital. When I was turning left at the stoplight after exiting the hospital parking lot, I saw a man walking toward the cross walk in front of me from the opposite left hand side of the street, then the image started pacing back and forth and then, what I seem to think happened was this image literally formed into blackness, and seemed to gather into my eye. After this a few months later, I myself was visiting with the same family member at their home, and when I was becoming restless with the visit, I went into the kitchen and started pacing back and forth; much like the man in this vision I had months earlier when driving away from the hospital. I should say I learned how to pace like this, during my six month sentence, while I was in prison in 2012 A.D., it is one way of keeping occupied, staying out of trouble, and getting some exercise in otherwise cramped quarters, we did this on the dorm "range" usually. Although some of these experiences may sound quite extraordinary, and even unbelievable, you are not alone, because I am in doubt of some of my comprehension of my life experience as well (Luke 12:29, Gal 4:20). And I have had other experiences similar to these, but I will not go into detail about them. Nevertheless, the apostle, Paul, seems to help explain this experience quite well in His epistle to the Galatians. He says, "For the flesh lusteth against the Spirit, and the Spirit against the flesh: and these are contrary the one to the other: so that ye cannot do the things that ye would." (Gal. 5:17). The point of bringing these experiences up is to open the readers mind to the possibilities of how we experience this world. But I will say one thing for certain; the Holy Bible of God has all of the answers for us. Alleluia and praise the LORD. Amen and Amen. Read on to learn more about the ideas of aliens, strangers and our own life experience here on earth, and God willing, everlasting life in the "world to come". Alleluia and praise the LORD. Amen and Amen.

Aliens, Strangers and Pilgrims

Ezekiel 23 speaks of Aholibah and Aholah, these are references to Jerusalem and Samaria, which describe the tribe of Judah, and the Northern 10 tribes of Israel in their rebellion to God Almighty (Ezek. 23:4). The northern tribes were taken into captivity by Assyria in approximately 700 B.C. and Judah was taken captive into Babylon in approximately 600 B.C. (1 Kings 17, 2 Kings 22). Ezekiel was likely writing his testimony around the time of the Babylonian captivity, when both the northern and southern tribes had already fallen into idolatry, and abominations of all kinds according to the strange customs of the nations around them (1 Kings 17, 2 Kings 22). Also, Jeremiah, another one of the Old Testament prophets, laments of the loss of Israel's possessions and property to aliens and strangers in Lamentations 5:2. The point here is that God speaks of our mind having been alienated from Him because of our sin (Eph. 4:17-19, Col. 1:21, 22). This is exactly what happens to anyone whom disobeys God; we become alienated from a sound mind, peace, joy and happiness (2 Tim. 1:7, Gal. 5:22, 23). Deuteronomy 27 and 28 speak of the curses that would come on the tribes of Israel and their descendants, if we disobeyed God and this includes diseases of the mind (Deut. 28:28, 29). The good news is that we have an advocate with God in Jesus Christ of Nazareth, whom came to lead us back to the Father, by His teachings to love one another and to repent and believe in His offering made on the cross for the forgiveness of our sins (John 13:34, 15:12, 17; Rom. 13:8, 1 John 4:10, 11; 5:2, 3). He came to give us life and life more abundantly (John 10:10). He came to forgive us our sins, not only this but He died on the cross for the forgiveness of our sins, He was buried and arose the third day to give us the hope and promise of eternal life in His Holy name. Alleluia and praise the LORD. Amen and Amen.

Next, if you would go through the Holy Bible and search for the word alien, you will find a few references in the Old Testament and in the New as well. Some are talking about foreigners from nations outside of Israel, and others speak of some of the Israelite prophets, namely David and Job, calling themselves aliens because of their separation from God and mankind because of their sin and persecution (Job 19:15, Ps. 69:8). In Deuteronomy it speaks of selling an animal that dies of itself to an "alien", or giving it to the stranger within the owner's gates (Deut. 14:21). And the Hebrew words used to describe the English word of alien are; "ger" and "neker", which mean stranger or foreigner, etc. (Deut. 14:21, Isa. 61:5). It is interesting to note that a derogatory word used in the past to describe people of "African" descent is very similar to the Hebrew word for alien or stranger, which if I had to guess, is likely where that "English" word has its roots from. Nevertheless, the point in all of this is that when God speaks of aliens in the Holy Bible, He is no doubt speaking of foreigners from a different nation, tribe or tongue. The reality is that even the Israelites as I had mentioned with David and Job, could become separated from their brethren because of persecution and sin. And in reality that was a command of God to separate or cast out or even stone to death the Israelites or strangers among them whom transgress certain laws given to Israel in the wilderness by God through Moses, namely if they blasphemed God's name, but there were other reasons as well (Lev. 24:15, 16). Ephesians 2:11-13 says, "Wherefore remember, that ye *being* in time past Gentiles in the flesh, who are called Uncircumcision by that which is called the Circumcision in the flesh made by hands; That at that time ye were without Christ, being aliens from the commonwealth of Israel, and strangers from the covenants of promise, having no hope, and without God in the world: But now in Christ Jesus ye who sometimes were far off are made nigh by the blood of Christ.". The point is that we have Jesus Christ of Nazareth, whom came for the lost sheep of Israel, and for other sheep, "…not of this fold…" (Matt. 15:24, John 10:16). Jesus came for both the lost children of Israel, and for the whole world (John 3:16). He came to reveal to us the kingdom of God, He came to teach us about God, the Father, and He came to forgive us our sin, heal us, and give us a better hope and promise of life more abundantly and eternal life in His Holy name. Alleluia and praise the LORD. Amen and Amen.

Last, I will speak more liberally now about the idea of aliens, spaceships and abductions, that have been depicted in movies, television shows and in written formats, as of the date of writing this book in 2018 A.D.; shedding the light of the gospel of Jesus Christ of Nazareth and the kingdom of God on these ideas (Matt. 5:15, Mark 4:22, Luke 11:33). The apostle, John's, experience likely in vision is the best example of "abductions" according to the Holy Bible, although Elijah was said to be caught up in a whirl wind to heaven (2 Kings 2:11, Rev. 1:9, 10). However, Elijah may still have been on earth afterward, as a letter was written by him to King Jehoram of Judah, in 2 Chronicles, although it could also have been sent before he was taken up, or the letter could have been sent by the hand of Elisha or another messenger after Elijah was taken up, God knows, and of course Elijah and Moses spoke with Jesus at Jesus' transfiguration (2 Kings 2:16-18, 2 Chr. 21:12, Matt. 17:2, 3; Mark 9:2-4, Luke 9:29-31). Nevertheless, John likely had a vision. It is the book of Revelation in the Holy Bible, that describes the latter part of earth's history, some of which was spoken of in this book, namely regarding the "...new heaven(s) and the new earth..."; that being said, Isaiah, a prophet of the Old Testament also prophesied of them, and the apostle, Peter, mentioned them in one of his epistles (Isa. 65:17, 66:22; 2 Pet. 3:13, Rev. 21:1). Nonetheless, occasionally when we have dreams it can seem like we are out of the body, or are somewhere else, they seem so real. I am not suggesting they are not real, but that it is possible that some of these, so called abductions may be dreams or visions, rather than actual physical experiences, again God knows (Gen. 6:5, 8:21; Matt. 15:18-20, Mark 7:20-23). Also, the idea of a spaceship beaming down light to pick up an abductee, does have some similitude to Jesus calling the disciples to be fishers of men, casting their nets out to reap the harvest for the kingdom of God (Matt. 4:19, 13:47, 48). And last, as I have seen on one particular person's website, there are pictures of people that have heads very similarly shaped to those of different alien depictions.[2] These likely come from someone whom has had hydrocephalus or someone whom has had their head bound to elongate it because of ancient customs past down from their ancestors, as of the date of writing this book in 2018 A.D.. Possibly to stretch their skin, to maintain youthfulness or elongate their head for a status symbol or possibly because of the belief that a bigger head meant a bigger person, I do not know for certain. Other body modification customs have been seen in the past in the binding of the feet of women in the orient as well as using rings to elongate the neck of a person, as of the date of writing this book in 2018 A.D.. The creatures in the 1986 movie "Aliens", by James Cameron come to mind, when thinking about all of these body modifications. Nevertheless, the truth of these customs and diseases are likely the reality of where the concepts of aliens in fictitious programs come from, along with other inspiration from God's creation here on earth. As I had said above, regardless, our reality is in Jesus Christ of Nazareth, and we do not need to change our bodies or images to be loved by God, God created us and loves us the way that we are. Alleluia and praise the LORD. Amen and Amen.

Overcome

Regardless of all of this, God calls His chosen people pilgrims and strangers on this earth (Heb. 11:13, 1 Pet. 2:11). The reality is that our fleshly bodies are only temporary, at least in this life, as the Holy Bible says, "...it is appointed unto men once to die, but after this the judgement..." (Heb. 9:27). So the "bigger picture" is that there is life in us through Christ Jesus of Nazareth, God, the Father, and the Holy Spirit, but because of God's omnipresence, He is everywhere. Is there life on other planets and in other solar systems? It is possible, but as the Holy Bible says of God, "...the heavens are not clean in his sight." (Job 15:15). And God said that there would be lying signs and wonders caused by the fallen spiritual forces of this world (Matt. 24:24, Mark 13:22, 2 Thess. 2:9, 10; Rev. 12:9). But we

---

[2] https://theearthexpanded.com/welcome-to-the-earth-expanded-com/gods-love-and-ufos/, retrieved 24/01/ 2022

can and will overcome the evil with good (Rom. 12:21). Ephesians 4:17-24 says, "This I say therefore, and testify in the Lord, that ye henceforth walk not as other Gentiles walk, in the vanity of their mind, Having the understanding darkened, being alienated from the life of God through the ignorance that is in them, because of the blindness of their heart: Who being past feeling have given themselves over unto lasciviousness, to work all uncleanness with greediness. But ye have not so learned Christ; If so be that ye have heard him, and have been taught by him, as the truth is in Jesus: That ye put off concerning the former conversation the old man, which is corrupt according to the deceitful lusts; And be renewed in the spirit of your mind; And that ye put on the new man, which after God is created in righteousness and true holiness.". In the name of Jesus Christ of Nazareth we are more than conquerors (Rom. 8:37). As the apostle, Paul, says, "For I am persuaded, that neither death, nor life, nor angels, nor principalities, nor powers, nor things present, nor things to come, Nor height, nor depth, nor any other creature, shall be able to separate us from the love of God, which is in Christ Jesus our Lord." (Rom. 8:38, 39). And this is the reality of life and all the abundance of it, it is that we have a loving God that sent His only begotten Son, Jesus Christ of Nazareth, conceived of the Holy Spirit and born of the virgin, Mary, espoused to Joseph, to die on the cross for the forgiveness of our sins; not only for the forgiveness of our sins, but for the whole world's sins, He was buried and He was raised up the third day to give us the hope and promise of eternal life in His Holy name (John 3:16). God loves us and we have hope in His only begotten Son, the hope of everlasting life in Jesus Christ of Nazareth's Holy name. Alleluia and praise the LORD. Amen and Amen.

In Zechariah 12:1, it says, God "...formeth the spirit of man within him.". Jesus spoke of there being weeping and gnashing of teeth outside of the kingdom of God, and a devil possessed boy gnashed his teeth (Matt. 8:12, Mark 9:18). This should be a clear sign of the difference between God's kingdom and the kingdom of darkness (Eph. 6:12, Col. 1:13, 1 Thess. 5:5, 1 Pet. 2:9, 10; 2 Pet. 2:4, 17; 1 John 1:5-12, Jude 1:7, 13). That being said, when we eat the bread in remembrance of Christ's offering up of His body on the cross for the forgiveness of our sins, we do gnash the bread with our teeth, and on occasion we may weep, either tears of repentance over our sins or tears of joy for Christ's offering of forgiveness for our sins. Alleluia and praise the LORD. Amen and Amen. The religious authorities in Jesus' generation were called "...vipers..." by John the Baptist and Jesus (Matt. 3:7, 12:34, 23:33; Luke 3:7). The Holy Bible speaks of some before ordained to this condemnation, Judas Iscariot and the religious authorities whom betrayed Jesus were examples of this, and of course Peter was an example of sort as well, denying that he knew Jesus, which Jesus said would happen beforehand (Matt. 26:14-16, 33-35, 59-61, 69-75, Jude 1:4). Jesus spoke a parable about servants given talents to steward, including the "...unprofitable servant..." accused of such for not being a good steward with the talent given to him, whom was to be cast into outer darkness (Matt. 25:30). The Holy Bible also speaks of all that ought to be called "...unprofitable servants..." because we only did what we are told to do (Matt. 8:12, Luke 17:10). Romans 3:12 says, "They are all gone out of the way, they are together become unprofitable; there is none that doeth good, no, not one.". This is why we need the grace of God in Jesus Christ of Nazareth to keep us in this life, save us and redeem us unto eternal life in His Holy name. Alleluia and praise the LORD. Amen and Amen. The apostle, Paul, also speaks of our predestination and our works before ordained for us by the will of God Almighty (Eph. 1:5, 6, 11, 12; 2:10). Alleluia and praise the LORD. Amen and Amen. Jesus spoke of many being called and few chosen (Matt. 20:16). This is also by the grace of God, and likely has something to do with the "elect", chosen of God, the saints (Matt. 24:22-24, 31; Mark 13:20-22, 27; Luke 18:7, Rom. 8:33, 9:11; 11:5, 7, 26-29; Col. 3:12, 13; 1 Thess. 1:4, 1 Tim. 5:21, 2 Tim. 2:10, Tit. 1:1, 1 Pet. 1:2, 2:6, 5:13; 2 Pet. 1:10, 2

John 1:1, 13). Nevertheless, we all have the opportunity of salvation in Jesus Christ of Nazareth's Holy name, "saint" or "sinner" (Matt. 5:44, 45; Acts 10:34, 35). God has given us the freedom to choose from the beginning (Gen. 2:16, 17; Ps. 54:6, Matt. 10:8). And He is still a God of miracles, whom heals whom He wills (Deut. 11:1-7, Mal. 3:6, John 2:11, 3:2). Alleluia and praise the LORD. Amen and Amen. So the reality is in Jesus Christ of Nazareth, whom was conceived by the Holy Spirit in the virgin, Mary, espoused to Joseph, born of the virgin, Mary, He was raised as a child of Israel, of the tribe of Judah, and had brothers and sisters (Matt. 1; 13:55, 56; Mark 6:3, Luke 2, Rev. 5:5). He began His ministry at the age of about thirty years of age, and for three and a half years healed, forgave and taught of the kingdom of God. He died on the cross for the forgiveness of our sins, shedding His Holy and righteous blood at Passover in 31 A.D., He was buried and the third day He arose to give us the hope and promise of eternal life in His Holy name. Alleluia and praise the LORD. Amen and Amen.

Judged by our works; Revelation 20:12 and 13 say, "And I saw the dead, small and great, stand before God; and the books were opened: and another book was opened, which is *the book* of life: and the dead were judged out of those things which were written in the books, according to their works. And the sea gave up the dead which were in it; and death and hell delivered up the dead which were in them: and they were judged every man according to their works.". Jesus says the work of God is to believe in the one whom He sent, that is, believe in the name of Jesus Christ of Nazareth, the only begotten Son of God (John 6:29). Alleluia and praise the LORD. Amen and Amen. After judgement, death and hell are cast into the lake of fire, this is the second death (Rev. 20:14). The prophet Hosea says of God, "I will ransom them from the power of the grave; I will redeem them from death: O death, I will be thy plagues; O grave, I will be thy destruction: repentance shall be hid from mine eyes." (Hos. 13:14). In Deuteronomy, God is said to be, "...a consuming fire, *even* a jealous God." (Deut. 4:24). And Jesus came to baptize with the Holy Spirit and fire (Matt. 3:11, Mark 9:49, Luke 3:16). After this all those not found written in the book of life are cast into the lake of fire (Rev. 20:15). The apostle, Paul, speaks of our works being burned up, but our own life being saved alive. 1 Corinthians 3:15 says, "If any man's work shall be burned, he shall suffer loss: but he himself shall be saved; yet so as by fire.". Jude speaks of saving some by fear, plucking them out of the fire, hating even the garment spotted by the flesh. Jude 1:23 says, "And others save with fear, pulling *them* out of the fire; hating even the garment spotted by the flesh.". In the end we must remember that God is full of mercy, grace and truth (John 1:14, Jam. 3:17). Jesus came to die for the forgiveness of the sins of the whole world, not just my sin or yours, but all of our sin (John 3:16). So we need to consider all of this when receiving forgiveness in Jesus Christ of Nazareth's Holy name. Jesus said, "Judge not, and ye shall not be judged..." (Luke 6:37). Jesus also said, "For God sent not his Son into the world to condemn the world; but that the world through him might be saved." (John 3:17). So I will leave it up to you to decide, where your eternal destination is, and how you plan to get there. As Jesus says of Himself, "...I go to prepare a place for you." (John 14:2). Jesus is already preparing a place for us in eternity, and no doubt that includes today, tomorrow, and forever more after that. Alleluia and praise the LORD. Amen and Amen.

UFO's, Revelation 12 and Daniel 12

To take the idea of aliens a step further, let us talk about the space programs of this world, along with the idea of UFOs, as of the date of writing this book in 2018 A.D.. To start, let us look back in history, Adam's son, Cain, and his children had knowledge of all kinds of metal work and other trades, and this was over five thousand years ago (Gen. 4:20-22). After the flood, Nimrod, a descendant of Ham through Cush, and the rebellious people of that time desired to build a tower to heaven and God confounded their language because of this rebelliousness (Gen. 10:9-10, 11:1-9). Because there is no new thing under the sun, should we believe this world is any different today (Eccl. 1:9)? Let us look now at the space program as the "new", tower of Babel; the Holy Bible of God does describe Babylon's sins reaching to heaven (Rev. 18:5). Fireworks are a sort of ancient alchemy, and no doubt this is where rocket propelled anything has its roots from.[3] Of course we have various examples in nature of free flying creatures of many kinds, and other natural phenomena, that man has mimicked. But this is where the first and second command of the ten commandments of God become relevant, "Thou shalt have no other gods before me. Thou shalt not make unto thee any graven image, or any likeness *of any thing* that *is* in heaven above, or that *is* in the earth beneath, or that *is* in the water under the earth. Thou shalt not bow down thyself to them, nor serve them: for I the LORD thy God *am* a jealous God, visiting the iniquity of the fathers upon the children unto the third and fourth *generation* of them that hate me; And shewing mercy unto thousands of them that love me, and keep my commandments." (Ex. 20:3-6). In 20th century A.D. history, Nazi Germany had the V2 rocket and other weapon systems used against the allied forces, namely these rockets were aimed at Great Britain and London specifically from mainland Western Europe in World War II. After this we have German scientists and technology being exported to Russia and the United States of America.[4] Whom at least one online reference has suggested influenced the air craft programs at the infamous Area 51, a U.S. air force base.[5] Then we have the "space race", which it seems Russia heavily influenced in its early days with the first satellite, Sputnik and rocket technology, and then the Luna, lunar orbital satellites, all in the 1950's.[67] In North America, namely in Canada, the Avro arrow project was being worked on in the 1950's.[8] And then the project was dismantled, no doubt the technology and knowledgeable minds from the Avro arrow project directly influenced the subsequent group of fighter jet technologies, like the harrier jet, F16's and the like, as well as rocket technology and the U.S. space program in general in the 1960's and in following years.[9] One thing should be said about Area 51 and UFO sightings in the area, according to one online reference, many of the sightings were likely of government classified air plane technology, that were air planes built with aluminum, titanium, or other highly reflective metal surfaces, that according to one reference, suggested that in the light of the sun, looked "fiery", and reportedly some of these vehicles moved at very high speeds.[10] Last we have the moon landing, with Apollo 11, other space probes orbiting other planets, telescopes viewing images of deep space like, Hubble, and other possible projects into the future, as of the date of writing this book in 2018 A.D.. Although I do not necessarily agree with all of these ideas, I will say, "Our Father which art in heaven, Hallowed be thy name. Thy kingdom come, Thy will be done in earth, as *it is* in heaven." (Matt. 6:9, 10). Alleluia and praise the LORD. Amen and Amen.

---

[3] https://en.wikipedia.org/wiki/Fireworks#History, retrieved 01/02/2018

[4] https://en.wikipedia.org/wiki/V-2_rocket, retrieved 01/02/2018

[5] https://warningilluminati.wordpress.com/the-most-powerful-man-in-the-world-the-black-pope/, retrieved 01/02/2018

[6] https://en.wikipedia.org/wiki/Sputnik_1, retrieved 01/02/2018

[7] https://moon.nasa.gov/exploration/history/, retrieved 01/02/2018

[8] https://en.wikipedia.org/wiki/Avro_Canada_CF-105_Arrow, retrieved 01/02/2018

[9] https://en.wikipedia.org/wiki/Avro_Canada_CF-105_Arrow#Operational_history, retrieved 01/02/2018

[10] https://en.wikipedia.org/wiki/Area_51#UFO_and_other_conspiracy_theories, retrieved 01/02/2018

Now, Revelation 12:1 and 2 say, "And there appeared a great wonder in heaven; a woman clothed with the sun, and the moon under her feet, and upon her head a crown of twelve stars: And she being with child cried, travailing in birth, and pained to be delivered.". First off, this is speaking of Mary, mother of Jesus Christ of Nazareth, preparing to give birth to our Saviour, Jesus Christ of Nazareth, which indeed happened in 4 B.C., some have suggested that this sign was actually shown in heaven in the constellations, during that time. The sun could be a sign of Joseph, Mary's espoused husband, and God's Holy Spirit protecting them and Jesus in general, but also likely is representative of Jesus Christ of Nazareth's presence in general (Rev. 12:1). The twelve stars likely represent the tribes of Israel, and God's presence with them, and the twelve apostles with the New Testament Church of God (Acts 7:8, Rev. 12:1, 21:14). Revelation 12:3 and 4 continue, "And there appeared another wonder in heaven: and behold a great red dragon, having seven heads and ten horns, and seven crowns upon his heads. And his tail drew the third part of the stars of heaven, and did cast them to the earth: and the dragon stood before the woman which was ready to be delivered, for to devour her child as soon as it was born.". This is representative first, of Satan's fall from heaven, and the angels he took with him, and also his desire to destroy God's plan and work (John 10:10). Because Jesus Christ was born for just the opposite purpose of Satan, that is, Jesus Christ of Nazareth was born to destroy the works of Satan (1 John 3:8). Alleluia and praise the LORD. Amen and Amen. But it is also representative of Satan's influence over this world in the various empires that have existed, this includes Herod, the Roman Governor of Jerusalem, whom literally attempted to kill Jesus Christ as a child, sometime after His birth, because Jesus is our eternal King, of course Herod did not succeed and he died shortly after the attempt (Matt. 2:13, 15, 19). Alleluia and praise the LORD. Amen and Amen. Revelation 12:5 and 6 say, "And she brought forth a man child, whom was to rule all nations with a rod of iron: and her child was caught up unto God, and *to* his throne. And the woman fled into the wilderness, where she hath a place prepared of God, that they should feed her there a thousand two hundred *and* threescore days.". This is referencing Jesus' birth, death on the cross for the forgiveness of our sins, burial, resurrection and ascension into heaven, to God's throne, to sit at the right hand of the Father until all of His enemies are made His footstool (Heb. 10:12, 13). Alleluia and praise the LORD. Amen and Amen. And then verse six speaks of the Church of God going into the wilderness, first of Judea, then unto the lost tribes of Israel, as true followers of Christ shared and share the gospel of God and Jesus Christ of Nazareth, His only begotten Son, with one another and the world throughout the centuries unto today (Jam. 1:1). Strictly speaking the time of one thousand two hundred and threescore days, has been suggested to be from the time of the council of Nicaea, 325 A.D., until about 1585 A.D., after the printing press was invented, and while the "Christian" reformation was taking place and the Holy Bible of God was being translated and made readily available to the common people in the English language. This also likely has everything to do with Jesus' ministry from late 27 A.D. to early 31 A.D., and very possibly the "Great Tribulation", which has not likely taken place yet as of the date of writing this book in 2018 A.D., as the Holy Bible speaks about it, and I have written a book about it (Matt. 24:21, Rev. 2:22). Alleluia and praise the LORD. Amen and Amen.

Revelation 12:7- 12 says, "And there was war in heaven: Michael and his angels fought against the dragon; and the dragon fought and his angels, And prevailed not; neither was their place found any more in heaven. And the great dragon was cast out, that old serpent, called the Devil, and Satan, which deceiveth the whole world: he was cast out into the earth, and his angels were cast out with him. And I heard a loud voice saying in heaven, Now is come salvation, and strength, and the kingdom of our God, and the power of his Christ: for the accuser of our brethren is cast down, which accused them before our God day and night. And they overcame him by the blood of the Lamb, and by the word of their testimony; and they loved not their lives unto the death. Therefore rejoice, *ye* heavens, and ye that dwell in them. Woe to the inhabiters of the earth and of the sea! For the devil is come down unto you, having great wrath, because he knoweth that he hath but a short time.". The good news in all of this is that my Saviour and yours, God willing, has overcome already. Alleluia and praise the LORD. As I had mentioned briefly earlier, Jesus Christ of Nazareth asks us to pray, "Our Father which art in heaven, Hallowed be thy name. Thy kingdom come. Thy will be done in earth, as *it is* in heaven…." (Matt. 6:9, 10). So ultimately, Jesus Christ of Nazareth, has already overcome all of the works of the Devil, Satan, that old serpent, and will continue to destroy them, as Christ wills it and we accept Him as our Lord and Saviour (John 16:33, 1 John 3:8). Alleluia and praise the LORD. Amen and Amen. Revelation 12:13-17 says, "And when the dragon saw that he was cast unto the earth, he persecuted the woman which brought forth the man *child*. And to the woman were given two wings of a great eagle, that she might fly into the wilderness, into her place, where she is nourished for a time, and times, and a half a time, from the face of the serpent. And the serpent cast out of his mouth water as a flood after the woman, that he might cause her to be carried away of the flood. And the earth helped the woman, and the earth opened her mouth, and swallowed up the flood which the dragon cast out of his mouth. And the dragon was wroth with the woman, and went to make war with the remnant of her seed, which keep the commandments of God, and have the testimony of Jesus Christ.". The woman flying into the wilderness on two wings of a great eagle, likely represents the Church of God being in the world, in the governing nations of the empires of this world, but not of them, as Jesus says (John 15:19). The serpent and the flood has been referenced as military forces, this would include likely the Papal Bull's that brought much persecution on the seventh day Sabbath keeping Church of God, during the middle ages, and still does to some extent today, as there is nothing new under the sun, as of the date of writing this book in 2018 A.D. (Eccl. 1:9). The good news is, again, that we overcome the dragon, Satan, that old serpent, by the blood of Jesus Christ of Nazareth and our testimony of His life; He is alive (Rev. 12:11, 17:14). Alleluia and praise the LORD. Amen and Amen.

Daniel 12:1-4 says, "And at that time shall Michael stand up, the great prince which standeth for the children of thy people: and there shall be a time of trouble, such as never was since there was a nation *even* to that same time: and at that time thy people shall be delivered, every one that shall be found written in the book. And many of them that sleep in the dust of the earth shall awake, some to everlasting life, and some to shame *and* everlasting contempt. And they that be wise shall shine as the brightness of the firmament; and they that turn many to righteousness as the stars for ever and ever. But thou, O Daniel, shut up the words, and seal the book, *even* to the time of the end: many shall run to and fro, and knowledge shall be increased.". Michael, as I mention in appendix F, likely represents the risen Lord, Jesus Christ of Nazareth, as Jesus Christ of Nazareth is indeed the great prince, the Prince of peace, etc., whom stands for His chosen and faithful followers (Isa. 9:6, Acts 3:15, 5:31; Rev. 1:5). Alleluia and praise the LORD. Amen and Amen. This "time of trouble", which was also spoken of by other Holy prophets of the Holy Bible's writings, one of which known as the "time of Jacob's trouble", is no doubt the "great tribulation" that Jesus Christ spoke of during the Monday of the final week of His earthly ministry before He died on the cross, Wednesday afternoon, at Passover in 31 A.D., for the forgiveness of our sins, shedding His Holy and righteous blood, He was buried and then He was raised up the third day to give us the hope and promise of eternal life in His Holy name (Jer. 30:7, Matt. 24, 27, 28). Alleluia and praise the LORD. Amen and Amen. But this also could refer to His earthly ministry of three and a half years in the early first century A.D., and if you are willing to receive it, this three and a half years of "great tribulation", could be condensed down to the three and a half days, Jesus Christ of Nazareth, was hidden from this world in the grave (Matt. 12:40, 28:1-7). If He died on the cross at Passover, Wednesday afternoon about 3 pm in 31 A.D., receiving the full penalty of our sins, the wrath of God, on Himself for us until Sunday morning, after His physical resurrection (Matt. 27:46, 28:1-7). At His giving up the ghost, there was an earth quake that tore the temple veil in two, the graves were opened and many bodies of the saints whom slept arose after His spiritual resurrection and appeared to many in the Holy city (Matt. 27:50-54). The nations of the people were fighting over Him at that time, at His betrayal, during the trial, even on the cross, and after His physical death and burial (Matt. 26:46-75; 27:1, 2, 12, 29, 30, 39-44, 62-66). The sun, the moon and the sky were darkened at his crucifixion (Matt. 27:45). And these are all signs of the "the great and terrible day of the Lord" (Joel 2:10, 11; 3:15, Matt. 24:29, Rev. 6:12, 13; 8:12, 9:2, 21:23, 22:5). So there may be a "great tribulation" yet to come, but understand this, that Jesus has indeed fulfilled these Scriptures on the cross, and if you have the testimony of Jesus Christ of Nazareth, and have accepted His blood offering of His Holy and righteous blood shed on the cross for the forgiveness of your sins, and the whole world's sins, you will in no uncertain terms be protected miraculously, by God, in Christ, through the Holy Spirit from evils of all kinds in this world, including during the possibly yet to come, "Great Tribulation", at least as of the date of writing this book in 2018 A.D.. Alleluia and praise the LORD. Amen and Amen.

Conclusion

In the book of Daniel, it speaks of there being an end to sin, it says, "Seventy weeks are determined upon thy people and upon thy holy city, to finish the transgression, and to make an end of sins, and to make reconciliation for iniquity, and to bring in everlasting righteousness, and to seal up the vision and prophecy, and to anoint the most Holy." (Dan. 9:24). This was in reference to the four hundred and ninety years from the decree to build the second temple, first by Cyrus, then Darius, then Artaxerxes and more importantly to restore and rebuild the city and walls of Jerusalem by about 457 B.C. to Jesus Christ of Nazareth's ministry (Ezra 5:13, 6:1-12, 7; Neh. 2). But the issue is that Jesus was "cut off" three and a half years into His ministry, as Daniel says, "And after threescore and two weeks shall Messiah be cut off, but not for himself: and the people of the prince that shall come shall destroy the city and the sanctuary; and the end thereof *shall be* with a flood, and unto the end of the war desolations are determined." (Dan. 9:26). The second part of this prophecy, was fulfilled by the destruction of the temple in about 70 A.D., by the Romans, but may have some future fulfillment as well, spiritually and/or physically, God only knows, as of the date of writing this book in 2018 A.D.. Daniel 9:25 says, "Know therefore and understand, *that* from the going forth of the commandment to restore and to build Jerusalem unto the Messiah the Prince *shall be* seven weeks, and threescore and two weeks: the street shall be built again, and the wall, even in troublous times.". This again began around 457 B.C., when Nehemiah and those whom went back to Jerusalem from captivity in Babylon, built the walls of Jerusalem, while under threat from foreign inhabitants of the land around Jerusalem, and other social turmoil from within the camp (Neh. 4-6). And last, Daniel 9:27 says, "And he shall confirm the covenant with many for one week: and in the midst of the week he shall cause the sacrifice and the oblation to cease, and for the overspreading of abominations he shall make *it* desolate, even until the consummation, and that determined shall be poured upon the desolate.". The reality is that Jesus Christ of Nazareth's earthly ministry likely started around the fall Holyday feasts in 27 A.D., He was "cut off" and "...cause[d] the sacrifice and the oblation to cease..." at Passover 31 A.D. (Dan. 9:26, 27). That would be about three and one half years or using the day for a year principle mentioned in the Holy Bible, three and a half days, that is the "midst of the week" (Ezek. 4:6, Dan. 9:26, 27). Not only this but Jesus literally was "cut off" in the "midst of the week", that is, He died on a Wednesday at about three in the afternoon, on the cross, shedding His Holy and righteous blood on the cross for the forgiveness of our sins, He was buried and He was raised up the third day, that is Saturday afternoon, but did not reveal Himself to His disciples until Sunday, the first day of the week (Matt. 28:1-7). Jesus did indeed "…confirm the covenant with many for one week…" (Dan. 9:27). He rode into Jerusalem meekly on an donkey's colt, the Sunday before the crucifixion, with much people coming to meet Him, calling Him, King of Israel (John 12:12-15). He prophesied of things to come, namely the "great tribulation", spoken of in Matthew 24, Mark 13, Luke 21, thoroughly in the book of Revelation and elsewhere in the Old Testament and New Testament's of the Holy Bible, which I have also written a book about. And He was anointed for His burial by a woman with spikenard, whom anointed His head with the oil (Matt. 26:7-12). But ultimately we must remember that He came to forgive, not to condemn, He came to give us life and life more abundantly, and not to judge us (John 3:17, 8:15, 10:10). Alleluia and praise the LORD. Amen and Amen.

Regarding all of these ideas, we should remember the spies of Israel and their evil report, that is a report that was not to be trusted, because it came from a place of fear (Num. 13:32). A psalmist speaks of God searching out wickedness until He find's none (Ps. 10:15). The Spirit that God has put in you and I, some may call it our conscience; searches our heart to reveal to us what our thoughts and desires are (Ps. 77:6). This is God's grace in Christ Jesus of Nazareth's Holy name. Alleluia and praise the LORD. Of course, the apostle, John, says in 1 John 1:10 about us and our relationship with God and His only begotten Son, Jesus Christ of Nazareth, "If we say that we have not sinned, we make him a liar, and his word is not in us.". This is the reality; that we have all sinned, and we have all come short of the glory of God (Rom. 3:23). As the Holy Bible says, "They are all gone aside, they are *all* together become filthy: *there is* none that doeth good, no, not one." (Ps. 14:3). But in Christ Jesus of Nazareth, by His Holy blood spilt on the cross for the forgiveness of our sins, His death on the cross, His burial and His resurrection three days later we have the hope and promise of eternal life in His Holy name. Alleluia and praise the LORD. Amen and Amen. God admonishes us, not to sin, but to seek out the truth in any situation (Matt. 6:33, 7:7, 8). And reveal it as He wills it to the world (Matt. 5:14-16). Jesus does admonish us to be perfect, even as He is perfect (Matt. 5:48). He also says that our righteousness must exceed that of the Pharisees, or else we are not worthy of the kingdom of God (Matt. 5:20). But again, try and try we may, nevertheless we will indeed all come short under our own strength and effort (Rom. 3:23). It is only by Jesus Christ of Nazareth that we are saved, and it is only by His working in us, through His Holy Spirit, that we can even attempt to attain perfection (Acts 4:12). The goal is sanctification, and that comes by the forgiveness of our sins, by accepting Jesus Christ of Nazareth as our LORD and Saviour. Alleluia and praise the LORD. Amen and Amen. At the temple during Jesus' dedication, as a child of Israel, Simeon told Mary, the mother of Jesus Christ of Nazareth, that a sword would pierce her own soul, that the thoughts of many hearts may be revealed (Luke 2:35). Because she is no doubt the "elect lady", and part of the body of Christ, she experienced this through the death of her firstborn son on the cross, Jesus Christ of Nazareth (2 John 1:1). But also has eternal life in the hope and promise we all have through Jesus' death on the cross for the forgiveness of our sins, His burial and His miraculous resurrection from the grave three days later. Alleluia and praise the LORD. Amen and Amen. Not only this, all whom are in Christ have or will experience this no doubt, as we are all of the body of Christ, if we have accepted Him as our Lord and Saviour (1 Cor. 12:27). Have you?

Appendix F

Angels
Introduction

In this appendix, I will talk about the subject of angels and their existence, but first I would like to give a personal experience to the reader to possibly put the subject into a proper light. In early 2012, about a month or so before I was imprisoned, I was helping out a local farmer with his lambing season. That is the time of year when the ewe sheep, give birth to their young lambs. On this particular day, one ewe, a female sheep, was struggling with giving birth. The farmer had his hands in the womb of the ewe, attempting to help the birth along, but to no avail, so He asked that I attempt to assist with the birth. And I did, but what I felt when my hands went into the womb, confounded me (1 Cor. 1:26-29, 1 Pet. 2:6). I felt two legs, which were already protruding to the exterior of the ewe's womb, and about a quarter of the body of the lamb, and then a smooth transition to the side wall of the mother's womb. I told the farmer what I had felt, and he said, that is not possible, so I pulled out my hands and then checked one more time, but nothing had changed. Because this was all new to me anyhow, I could only think of a few options I knew of to solve this seeming problem at the time, which would have been to possibly slaughter the ewe if something did not change, and then deal with this strange, unexplainable event; or wait for something to change by itself; or the third option, which was to pray. I pulled my hands out, and he put his hands in, and I prayed fervently, as if life depended on it, not out loud, if I remember correctly and I did not even mention what I was doing to him or the other assistant that was there at the time. And thanks be to God, the baby lamb came out, albeit it was still born, from what I remember, but the ewe did indeed survive the event. To God be the Glory. Alleluia and praise the LORD. Amen and Amen. The point in all of this is to explain to the reader, albeit you may have had your own unexplainable experience or experiences in this life, that God is indeed a God of miracles, and wonderment and He answers prayer, quickly (Ps. 51:6). Alleluia and praise the LORD. Amen and Amen. As Jesus said, "Behold, I come quickly…" (Rev. 3:11, 22:7). Nevertheless, the remainder of this appendix will speak about the subject of angels, so keep an open mind when reading, and ultimately, believe that God answers prayer, and He is a God of miracles. Alleluia and praise the LORD. Amen and Amen. To God be the glory. Alleluia and praise the LORD in the name of His only begotten Son, Jesus Christ of Nazareth. Amen and Amen.

Michael, Gabriel and the Angel of the Lord

Two names are mentioned that seem to represent "angels" mentioned both in the New Testament and the Old Testament, they are Gabriel and Michael (Dan. 8:16, 9:21, 10:13, 21; 12:1; Luke 1:19, 26, Jude 1:9, Rev. 12:7). Gabriel means "man of God", Strong's number 1403. He spoke to Daniel in vision (Dan. 8:16, 9:21). He also spoke to Zechariah and Elisabeth, the parents of John the Baptist, as well as Mary the mother of Jesus (Luke 1:19, 26). He was the "man of God" speaking of the "Son of man" coming to save the world (Dan. 9:21, Luke 1:26). And was spoken of as an angel of the Lord (Luke 1:11, 19). Michael means "who is like God?", Strong's number 4317. And the answer is Jesus Christ of Nazareth is like God (John 10:30). Michael was also the name of multiple Israelites from at least eight of the tribes of Israel; Asher (Num. 13), Naphtali (1 Ch. 5:14), Gad (1 Ch. 5:13), Levi (1 Ch. 6:40), Issachar (1 Ch. 7:3, 1 Ch. 27:18), Benjamin (1 Ch. 8:16), Manasseh (1 Ch. 12:20) and Judah (2 Ch. 21:2, Ezra 8:8). In some cases these people were chiefs of their tribes, namely I believe Asher and Issachar, but possibly others as well (Num. 13, 1 Ch. 7:3, 27:18). The Michael named of Judah may have a particular role in the visions of Daniel, while in Babylon as the person whom visited him in vision, likely Jesus, spoke of a Michael, as someone being involved with a situation with the prince of Persia (Ezra 8:1, 8; Dan. 10:13). There was a son of a man named Michael, whom came out of Babylon back to Jerusalem around the same time (Ezra 8:8). And there was a Michael who was a son of Jehoshaphat, king of Judah, but he was killed by his brother Jehoram, whom succeeded Jehoshaphat as king of Israel, actually king of Judah, but his actions were of an Israelite king, i.e. idolatry, wickedness, etc. (2 Ch. 20:35, 21:2, 4). Daniel 10:13 says, "But the prince of the kingdom of Persia withstood me one and twenty days: but, lo, Michael, one of the chief princes, came to help me; and I remained there with the kings of Persia.". This could be referring to one of the men named Michael mentioned above, and this "messenger" of God that was speaking with Daniel in vision, may have been working with one of the chief princes, Michael, like He was with Daniel in vision; whom was also possibly in captivity in Babylon and Persia, as the empires were successive (Dan. 2:36-39, 5:18-31, Ezra 8:1, 8). Or it could be that, this Michael, was indeed an angel of God, God only knows. Nevertheless, to God be the glory in the truth of these interpretations. Alleluia and praise the LORD. Amen and Amen.

In the New Testament, Michael is spoken of contending with Satan over the body of Moses (Jude 1:9). In Deuteronomy 34:5 and 6, it says, "So Moses the servant of the LORD died there in the land of Moab, according to the word of the LORD. And he buried him in a valley in the land of Moab, over against Bethpeor: but no man knoweth of his sepulchre unto this day.". The question would be, who is the "he", whom buried Moses, it seems to be speaking of God, it could have been an angel of the Lord, named Michael, but it is not specific (Deut. 34:4-12). This Michael, mentioned in the epistle of Jude said, "…The LORD rebuke thee." to the devil (Jude 1:9). It is interesting that he said this, because Jesus said something very similar to Satan, when He was in the wilderness being tempted forty days and forty nights (Matt. 4:7, 10; Luke 4:12). Jesus was likely contending over the body of Moses as well, because He had to defend the laws and the prophets, as they spoke of Jesus, and prophesied of His kingship (Deut. 18:18, 19; John 5:39). So Satan and Jesus literally had to spiritually fight it out over the true testimony of not only Moses, but of His own life spoken of by all the prophets, namely in Deuteronomy 18:18 and 19, that speaks of a Prophet, that will be raised up among Israel, that will speak God's words to Israel, and those who do not listen, God will require it of them (Deut. 18:18, 19). This Prophet is Jesus Christ of Nazareth. Also, the LORD said the same thing as this Michael, in Jude 1:9, to Satan in Zechariah 3:2. It says, "And the LORD said unto Satan, The LORD rebuke thee, O Satan; even the LORD that hath chosen Jerusalem rebuke thee: is not this a brand plucked out of the fire?" (Zech. 3:2). Last, Michael is spoken of in contending with Satan in heaven with his angels in the book of Revelation, and Satan and his angels are cast out into the earth and "…neither was their place found any more in heaven." (Rev. 12:7-9). This is also a vision, but it likely was fulfilled when Jesus Christ of Nazareth overcame the world during His ministry in the early first century A.D. and all power in heaven and in earth was given to Him after His resurrection (Matt. 28:18, Luke 10:18, John 1:51, 16:33). Alleluia and praise the LORD. Amen and Amen. Nevertheless, the reality is in Jesus Christ of Nazareth (John 1:51, Eph. 4:20-24). Jesus is that man child mentioned in the prophecy in the book of Revelation, and the Body of Christ, the Church of God, are the children of God, and the children of Jesus Christ of Nazareth and the saints, the remnant of her seed in the wilderness (Rev. 12:6, 14-17). The reality is that we have an advocate with God, our Father, in Jesus Christ of Nazareth, God's only begotten Son, protecting us and defending us from evil (Matt. 28:20, John 14:18). This is the power of the cross of Jesus Christ of Nazareth (Matt. 28:18). He has conquered death, and He desires us to as well in His Holy name. Alleluia and praise the LORD. Amen and Amen.

Jesus describes Himself as the Alpha and the Omega, Beginning and the End, and First and the Last (Isa. 44:6, 48:12; Rev. 1:8, 11, 17; 2:8, 21:6, 22:13). There is also the milk and meat of the word, the milk is the simple truth of our salvation in Jesus Christ of Nazareth, and His coming again to receive us into eternal life with Him forever (1 Cor. 3:2, Heb. 5:12, 13). The meat is the greater details of how this has all been worked out in history, today and prophetically in things yet to come (Heb. 5:14). Knowing that we are not only flesh, but we have a soul and spirit as well, may help us understand how we live in the "bigger picture" of God's creation (Gen. 2:7, Job 32:8, Ps. 78:39). As God is a Spirit, as Jesus said, but He came in the flesh through Jesus Christ of Nazareth, and He dwells in us as well through His Holy Spirit, as we accept Him and His truth of salvation and love, in Jesus Christ of Nazareth's Holy name, the name above all names (John 4:24, Acts 4:12). Alleluia and praise the LORD. Amen and Amen. Jesus said, "And he saith unto him, Verily, verily, I say unto you, Hereafter ye shall see heaven open, and the angels of God ascending and descending upon the Son of man." (John 1:51). Jesus is the ultimate ladder to heaven, seen in vision by Jacob, and experienced by us in spirit and in truth (Gen. 28:12, John 1:51). Jesus was with Israel in the wilderness, dwelling with them, as the disciple of Christ, Stephen says, "Our fathers had the tabernacle of witness in the wilderness, as he had appointed, speaking unto Moses, that he should make it according to the fashion that he had seen. Which also our fathers that came after brought in with Jesus into the possession of the Gentiles, whom God drave out before the face of our fathers, unto the days of David; Who found favour before God, and desired to find a tabernacle for the God of Jacob." (Acts 7:44-46). Although this reference to "Jesus", is likely speaking of Joshua, the son of Nun, whom brought the Ark of the Covenant and the tabernacle into Canaan, with Israel (Deut. 3:28, 34:9). No doubt Jesus was with them in Spirit (John 8:58). The apostle, Paul, also spoke of Jesus being with the Israelites in the wilderness. He said, "And did all drink the same spiritual drink: for they drank of that spiritual Rock that followed them: and that Rock was Christ." (1 Cor. 10:4). Nevertheless, the reality is in Jesus Christ of Nazareth, whom died on the cross for the forgiveness of our sins, He spilt His righteous and Holy blood on the cross, He was buried and the third day He arose to give us the hope and promise of eternal life in His Holy name. Alleluia and praise the LORD. Amen and Amen.

Two cherubim and the Ark of the Covenant of the Lord

Regarding the two cherubim on the Ark of the Covenant of the Lord, Moses had made for Israel, as a testimony to them of God and His promises, which contained the Ten Commandments, and the law, and was carried with Israel during the wilderness journey and into Canaan, into Shiloh, until its resting place in the temple of God, Solomon built in Jerusalem (Ex. 25, Deut. 31:25, 26; Josh. 3:6, 1 Sam. 4:3-5, 1 Kings 3:15, 8:6). I would say that the cherubim on the ark and the ark as a whole tell a brief account of the history of mankind in our relationship with God, using the Scriptures of the Holy Bible to bring that account to light (Ex. 25). Gabriel likely represents the cherub on the left side, as the "man of God", and Michael on the right hand side represents redeemed mankind, through Jesus Christ of Nazareth (Ex. 25:18, Dan. 9:21, 12:1; Luke 1:19, Jude 1:9, Rev. 12:7). They could very well be representative of the fleshly "man of God", and the redeemed, spiritual "man of God", in Christ Jesus of Nazareth's Holy name (Matt. 8:20, 14:33; John 3:1-7). I should note that there is a claim that Jesus' blood flowed down from the cross, into a crack in the rock of the crucifixion site after the earth quake, and landed on the mercy seat of the Ark of the Covenant (Heb. 9:12). Claimed to be located in a chamber under the crucifixion site, after being hidden and kept there, from before the Babylonian destruction and pillage of the temple around 525 B.C. (2 Chr. 36:19, Jer. 52:13). And the apostle, Paul, spoke of this atonement physically, either knowingly or not, I do not know. Hebrews 9:12 says, "Neither by the blood of goats and calves, but by his own blood he entered in once into the holy place, having obtained eternal redemption *for us*.". This has been claimed by Ron Wyatt a biblical archaeologist, whom claims to have found the Ark of the Covenant under Jesus' crucifixion site, https://www.ronwyatt.com/ark_of_the_covenant.html, retrieved 19/02/2018. If this is true, and I believe it must be, it just goes to show us the height, width, length, and depth to which God is willing to go to show us His love for us. It is the truth, God Almighty does indeed love us, and He desires us to be with Him forever by the forgiveness of our sins in the name of Jesus Christ of Nazareth, His only begotten Son (John 3:16). Whom died on the cross for the forgiveness of our sins, spilling His Holy and righteous blood, entering the most Holy place by His own Holy blood, forgiving us our sins, He was buried and the third day He arose giving us the hope and promise of eternal life in His Holy name. Alleluia and praise the LORD. Amen and Amen.

In reality this same representation of the Ark of the Covenant and the cherubim is seen at the cross, with Jesus and the two "angels", albeit accused criminals, on the crosses on His left and right side (Matt. 27:38). The one on the left representing the fleshly unbelieving and fallen man, and the one on the right defending Jesus in His trial, being commended by Jesus that, "…To day shalt thou be with me in paradise." (Luke 23:43). So just like the cherubim or angels on either side of the Ark of the Covenant, with the mercy seat in between them, you have the two men on their crosses, with the merciful Son of God, dying for our sins and theirs on the cross in between them (Ex. 25:18, Matt. 27:38). Not only this, but the ark is literally under Jesus Christ of Nazareth on the cross, according to Mr. Ron Wyatt, as mentioned, acting as His footstool (Heb. 9:12). If this does not prove physically Jesus Christ of Nazareth, fulfilling the earthly life of God, Immanuel, I do not know what would (Isa. 7:14, Matt. 1:23). Not only this, but it is claimed that blood was found on the mercy seat, as mentioned above, and was tested and found to have only twenty four chromosomes twenty three from the virgin birth, and one y chromosome from God, and it was alive. Our DNA has forty six chromosomes, twenty three from our father and twenty three from our mother. If this blood only had twenty four chromosomes, this would prove that it was of a person with only "one" earthly parent (Matt. 1:18-24)[11]. That person is Jesus Christ of Nazareth, the only begotten Son of God (John 1:14, 18; 3:16). Alleluia and praise the LORD. Amen and Amen. This representation is repeated again at the discovery of the empty tomb by Mary Magdalene, with two angels sitting at either end of where Jesus had laid, with Jesus revealing Himself nearby, as the risen Lord (Mark 16:9, John 20:1). John 20:11-17 says, "But Mary stood without at the sepulchre weeping: and as she wept, she stooped down, *and looked* into the sepulchre, And seeth two angels in white sitting, the one at the head, and the other at the feet, where the body of Jesus had lain. And they say unto her, Woman, why weepest thou? She saith unto them, Because they have taken away my LORD, and I know not where they have laid him. And when she had thus said, she turned herself back, and saw Jesus standing, and knew not that it was Jesus. Jesus saith unto her, Woman, why weepest thou? whom seekest thou? She, supposing him to be the gardener, saith unto him, Sir, if thou have born him hence, tell me where thou hast laid him, and I will take him away. Jesus saith unto her, Mary. She turned herself, and saith unto him, Rabboni; which is to say, Master. Jesus saith unto her, Touch me not; for I am not yet ascended to my Father: but go to my brethren, and say unto them, I ascend unto my Father, and your Father; and *to* my God, and your God.". Jesus standing outside speaking with Mary and the angels still in the tomb at His former resting place is representative of the freedom we all have in Jesus Christ of Nazareth's life giving offering on

---

[11] https://www.youtube.com/watch?v=7UyqxzuSMCo, minute 5:55-8:35, retrieved 24/01/2022

the cross. Jesus has ascended to God, the Father, and sits at His right hand, until all His enemies are made His footstool (Acts 2:32-36). And we have that resurrection freedom in the Holy Spirit of God, in the name of Jesus Christ of Nazareth, poured out at Pentecost 31 A.D. (Acts 2). All we need to do is repent and believe in the gospel of Jesus Christ of Nazareth and the kingdom of God Almighty, that is, receive forgiveness for our sins and eternal life in Jesus Christ of Nazareth's Holy name. Alleluia and praise the LORD. Amen and Amen.

This representation can also be carried over to the temple in the "Messianic Age", as mentioned in Ezekiel 41:17-20 it says, "To that above the door, even unto the inner house, and without, and by all the wall round about within and without, by measure. And *it was* made with cherubims and palm trees, so that a palm tree *was* between a cherub and a cherub; and *every* cherub had two faces; So that the face of a man *was* toward the palm tree on the one side, and the face of a young lion toward the palm tree on the other side: *it was* made through all the house round about. From the ground unto above the door *were* cherubims and palm trees made, and *on* the wall of the temple.". Also, Ezekiel 41:25 says, "And *there were* made on them, on the doors of the temple, cherubims and palm trees, like as *were* made upon the walls; and *there were* thick planks upon the face of the porch without.". If we look at an individual set of this design, there will be a cherub with a face of a man on the one side of the palm tree, and a cherub with the face of a young lion on the other side of the palm tree, both facing the palm tree in the middle, this reflects the likeness in all of the other imagery of the ark, Christ and the criminals at the cross, and the resurrection scene at the tomb, etc. (Ex. 25:10-22, Ezek. 41:18, 19; Matt. 27:38, John 20:12). Jesus would be in the centre as the "tree of life", the palm tree, with the grown man of God, the cherub with a man's face, on the one side of the palm tree looking at the palm tree, and the young lion, the child of God, looking at the palm tree, the risen Lord, Jesus Christ, from the other side (Ezek. 41:18, 19; John 12:13). This again is and will be a reminder, especially if the Ezekiel temple is to be built in the "Messianic Age", that Jesus Christ of Nazareth is the "Risen Lord" and He is the tree of life (Gen. 3:24, Ezek. 41:18, 19; John 12:13). The Scriptures talk about trees growing on the riverside in Ezekiel's description, but they are also spoken of in the book of Revelation to John (Ezek. 47:7-12, Rev. 22:2). Psalm 92:12 says, "The righteous shall flourish like the palm tree: he shall grow like a cedar in Lebanon.". In Song of Solomon, Solomon's wife is also referred to as having a stature of a palm tree, "This thy stature is like to a palm tree…" (Song 7:7). Which would also bring up the "male" and "female" component of God, this is mentioned in Jeremiah, as the Branch, "he", "the LORD OUR RIGHTEOUSNESS", and, "she", "the LORD our righteousness" (Jer. 23:6, 33:16). The Ark and the "like" signs after it truly represent the marriage of the man and woman of God, and with God, from Adam and Eve until the spiritual marriage supper of the Lamb of God, Jesus Christ of Nazareth with His bride the Church in the resurrection and forever more in the "world to come" (Lev. 23:40-43, 1 Kings 6:29, Rev. 7:9, 19:7-9, 21:2, 9; 22:17). As we as covenant partners, stand beside the covenant commands, and now the New Covenant in Christ, watching, and guarding it with our lives, our backs turned from the world around us and our eyes and minds fixated on the commands and promises of God in Jesus Christ of Nazareth (Matt. 7:13, 14; Matt. 22:37). Coming together as God wills it to fulfill our part in the marriage ceremony to produce much fruit, to be fruitful and multiply, in Christ Jesus of Nazareth's Holy name (Gen. 2:4, Mal. 2:15, Matt. 9:5, 6). The point is that the palm tree is used to describe Jesus Christ of Nazareth, the marriage between man and wife, and God's righteousness in His Old covenant and New covenant promises in general (Gen. 2:21-25, Ps. 92:12, Song 7:7, Rev. 7:9). Alleluia and praise the LORD. Amen and Amen.

Angels in realistic terms

One of the words for "angel" in the Hebrew language is "ab-beer'", and it comes from Psalm 78:25, and means; angel, bull, chiefest, mighty, stout, strong or valiant. It is interesting to note that some of the words that surround this word in Strong's concordance are similar, like "'abar", and "'eber", and mean to soar, fly and a pinion, winged, respectively. Also, Abram, one of the forefathers of Israel, is mentioned in the same area of the concordance. If one of the root words for "angel" is related to a word similar to "Hebrew", wings, feather and flight; is it not possible, that this is why these men on either side of the Ark were shown with wings, to be considered "cherubim" (Ex. 25:20)? It is sign of our desire to be "free", but also, always beholding the face of God, with the cherubim looking toward the mercy seat (Ex. 25:20, Ps. 11:1, Isa. 40:31, Matt. 18:10). Moses even mentioned being a sleep, and flying away in Psalm 90, and the Holy Bible says that he was to sleep with the fathers who went before him until his resurrection (Ps. 90:10, Deut. 31:16). Cherub "wings"; the other word for "wings" in the Holy Bible is used as skirt, or the edge of a garment (Deut. 22:12, 22:30, 27:20; Ruth 3:9, 1 Sam. 15:27, 24:4, 5, 11). Think in modern terms of someone spreading out their arms while wearing a poncho or some other draped garment. This would create the similitude of "wings"; this is no doubt where the idea of "wings" for a human like angel comes from. These "cherub" were also described for the workman whom did the work on the tabernacle in the wilderness itself (Ex. 26:1, 31; 36:8, 35). In this light the promise of trusting in "…the shadow of thy wings…" is also made clear by the shadow of the cross of Jesus Christ of Nazareth, with His arms outstretched suffering for our salvation (Ps. 17:8, 36:7, 57:1, 61:4, 63:7). He also suffered the children to come to Him during His earthly ministry, to abide in His "shadow", under His arms, as all fathers and mothers are called to nurture, love and care for their children throughout their life (Matt. 19:13-15, Mark 9:36, 37; 10:13-16, Luke 18:15-17). As well, David prophesied of this in 2 Samuel 22:11, "…rode upon a cherub…". Jesus was and is that true cherub, the perfect vessel God used to save us from our sins (Gal. 4:14, 1 Thess. 4:16, 17). As well if we were made in the image of God, and Jesus is the only begotten Son of God, why was there never spoken of "wings" on Jesus at His resurrection? Nor were mentioned to be seen on Moses or Elijah during the transfiguration (Matt. 17:1-8, Mark 9:2-9)? I strongly believe that the reality is that the "winged" cherubim, and idols that are made by man's hands in this life are merely figurative, if anything. Because when we are resurrected, we are going to be spirit, first and foremost, why would we need wings to get around if we are a spirit? Nevertheless, the reality is that we cannot run from our Creator, Jesus Christ of Nazareth is our Creator, and ultimately, He has authority over us, and that authority has been given to Him by God, the Father, for Jesus', God's only begotten Son's, righteous act on the cross (Matt. 28:18, John 1:1-3). However we move around in the next life, I do not believe it will be any different than how man has throughout history in this life, unless we are in spirit form for some length of time. If Jesus is the truth and we are to follow Him. He revealed Himself after His resurrection, without wings on all accounts, why should we believe that we are going to be any different than Him? He ascended into the clouds, but the Holy Bible did not say He flew into the clouds, it is by the miraculous power of God that He ascended (Mark 16:19, Luke 24:51, Acts 1:2). Alleluia and praise the LORD. Amen and Amen.

I will be honest in saying that I had never intended originally in talking in this detail about the subject of the "Ark of the Covenant" and the significance at the crucifixion, burial, and resurrection of Jesus Christ of Nazareth. But as the Holy Bible says, "Ask, and it shall be given you; seek, and ye shall find…", and "…the truth shall make you free." (Matt. 7:7, John 8:32). It is interesting that the Ark, if located under the crucifixion site, is representative of the ten commandments being in the "Ark" hidden from eye sight, and now the Ark is underground hidden from our eye sight. In the Scriptures it says "…in those days, saith the LORD, they shall say no more, The ark of the covenant of the LORD: neither shall it come to mind: neither shall they remember it; neither shall they visit it…" (Jer. 3:16). That is likely because it has been found, as well, with this evidence of Jesus Christ of Nazareth's works in His earthly life in the early first century A.D., finishing with spilling His Holy and righteous blood on the cross for the forgiveness of our sins, His death on the cross, His burial and His resurrection three days later, as the New Covenant promise of eternal life in His Holy name, we no longer require the "letter" of the law to save us (John 3:16, 5:36, 6:29, 9:3, 4; 14:10). But it is the living Word of God, Jesus Christ of Nazareth, whom has given us salvation in His righteous and Holy blood atonement for our sins on the cross. Alleluia and praise the LORD. Amen and Amen. There is some discussion surrounding the "Ark of the Covenant", its where about' with its role in fulfillment of prophecy to come, as of the date of writing this book in 2018 A.D.. Namely the idea of building the temple spoken of in Ezekiel 40-46, sometime referred to as the temple in the "Messianic Age", during the 1000 year rule of Christ with His saints (Rev. 20:4). However there are two proofs that negate the need for the Ark to be in this temple, the first is that Jeremiah speaks of a prophecy regarding the "Ark of the Covenant", as mentioned earlier, "And it shall come to pass, when ye be multiplied and increased in the land, in those days, saith the LORD, they shall say no more, The ark of the covenant of the LORD: neither shall it come to mind: neither shall they remember it; neither shall they visit it; neither shall that be done any more." (Jer. 3:16). Also, there is no need for the Ark of the Covenant in this "Messianic Age" temple, because there is no need for blood to be placed on it, during the "Day of Atonement", the first fall Holy day, because Jesus Christ has spilt His Holy and righteous blood for us on the cross, and onto the mercy seat, once for all of our sins (Lev. 16:14, 15; Heb. 9:12). The Messianic Age temple is, if or when built, God willing, used to prove God's promises to Israel, and the world, fulfilling prophetic Scripture (Ezek. 40-48). It is also used as a gathering place to bring God's people to, from around the world, in the 1000 year reign of Christ with the saints, the "Messianic Age", to worship God (Zech. 14:16, Rev. 20:4). This would continual fulfill the literal ingathering of God's people before the final spiritual harvest at the "last great day", at the end of that age, the 1000 years, mentioned in Revelation 20 (Rev. 20:11-15). You can learn more about the idea of the "Messianic Age", in the Holy Bible of God, and I have written a book about it as well called, "The Day Star and Us" (Ezek. 40-48, Zech. 14:16-21, Rev. 20:4). That all being said, for today and throughout the "Messianic Age", if or when it comes, we must remember that Jesus did say, "But the hour cometh, and now is, when the true worshippers shall worship the Father in spirit and in truth…." (John 4:23). This is the freedom that we have in Jesus Christ of Nazareth today. Alleluia and praise the LORD. Amen and Amen.

During Jesus' forty day trial in the wilderness being tempted by Satan at the beginning of His ministry, angels ministered to Him (Mark 1:13). The gospel according to Luke says, "And Jesus returned in the power of the Spirit into Galilee…" (Luke 4:14). Between the two of these verses, the relationship between the Spirit and the angels can be seen; likely they are closely related (Acts 23:9). According to the apostle, Paul, God will be and is "…all in all." (1 Cor. 12:6, 15:28; Eph. 1:23). Jesus said, "… he shall come in his own glory, and in his Father's, and of the holy angels." (Luke 9:26). Jesus also said, "Whosoever shall confess me before men, him shall the Son of man also confess before the angels of God: But he that denieth me before men shall be denied before the angels of God." (Luke 12:8, 9; Rev. 3:5). If the angels are the saints, or at least a portion of them, as will be spoken of below, the

Holy Bible does say that the saints will be given judgement, Jesus made this clear when speaking to the twelve apostles (Matt. 19:28, Luke 22:30, 1 Cor. 6:3). This would also make the judgement given to the saints an easy one, because Jesus would be doing all of the work. As the Holy Bible says, "This is the work of God, that ye believe on him whom he hath sent." (John 6:29). Jesus was true in saying that all judgement has been given to Him (John 5:22, 23). Praise the LORD God Almighty and Jesus Christ of Nazareth, His only begotten Son. Alleluia and praise the LORD. Amen and Amen. I suppose this is why, "And whosoever shall speak a word against the Son of man, it shall be forgiven him: but unto him that blasphemeth against the Holy Ghost it shall not be forgiven." (Luke 12:10). It is God's Holy Spirit that gives us life, and life everlasting in Jesus Christ of Nazareth's Holy name. In the end, we are not to worship angels, even these messengers in the Holy Bible say this (Gal. 1:8, Rev. 14:6, 7; Rev. 22:8, 9). It is God that we are to worship, even Jesus said this, He said, "...*there is* none good but one, *that is,* God..." (Matt. 19:17). Whether there are two literal "chief angels" or not, we know we have Jesus Christ of Nazareth to save us, because "...there is none other name under heaven given among men, whereby we must be saved." (Acts 4:12). The apostle, Paul, said, "For I am persuaded, that neither death, nor life, nor angels, nor principalities, nor powers, nor things present, nor things to come, Nor height, nor depth, nor any other creature, shall be able to separate us from the love of God, which is in Christ Jesus our Lord." (Rom. 8:38, 39). This is the simple truth of the matter, Jesus loves you and I. And He died for you on the cross, to forgive you of your sins, He was buried and He was raised up the third day to give you the hope and promise of eternal life in His Holy name. Praise the Lord God Almighty and His only begotten Son, Jesus Immanuel Christ of Nazareth. Hallelujah and praise the LORD. Amen and Amen.

Saints

Enoch prophesied, "...the Lord cometh with ten thousands of his saints," (Jude 1:14). Jesus spoke of coming in the glory of His Father with His angels (Matt. 16:27, Mark 8:38). No doubt the saints will have glorified, resurrected bodies like Jesus has, at His coming again (Ps. 104:4, 2 Thess. 1:7-10, 2 Pet. 1:14). Albeit, He proved that our flesh will survive the grave, as His did (John 20:27). We need to remember that God is a Spirit first and foremost (John 4:24). Jesus mentions the angels gathering the elect, as will be mentioned, this is related to the harvest and the preaching of the good news of Salvation in Jesus Christ of Nazareth's Holy name (Matt. 24:31, Mark 13:27). Jesus came for His lost sheep, and this is what He desires His followers to do, gather His sheep to Him, and the Father Almighty, through repentance, and forgiveness of sin, the indwelling of the Holy Spirit, obedience to Him, and praise and worship of God Almighty forever more (Matt. 10:6, 15:24; John 10:16). Alleluia and praise the LORD. Amen and Amen. As Jesus said, "Likewise, I say unto you, there is joy in the presence of the angels of God over one sinner that repenteth." (Luke 15:10). The saints, at least in part, are likely the angels Jesus is speaking of when the fields of the earth are ready for harvest (Matt. 13:39, 41, 49; 2 Thess. 1:7-10, 1 Tim. 5:21). The job of these angels is to separate the wicked from the just, and to feed the wicked into the furnace of fire (Matt. 13:41, 42, 49, 50). Of course this can be seen as both literal and spiritual in interpretation, but from the perspective of Jesus' teachings, He is not calling us to literally put someone into a furnace of fire, He is more likely talking about preaching the Word of God, and speaking truth to each other in the Holy Ghost of God (Matt. 28:19, 20; Mark 16:15, Luke 24:46, 47; John 8:32). However, there are a few parables where the fruit of the wicked is paid back to them (Matt. 21:41, Mark 12:9, Luke 19:27, 20:16). But, the Holy Bible also says that God is a consuming fire, even the angel of the Lord went up in a flame to heaven, from a fire kindled by the parents of Samson, a judge over Israel, whom the angel of the LORD was speaking with to tell them of their son's birth (Deut. 4:24, Jud. 13:20, 21). The apostle, Paul, said, "Therefore if thine enemy hunger, feed him; if he thirst, give him drink: for in so doing thou shalt heap coals of fire on his head." (Rom. 12:20). The Holy Bible also says our tongue is a flame (Jam. 3:6). The point is the truth and the Word of God are a fiery flame, and they devour the wicked works of this world (2 Pet. 3:10, 1 John 3:8). As Jesus said, "...The harvest truly *is* plenteous, but the laborers are few..." and "...look on the fields; for they are white already to harvest." (Matt. 9:37, John 4:35). He is speaking about us, His disciples doing the work of preaching of Salvation in Jesus Christ of Nazareth's Holy name, and the gospel of the Kingdom of God, eternal life in Jesus Christ of Nazareth's Holy name (Matt. 28:19, 20; Mark 16:15, Luke 24:46, 47). Alleluia and praise the LORD. Amen and Amen. This is every follower of Jesus' responsibility in this life, to share the good news with others, of Salvation in Jesus Christ of Nazareth's Holy name, and life everlasting in His Holy name. Alleluia and praise the LORD. Amen and Amen.

Of Abraham, Genesis 18:1-3 says, "And the LORD appeared unto him in the plains of Mamre: and he sat in the tent door in the heat of the day; And he lift up his eyes and looked, and, lo, three men stood by him: and when he saw *them,* he ran to meet them from the tent door, and bowed himself toward the ground. And said, My Lord, if now I have found favour in thy sight, pass not away, I pray thee, from thy servant:". If these three men were God, in the flesh, which may or may not be the case, they would certainly have represented God, the Father, His Son, Jesus Christ of Nazareth, and the Holy Ghost (Gen. 18:2, Matt. 28:19, John 8:16-18, 20:22, 23). The conversation Abraham has in Genesis 18 would certainly seem as if these three men were God. It even seems as if Abraham and Sara are speaking to all of them as if they are one person throughout the conversation (Gen. 18:3, 12, 15). Even these men spoke to Abraham and Sara as if they were one person (Gen. 18:5, 9, 10, 13-15). I do believe this conversation and the account of the two angels coming to Sodom to visit and save Lot and his family from the fiery destruction of the city may be a good indication of the relationship between God, man, and angels in general (Gen. 18, 19). Certainly if angels do exist, they are very purposeful in their existence. These men's faces looked toward Sodom, much like Jesus' face was set towards Jerusalem just prior to His crucifixion (Gen. 18:16, 22; Luke 9:51-53). They were sent for a purpose and they intended to fulfill that purpose. Actually they were sent for two purposes, the first was to confirm with Abraham and Sara the covenant God had made with them, that Sara would conceive a child and an heir to Abraham's inheritance in her old age (Gen. 17:15-21, 18:9-15). And the second was to see the "cry" of Sodom and Gomorrah, regarding their wickedness, and need of punishment for that wickedness (Gen. 18:16-22). I will say though, that there is a distinct point in the conversation, when these three men and the LORD, seem to be separated. Genesis 18:22 says, "And the men turned their faces from thence, and went toward Sodom: but Abraham stood yet before the LORD.". So I will leave it up to you to decide who was talking with whom, and how this conversation transpired, regardless, as Jesus said, we must remember that God is a Spirit, first and foremost, regardless of the reality of the flesh (John 4:24). As He said, "It is the spirit that quickeneth; the flesh profiteth nothing..." (John 6:63). Alleluia and praise the LORD. Amen and Amen. Also, the apostle, Peter, was visited by the angel of the Lord, and thought he was experiencing Him in vision, when he was lead out of prison and into the street (Acts 12:5-11). It should also be said that God is not a respecter of persons, in that both men and women are able to be "angels", saints, the elect, called and chosen (1 Pet. 3:7, 2 John 1:1). As well as the offering of eternal salvation in general by the blood of Jesus Christ of Nazareth, this is a free gift to all; male and female, and of every tongue and tribe and nation (John 12:50, Gal. 3:28, Eph. 2:8, 9; Rev. 7:9, 10). Alleluia and praise the LORD. Amen and Amen.

Us

Angel means messenger of God, in Hebrew pronounced, "malak", Strong's number 4397, the Hebrew word is also used to describe an earthly messenger as well in some places in the Old Testament (Gen. 16:7, 32:3, Mal. 3:1). If we have a message whether by a vision, dream or a thought that comes into our mind, and we believe it is of God, to speak to others about, are we not being used as a messenger of God, as an angel of the Lord (1 Sam. 29:9, 2 Sam. 14:7, 20, 27; Acts 6:15, Gal. 4:14)? But ultimately it is Jesus Christ of Nazareth working in, with and through us that does the work (Mark 16:20, Rom. 11:36, 1 Cor. 9:11, Eph. 4:6, Col. 1:29). Jesus said, "For in the resurrection they neither marry, nor are given in marriage, but are as the angels of God in heaven." (Matt. 22:30, Mark 12:25, Luke 20:35, 36). The apostle, Paul, also spoke of a similar situation for Christ's followers in his time, which could be applied to our lives as well as required. He said, "But this I say, brethren, the time *is* short: it remaineth, that both they that have wives be as though they had none..." (1 Cor. 7:29). This is similar to what Jesus was describing regarding His followers in the resurrection (Matt. 22:30). That being said, Paul also said just before that, "But and if thou marry, thou hast not sinned..." (1 Cor. 7:28). Nevertheless, it is hard to argue, that there are not "angels" in the heavenly sense, the Holy Bible of God certainly speaks a lot about them (Matt. 18:10, Mark 1:13, Luke 2:13-15, 22:43; John 5:4, 20:12; 1 Cor. 4:9, 1 Tim. 3:16, Heb. 12:22, 13:2; Rev. 1:20, 5:11; Rev. 7:1, 2, 11; Rev. 8:2, 3, 13; Rev. 9:11, 14; Rev. 10:1, 11:1, 14:6, 8, 9, 15, 17, 18; Rev. 15:1, Rev. 18:1, 21; Rev. 19:17, Rev. 21:1). That being said, they could also be referring to people, I do not know for certain. But for practical purposes, we are not to worship angels as mentioned earlier, because it is by Jesus Christ of Nazareth and God's Holy Spirit that we must live (Matt. 18:10, Gal. 1:8, Col. 2:18, Rev. 14:6, 7; Rev. 22:8, 9). Angels, if they exist in the heavenly, are simply servants of God, like us; as even these angels had said to various prophets in visions (Luke 24:23, Acts 10:3, Rev. 19:10). Also, we all have the opportunity to be "like" God, made in the image of God, through Jesus Christ of Nazareth's offering of forgiveness of our sins and eternal life in His Holy name, by His Holy and righteous blood spilt on the cross, dying for the forgiveness of our sins, He was buried and He was raised up the third day to give us the hope and promise of eternal life in His Holy name (Luke 20:36). By Jesus Christ of Nazareth's offering of His shed blood on the cross for the forgiveness of our sins, we have become adopted, sons and daughters of God, in Christ Jesus of Nazareth's Holy name (Luke 20:36). And we have the hope and promise of the resurrection through His death on the cross for the forgiveness of our sins, His burial and His resurrection three days later. Alleluia and praise the LORD. Amen and Amen.

Revelation 21:17 says, "And he measured the wall thereof, and hundred *and* forty *and* four cubits, *according to* the measure of a man, that is, of the angel.". I believe the number, 144, is a direct indication of the saints, the 144 000, the elect, and their relationship with God, in Christ Jesus of Nazareth's Holy name, as resurrected beings, as "angels spirits" (Ps. 104:4, Acts 23:9, Rev. 7:4). The Holy Bible of God even indicates that He makes His "angels spirits" (Ps. 104:4). And that is exactly what we will be at the resurrection first and foremost is spirit beings, like God, children of God, as God is a Spirit (John 4:24). Jesus proves this as He is the "Son of man" and "Son of God"; He was born into this world, conceived by the Holy Spirit in the virgin, Mary, born of the virgin, Mary, espoused to Joseph, but fully man, and fully the "Son of God" (Matt. 1:18-25, 8:20, 14:33). He died on the cross for the forgiveness of our sins, He was buried and He arose the third day for our hope and promise of eternal life in His Holy name, He continued to dwell on earth, speaking with the disciples for a period of time before His ascension near Pentecost 31 A.D. (Acts 1:2, 3). He was even touched by doubting

Thomas, and ate with His first century A.D. disciples as He had flesh on His resurrected body (Luke 24:36-43, John 20:24-31). The point is we have Jesus Christ of Nazareth, the risen Lord whom will protect us, comfort us and dwell with us all, and in us all through His Holy Spirit of God, to the end of the world and forever more in the "world to come" (Matt. 28:20, John 14:16-18). Alleluia and praise the LORD. Amen and Amen. Jesus is the chief of the angels of God; He is the head of the Church and the Almighty, King of kings and Lord of lords (John 1:51, 1 Thess. 4:16, 17, Heb. 1, 1 Pet. 3:22, Rev. 1:1, 22:6, 16). The apostle, Paul, says of Jesus, "Being made so much better than the angels, as he hath by inheritance obtained a more excellent name than they." (Heb. 1:4). Glory be to God Almighty and His only begotten Son, Jesus Christ of Nazareth. Alleluia and praise the LORD. Jesus said, "For where two or three are gathered together in my name, there am I in the midst of them." (Matt. 18:20). This is the continuation of the representation of the Ark of the Covenant, and the like, when we come together in the name of Christ, Jesus Christ of Nazareth is with us. Alleluia and praise the LORD. Amen and Amen.

Conclusion

The apostle, Paul, admonishes us to, "Be not forgetful to entertain strangers: for thereby some have entertained angels unawares." (Heb. 13:2). Of course, Abraham seems to have done this before the angels went to Sodom and Gomorrah to smite it with fire and brimstone, as mentioned (Gen. 18, 19). Jesus spoke of the angels ascending and descending on the Son of man, as mentioned in the body of this appendix (John 1:51). Jesus ultimately is the person, angelically, spiritually, in the flesh, and in the Holy Bible of God, the written Word of God, that we ought to believe in and follow (John 5:39). And He has given us His Holy Spirit to teach us all things (John 14:26). It is this same Holy Spirit that Jesus was conceived of, grew in as a child, and had received in the flesh after His baptism in 27 A.D. by John the Baptist in the river Jordan (Matt. 1:20, 3:13-17; Luke 2:40, 3:21-23). And He ultimately gave His Spirit up on the cross for the forgiveness of our sins, dying on the cross for forgiveness of our sins, saying "…Father, into thy hands I commend my spirit: and having said thus, he gave up the ghost." (Luke 23:46). He spilt His Holy and righteous blood on that cross, dying for the forgiveness of all of our sin, He was buried and the third day He arose giving us the hope and promise of eternal life in His Holy name. Alleluia and praise the LORD. Amen and Amen. As mentioned earlier, as the apostle, Paul, says in his letter to the Romans, "For I am persuaded, that neither death, nor life, nor angels, nor principalities, nor powers, nor things present, nor things to come, Nor height, nor depth, nor any other creature, shall be able to separate us from the love of God, which is in Christ Jesus our Lord." (Rom. 8:38, 39). This is the simple truth in the matter of angels, and all other things; that Jesus, God's only begotten Son, loves us, and God, the Father, loves us, and they two are One (John 3:16, 10:30, 15:13). And God showed His love for us by giving us His only begotten Son, Jesus Christ of Nazareth, born of the virgin, Mary, espoused to Joseph, raised as a child of Israel (Matt. 1:18-25, Luke 2:41-52, John 3:16). He ministered to the world, set His face toward Jerusalem, was delivered up to the cross without cause, and died on that cross spilling His Holy and righteous blood for the forgiveness of our sins (Matt. 20:28, Luke 9:51, 23:4). He entered into the most Holy place by His righteous and Holy blood to atone for our sins, once for all, He was buried and the third day He arose to give us all the hope and promise of eternal life in His Holy name (Heb. 9:12). Alleluia and praise the LORD. Amen and Amen. Repent and believe in the gospel of the Kingdom of God, and salvation in the name of Jesus Christ of Nazareth, God's only begotten Son. Alleluia and praise the LORD. Amen and Amen.

Appendix G

Mark of the beast or mark of God?
Introduction

This interpretation comes from experience of my lifetime here on earth for the last thirty four years. I will say that it is exactly that an interpretation, and some of the interpretation may be more relevant to my experience here on earth, where someone else may be able to interpret "the mark of the beast", from your own perspective. And the Scriptures do admonish us to "count" the number, meaning likely interpret, etc. (Rev. 13:18). But for the sake of this book and in general, I will explain to you what I think I understand about it. You can be the judge on the truth of the matter. To keep it simple though, I will say that I wrote a blog post about it a couple of years ago, as of the date of writing this book in 2018 A.D., and basically interpreted it as being selfishness (Ezek. 8:12). The apostle, Paul, mentions in the last days people would be "…lovers of their own selves…" (2 Tim. 3:2). I will also say that Jesus took this mark upon Himself at His death on the cross, that is, He died for the forgiveness of our sins on the cross, including our selfishness, this is where the "mystery of iniquity" and "mystery of God" meet, at the cross of Jesus Christ of Nazareth (Matt. 19:30, Col. 2:2, 2 Thess. 2:7, 1 Tim. 3:16, Rev. 10:7). He is the "…Lamb of God, which taketh away the sin of the world." (John 1:29). Again, this is an interpretation, but the reality is in the living Christ, the resurrected Jesus Christ of Nazareth, whom overcame the "mark of the beast". He died on the cross for the forgiveness of our sins, spilling His righteous and Holy blood to cleanse us of all our iniquity, He was buried and the third day He arose to give us all the hope and promise of eternal life in His Holy name. Alleluia and praise the LORD. Amen and Amen. With this all being said, if you desire to come with me another "mile", let me speak of the subject a little further in this appendix (Matt. 5:41). And I will leave the rest up to you to decide what you believe. All glory and thanks be to God Almighty and His only begotten Son, Jesus Christ of Nazareth. Alleluia and praise the LORD. Amen and Amen. Who live and reign forever and ever. Amen and Amen.

Mark of the beast and animals, "nature", and sacrifice

Beasts do not have understanding, this is why people whom have the mark, would likely not know they have it, nor would they readily admit to having the mark (Ps. 32:9). God only knows for certain. Albeit, in the book of Job it says, "But ask now the beasts, and they shall teach thee; and the fowls of the air, and they shall tell thee: Or speak to the earth, and it shall teach thee: and the fishes of the sea shall declare unto thee. Who knoweth not in all these that the hand of the LORD hath wrought this? In whose hand *is* the soul of every living thing, and the breath of all mankind." (Job 12:7-10). Nevertheless idolizing animals, worshipping creation instead of our Creator, following after "nature", wondering over the seasons, and the beasts that follow migratory patterns, etc., are all likely indicators of the "mark" of the beast (Rev. 13:3). Nimrod and Esau were hunters; this idea of "self" preservation and "self" reliance is in no doubt related to the mark of the beast (Gen. 10:9, 25:27). What we need to do is be thankful to God Almighty for creating His creation in the "woods" and in the "cities", in the "fields" and in the "highways", in the "waters" and in the "heavens", and in the "deeps" of the earth (Ps. 50:10, 11; 147:9, 148:7, 10, 13; Isa. 43:20, 63:14). All of this exists by the Almighty God of Jacob, Isaac and Abraham, by the Creator, in Jesus Christ of Nazareth. Alleluia and praise the LORD. Amen and Amen. We ought to worship Him in Spirit and in Truth, not "wonder" after the creation He has created. He is after all "…Wonderful, Counsellor, The mighty God, The everlasting Father, The Prince of Peace." (Isa. 9:6). Jesus multiplied fishes and loaves; He ate the Passover supper with His disciples, so He does eat of the fruit of the land and seas, but our first love is God, not His Creation (Matt. 4:4, 14:17-21, 26:17-30; Mark 12:29, 30; 1 John 4:19, Rev. 2:4). He said to the Samaritan woman, "...the hour cometh, when ye shall neither in this mountain, nor yet at Jerusalem, worship the Father. ... But the hour cometh, and now is, when the true worshippers shall worship the Father in spirit and in truth..." (John 4:21, 23). John said that we are to love in "...deed and in truth." (1 John 3:18). And in the book of Esther, letters were sent in "...peace and truth..." (Esther 9:30). The reality is that God's kingdom is of peace, and this peace is a "deed" or work, the work of peace (Matt. 5:9, Mark 9:50, Luke 1:79, 2:14, 7:50, 19:38, 24:36; John 14:27, 16:33, 20:19, 21, 26). And "...This is the work of God, that ye believe on him whom he hath sent." (John 6:29). That is, to believe on His only begotten Son, Jesus Christ of Nazareth and all that He stands for. Praise the LORD God Almighty and His only begotten Son, Jesus Christ of Nazareth. Alleluia and praise the LORD. Amen and Amen.

The cross, our sins, our beast like nature without God, our "murder" of the Son of God on the cross is all a part of the "mark of the beast" (Eccl. 3:18). It is only by God's mercy in Jesus Christ of Nazareth that we are saved (Eph. 2:8, 9). It is by His sacrifice, His offering up of His body and His forgiveness of our sins, by His Holy and righteous blood spilt on the cross that we are saved. It is by His death on the cross, His burial, and His resurrection three days later, that we have hope, and it is by accepting His Holy Spirit into our body, mind and soul, that we receive the Mark of our God in our forehead, in the name of Jesus Christ of Nazareth, Saviour of the whole world and Redeemer of all mankind. Alleluia and praise the LORD. Amen and Amen. As mentioned in the introduction, the Mystery of God and mystery of iniquity meet at the cross of Jesus Christ of Nazareth (Matt. 19:30, Col. 2:2, 2 Thess. 2:7, 1 Tim. 3:16, Rev. 10:7). In the Old Testament, animals were offered for an atonement of sin (Lev. 16). And the Holy Bible speaks of the altar of stone not hewn by man's hands (Ex. 20:25). There is the man made four horned altar of the Old Testament sacrifices and in the prophecy of Ezekiel (Ex. 27:1, 2; Ezek. 43:13-18). But also the spiritual four horned altar of the book of Revelation, not hewn by man's hands (Rev. 9:13, 14). There are four beasts of the book of Revelation that worship God, as well as other beasts mentioned in the Holy Bible (Rev. 4:6, 8; 5:6, 8, 14; 6:6, 7:11, 14:3, 15:7, 19:4). But most importantly we must remember that Jesus Christ of Nazareth was and is the eternal Passover lamb, offered up on the cross for the forgiveness of our sins (John 1:29, 36; Rev. 5:6, 8, 12, 13; 6:1, 16; 7.9, 10, 14, 17; 12:11, 13:8, 14:1, 4, 10; 15:3, 17:14, 19:7, 9; 21:9, 14, 22, 23, 27; 22:1, 3). He was conceived by the Holy Spirit, in the virgin, Mary, espoused to Joseph (Matt. 1:20). He is the chief cornerstone, not hewn by man's hands (Eph. 2:20). In prophecy we have the "Messianic Age", Ezekiel temple with its offerings, etc. (Ezek. 40-48). Nevertheless, Jesus Christ of Nazareth said, "...learn what *that* meaneth, I will have mercy, and not sacrifice..." (Hos. 6:6, Matt. 9:13, 12:7). David in the book of psalms said, "For thou desirest not sacrifice; else would I give *it:* thou delightest not in burnt offering. The sacrifices of God *are* a broken spirit: a broken and a contrite heart, O God, thou wilt not despise. Do good in thy good pleasure unto Zion: build thou the walls of Jerusalem. Then shalt thou be pleased with the sacrifices of righteousness, with burnt offering and whole burnt offering: then shall they offer bullocks upon thine altar." (Ps. 51:16-19). Jesus is calling us to "die" to ourselves, our sinful flesh, and our sinful relationship with this world first and foremost, as of the date of writing this book in 2018 A.D. (Luke 14:33). All of the parables that He gave are spiritual in nature first and foremost (John 6:63). He desires us to understand them and follow them spiritually (Matt. 5:20). Alleluia and praise the LORD. Amen and Amen. It all starts in the "mind", the brain, the "forehead" (Matt 22:37, Rev. 7:3, 14:1, 22:4). Are we obedient to God Almighty or fallen mankind? Are we listening to the Holy Spirit or our own perverse minds and thoughts, that are evil, deceiving and outright wrong without

God's Holy Spirit (Rom. 8:7)? It is only by God's Holy Spirit in our mind, body and renewing our soul, giving us a "new" uncorrupt Spirit in us, that we have truth, understanding and life everlasting in the name of Jesus Christ of Nazareth, the only begotten Son of God (John 3:3-7, 1 Pet. 1:22, 23). Alleluia and praise the Lord. Amen and Amen.

Regarding the "Ezekiel Temple" in the Messianic Age, I wrote a book speaking of this time, and the temple in general, from a follower of Christ's perspective, but I never spoke about how it was going to be constructed. God works in mysterious ways and since having written another book and working on this one, God has revealed to me the Scriptures on the matter a little further. Common sense would say mankind would build the temple, like in time past, in the wilderness the congregation gathered to support the building of the tabernacle, and during David and Solomon's time they planned, prepared and built the temple in Jerusalem, and similarly the second temple after the exile into Babylon and return in around 486 B.C. (Ex. 5-27, 1 Kings 5-7, 2 Ch. 28, 29; Ezra, Neh.). The point is that there are four beasts mentioned in the book of Revelation that worship God, one like a lion, one like a calf, one like the face of a man, and one like a flying eagle (Rev. 4:7). They are "...full of eyes before and behind." (Rev. 4:6). And have "...six wings...full of eyes within...rest not day and night, saying, Holy, holy holy, Lord God Almighty, which was, and is, and is to come." (Rev. 4:8). Revelation 4:9-11 describes how when they worship God, that the twenty four elders before God's throne, "...fall down before Him that sat on the throne," (Rev. 4:10). Isaiah 6:2 and 3 describe a similar being, called a "seraphim" saying the same thing, "Holy, holy, holy, *is* the LORD of hosts: the whole earth *is* full of his glory.". And again, Ezekiel 1:5-10 is a similar description to Revelation 4:6-8, except they each have "four faces", one of which is an ox instead of a calf, they have "four wings" and these "living creatures" have "hands of a man under their wings" and went "straight forward" together (Ezek. 1:6-10). I see these four creatures as unconverted gentiles and young people in their relationship with God and others, and the twenty four elders of Revelation 4, as the experienced husband and wife, parents and grandparents, represented by the twelve tribes of Israel (Rev. 4:4). God works through all, and it would seem He even uses these unconverted or "simple" people and beasts to cause the elders, the married, the "experienced", the "wise", to worship God (Ezek. 10:8, 21; Rev. 4:9, 10). Ezekiel 10 brings this point to a conclusion; Ezekiel 10:11 and 22, describes the straightness of our path in life here on earth (Ezek. 1:10). Ezekiel 10:14 and 16 likely relates all of this back to the world and the daily "cycle" of life, the "wheels", which could be vehicles, communications technology and the like. Ezekiel 10:17 speaks of the "...spirit of the living creature..." being in these "cherubim" with similar description to the four beasts of Revelation 4 and Ezekiel 1, except that the one face is the face of a "cherub", instead of an "ox" or "calf" (Ezek. 10:14). This describes a sign of growth and maturity throughout these three descriptions. I think this is a sign of God's authority over life today and in the so called "Messianic Age" at the temple and throughout the world, through whomever He wills it (Ezek. 10:19). I also think it describes the use of common day construction equipment to build the "Messianic Age" temple, with manual labour as well (Ezek. 10:1-13). This only stands to reason, and may seem out of place in the subjects of this book, but this is where the interpretation came to me, as the Holy Bible says, "...here a little, *and* there a little..." (Isa. 28:10). The point is that we should not have any concern, anxiety, etc., over God's sovereign authority over all things, prophecy, our life today, and in the "world to come". All we need to do is worship Him, in the name of Jesus Christ of Nazareth, as the testimony of Jesus is the spirit of prophecy and God will lead us on the straight path to eternal life in the name of Jesus Christ of Nazareth (Rev. 19:10). Alleluia and praise the LORD

God Almighty. Amen and Amen. And as the Scripture says, "Behold, I come quickly: hold that fast which thou hast, that no man take thy crown." (Rev. 3:11).

Mark of the beast and family

Putting down "roots" or constant upheaval and moving around, following after our lusts, evil imaginations, etc. (1 Pet. 5:10, ref). The Holy Bible says, God will establish us, so that we will not be moved (1 Thess. 3:2, 3; 1 Pet. 5:10). Boxes have six sides, and of course they are used for transporting bulk items of all kinds. The "new Jerusalem", is also described to be in the shape of a "cube", but the roof, the temple, is made of God, the Father, and of the Lamb of God, Jesus Christ of Nazareth (Rev. 21:22). Nevertheless, the point is Jesus Christ said that the kingdom of God is within us, it does not come by observation (Luke 17:20, 21). Jesus Christ was and is and always will be the kingdom of God, in the flesh (Rev. 21:22). God's kingdom is of peace, and is everlasting, and is of the Holy Spirit, as God is a Spirit, first and foremost (John 4:24). As the Holy Bible says, "It is the spirit that quickeneth; the flesh profiteth nothing…" (John 6:63). It is by God's Holy Spirit in the name of Jesus Christ of Nazareth that gives us life and life everlasting, because there is no other name under heaven by which we can be saved (Acts 4:12). Regarding life and death and "enemies", Jesus said, "…bless them that curse you…and pray for them which despitefully use you, and persecute you;" (Matt. 5:44). He also said, "…I am come that they might have life, and that they might have *it* more abundantly." (John 10:10). Magicians and sorcerers can "mimic" miracles using "enchantments" to "give" life, but often at least in the system, as of the date of writing this book in 2018 A.D., they are taking life from somewhere else to give it to another (Ex. 7:11, 22; 8:7, 18). This seems to be a false life giving system, at least in part if not fully, the organ and blood donation system that exists today, as of the date of writing this book in 2018 A.D. (Rev. 13:3, 12). I am not outright judging this system, as we can do nothing but by God (John 1:3, Rev. 4:11). However, I trust Jesus Christ of Nazareth over the works of the hands of men, that is, God can still restore our bodies miraculously without the work of man's hands today (Dan. 2:34, 45). A perfect example is in the woman whom was healed of the issue of her blood, that no physician could heal and she spent all she had on them to heal her, but when she touched Jesus' garment, virtue, that is power, left Him, and by faith she was healed (Mark 5:25-34). Alleluia and praise the LORD. Amen and Amen. Jesus gave His own life for the forgiveness of our sins, dying on the cross, He was buried and He arose to give us hope and the promise of everlasting life in His Holy name. No other man here in earth or in heaven can do this (Acts 4:12). He raised the dead and healed the sick and so did His disciples in His Holy name (Matt. 4:24, 12:15, 14:14, 15:30, 19:2, 21:14; John 11:1-45, Acts 9:36-42, 14:19, 29; 20:7-12). This shows God's life giving Spirit is greater than man's hands and abilities. Alleluia and praise the LORD. Amen and Amen. Jesus Christ came to give life and life more abundantly (John 10:10). Alleluia and praise the LORD. Amen and Amen. Marrying a spouse, bearing children, teaching them God's way and the process continuing with their children and grandchildren is part of this "increase" or growing of the kingdom of God here on earth, and will be fully realized when we are resurrected unto eternal life in Christ Jesus of Nazareth's Holy name in the "world to come" (Mal. 2:15). Alleluia and praise the LORD God Almighty in the name of His only begotten Son, Jesus Christ of Nazareth. Alleluia and praise the LORD. Amen and Amen.

Disobedience to God, fornication, ungodly use of the body for self-gratification of all kinds; these are the works of the Sodomites of Sodom and Gomorrah, and have a later example in some of the children of Benjamin in the book of Judges (Gen. 13:13, 18:20, 21; 19:1-14; Jud. 19, 2 Pet. 2:6-10, Jude 1:7).

That all being said, the reality is that we are all sinners and we all need God's forgiveness through His only begotten Son, Jesus Christ of Nazareth (Ps. 14:3, 53:3; Rom. 3:23). If the wicked repent of their ways, they will be forgiven (Ezek. 18:21, 33:15, 19). Another abomination is parents not allowing children to "grow" up and start a family of their own. The commandment from the beginning is to leave father and mother and cleave to our spouse (Gen. 2:24). Jesus said, "He that loveth father or mother more than me is not worthy of me: and he that loveth son or daughter more than me is not worthy of me." (Matt. 10:37). The point here is, we must let our children "go" and have their own life in Christ Jesus of Nazareth's Holy name, with a spouse as God has intended, and as God wills it of course (Matt. 6:10, Mark 10:6-9). Jesus did mention that some are "eunuchs", of their own desire, some of God's desire, and some made by man, which would be another mark of the beast, man forcing man to be "celibate", as of the date of writing this book in 2018 A.D. (Matt. 19:12, Rev. 13:16, 17). But ultimately, whatever we do here on earth we must do it for God Almighty and His only begotten Son, Jesus Christ of Nazareth first and foremost (1 Cor. 10:31, Col. 3:17, 23). And as God wills it, He will provide a spouse for us, and children and a house and riches (Prov. 19:14, Matt. 19:14, 29). God is the Provider of all things. To God be the glory in the name of His only begotten Son, Jesus Christ of Nazareth. Alleluia and praise the LORD. Amen and Amen. This is where patience and obedience comes into play, as Jesus said, "In your patience possess ye your souls." (Luke 21:19). We all need patience, prayer, worship of the true God, in Christ Jesus of Nazareth's Holy name and all other things will be given to us (Matt. 6:33). This is the kingdom of God in Christ Jesus of Nazareth's Holy name. Jesus said of Himself, "Take my yoke upon you, and learn of me…For my yoke *is* easy, and my burden is light." (Matt. 11:29, 30). We have the living God with us by the Holy Spirit of God in the name of Jesus Christ of Nazareth. Learn from Him. Do not trust in my interpretations, understanding, etc. or anyone else's for that matter, but in Christ Jesus of Nazareth and God, the Father, the living God, through His Holy Spirit given to all whom receive Him. Alleluia and praise the LORD. Amen and Amen. Joshua said to the Israelites at the entering of the "promised land", "…choose you this day whom ye will serve…but as for me and my house, we will serve the LORD." (Jos. 24:15). I say the same thing to you. Jesus came to give us life here on earth today and more abundantly (John 10:10). Whom are you going to serve, man or Christ Jesus of Nazareth, the risen Lord? You choose. Alleluia and praise the LORD God Almighty in the name of Jesus Christ of Nazareth, His only begotten Son. All thanksgiving and glory and honour be unto our God. Amen and Amen.

Mark of the beast and governance

"Artificial intelligence", that is the "set it and forget it" attitude, the "automatic" life. In the Holy Bible we have the example of Ai, when the tribes of Israel, led by Joshua, were entering into the "promised land" (Jos. 7, 8). They could not defeat the city of Ai, until the camp of Israel had been cleansed of sin (Jos. 7). One man was hiding spoils from a previous battle, and he was found and killed for it (Jos. 7:1, 16-26). Then the encampment was successful at overcoming the city of Ai (Jos. 8). King Solomon had many strange wives and went into idolatry through them (1 Kings 11:8-10). King Solomon had six hundred threescore and six talents of Gold brought to him yearly for tribute from the kings of the earth (1 Kings 10:14). I would suggest this is related to the "tax" systems of the world, albeit, Jesus Christ said, "…Render therefore unto Caesar the things which are Caesar's…" (Matt. 22:21). For religion in general, some religious worship on the 6th day of the week, Friday, which may be an indication of the "mark of the beast" (Rev. 13:18). The reality is that the Sabbath is on the seventh day of the week, which was from the beginning of creation (Gen. 2:3). That is, if we have kept "time" correctly, the so called "Saturday", of the Gregorian calendar. No matter, the Holy Bible says, "Rejoice in the Lord alway…" (Phil. 4:4). There are "seven" churches mentioned in the book of Revelation, and are described by some as the "eras" of the church, that can actually trace their roots throughout the centuries to the first century church of Jesus Christ of Nazareth and the other founding apostles (Rev. 1-3). In the Old Testament, it says that seven women will desire to be named by one man (Isa. 4:1). No doubt this is prophecy of the seven churches, Ephesus, Smyrna, Pergamos, Thyatira, Sardis, Philadelphia and Laodicea, being led by God Almighty in the name of Jesus Christ of Nazareth, God's only begotten Son, by the Holy Spirit of God and Christ, throughout the centuries in the ages past, today, tomorrow, and in the "world to come" forever more (Rev. 2, 3). Alleluia and praise the LORD. Amen and Amen.

At Jesus' transfiguration, Elijah and Moses were seen with Jesus (Matt. 17:2, 3). Both had slain people, but God also wrought great "wonders", true miracles through them as well (Ex. 2:11, 12; 1 Kings 18:40). David also delivered Israel of the Philistine giant, Goliath, but He gave the glory and honour to God Almighty in the battle (1 Sam. 17:32-51). King Nebuchadnezzar became like the "beasts" of the field for seven years, after failing to give God the glory, but was restored by God (Dan. 4). Another ruler was destroyed by God for not praising Him and worshipping Him (Acts 12:22, 23). David acted as if he had lost his mind at one point in time in his life, pretending to be mad, even frothing at his mouth, which would explain the "acting" world of today in some respects, as of the date of writing this book in 2018 A.D. (1 Sam. 21:12-15). Nevertheless, the point here is that military force, weapons, etc., made by man's hands cannot overcome the enemy by themselves, we need God Almighty to be with us in our battles in this life, spiritually first and foremost, and if God wills it physically (Dan. 2:34, 45; 8:25). But God is a God of peace, and we are called to be peace makers in the name of Jesus Christ of Nazareth (Matt. 5:9). Military "forces" and "might", no doubt are related to the "mark of the beast" (Dan. 11:38). David was accused of being a "man of Belial", but the man, Shimei, was found to be in error whom did the accusing (2 Sam. 16:7-13; 19:16-23). Some of the men of David's company also were named similarly, as well as other people in the Old Testament, which was an indication of their greed and unbridled murderous ways, and general evil nature (Deut. 13:12-18, Jud. 19:22-28, 20:12; 1 Sam. 2:12, 10:27, 25:17, 25; 30:22; 2 Sam. 20:1, 23:6, 7; 1 Kings 21:10-14, 2 Cor. 12:7). The sons of Eli, a priest of the temple of God, were called "sons of Belial", after hastily and uncleanly handling the meat offerings of the temple of God, and treating the women coming to give offerings at the temple as harlots (1 Sam. 2:11-19, 22). This is an abomination to God Almighty. This is why they were removed from their priesthood, and Samuel replaced them, as a priest and prophet of God (1 Sam. 2:18-21). Killing may be a requirement by God using man's hands, namely of livestock for food consumption, but the reality is that it is God Almighty who has the ability to destroy both body and soul in hell (Matt. 10:28). There is no other man here on earth that can take or destroy our body and soul, and if they say they can, they are liars (Deut. 32:39). It is by the name of Jesus Christ of Nazareth that we live and die, and it is by the name of Jesus Christ of Nazareth that we have eternal life. Alleluia and praise the LORD. Amen and Amen.

God's image or the beast's image

Revelation 13:11-18 says, "And I beheld another beast coming up out of the earth; and he had two horns like a lamb, and he spake as a dragon. And he exerciseth all the power of the first beast before him, and causeth the earth and them which dwell therein to worship the first beast, whose deadly wound was healed. And he doeth great wonders, so that he maketh fire come down from heaven on the earth in the sight of men, And deceiveth them that dwell on the earth *by the means of* those miracles which he had power to do in the sight of the beast; saying to them that dwell on the earth, that they should make an image to the beast, which had the wound by a sword, and did live. And he had power to give life unto the image of the beast, that the image of the beast should both speak, and cause that as many as would not worship the image of the beast should be killed. And he causeth all, both small and great, rich and poor, free and bond, to receive a mark in their right hand, or in their foreheads: And that no man might buy or sell, save he that had the mark, or the name of the beast, or the number of his name. Here is wisdom. Let him that hath understanding count the number of the beast: for it is the number of a man; and his number *is* Six hundred threescore *and* six.". It is very possible that the "key" to understanding this prophecy is the word "should", it is mentioned three times referencing the "beast", and the "image", and the "life" of it. Simply put should starts with the letter "s", and it has six letters in the word. "Should" may indicate the "possibility", but not the "definitive", nature of a command. God's will is certain; we cannot "should" things into existence (Matt. 7:29, 28:18). I am not suggesting that the mark will not be fully realized in this world in the "Great Tribulation" as of the date of writing this book in 2018 A.D., as the Holy Bible says, "…with God all things are possible." (Matt. 19:26). But what I am saying is that God is merciful, kind, longsuffering, forgiving, loving, peaceful, joyful, etc. (Gal. 5:22, 23; Eph. 4:32). So we must not fear the "mark of the beast", nor the "name", nor the "number". If we are earnestly submitting our life to God in the name of Jesus Christ of Nazareth, our lives are His to do with as He pleases (John 1:3, Rev. 4:11). Receiving the mark of God means, we must be willing to give up our physical life, which is temporary to receive eternal life in the name of Jesus Christ of Nazareth (Matt. 10:39, 16:25; Gal. 6:17, Phil. 3:14). Alleluia and Praise the LORD. Amen and Amen.

The "image of the beast", may seem so similar to true Christ following that it would almost seem to be a "copycat", but it is a false witness (Matt. 15:19, 20; 2 Cor. 11:14). Which is the truth, Satan, and his "world", has none understanding, he is fallen, a "…liar, and the father of it.", and was a liar from the beginning (Gen. 3:1-5, John 8:44). It is only by the risen Lord, Jesus Christ of Nazareth, and God, the Father, through the Holy Spirit that we live and breathe, not by any other "image", "name", number, etc. (Gen. 2:7, Job 12:10, 27:3, 33:4; Ps. 33:6, Jer. 10:14, 51:17; Hab. 2:19). It is by the number of God, seven, that numbers are complete (Gen. 2:3, 7:2, 8:4). The lamb of the book of Revelation has seven eyes, and seven spirits, there are seven churches mentioned in the book of Revelation, representing the "eras" and "body" of Christ throughout the centuries and ages, and there is a stone with seven "eyes" in Old Testament prophecy as well, which no doubt is a reference to Jesus Christ of Nazareth (Zech. 3:9, Rev. 1:4, 11, 20; 5:6). Not the incomplete false witness, six hundred threescore and six, that comes short of the glory of God, the gold that rusts and is corrupted, the fallen monetary systems of this world and the like (1 Kings 10:14, Matt. 6:19, 1 Cor. 15:50, Gal. 6:8, 1 Tim. 6:5, Jam. 5:2, Rev. 13:18). But it is by God, the Father, Almighty in the name of Jesus Christ of Nazareth, God's only begotten Son, that we live, breath and are provided for in material things, and spiritual eternal things. To God be the Glory in the name of Jesus Christ of Nazareth, God's only begotten Son. Alleluia and praise the LORD. Amen and Amen. He lives and breathes and dwells with us, in us and through us forever and ever. Alleluia and praise the LORD. Amen and Amen. In the beginning we were made in the image of God, through our ancestors, Adam and Eve, and then we disobeyed Him and ate from the tree of knowledge of good and evil, listening to the "beast", the dragon, that old serpent, the devil (Gen. 3:1-19, Rev. 12:9). But now we are redeemed by the blood of the Lamb of God, the only begotten

Son of God, Jesus Christ of Nazareth. Alleluia and praise the LORD. Amen and Amen. Jesus Christ said, "But seek ye first the kingdom of God, and his righteousness; and all these things shall be added unto you." (Matt. 6:33). He said of Himself, "Take my yoke upon you, and learn of me…For my yoke *is* easy, and my burden is light." (Matt. 11:29, 30). This is the true example of living that we have in this life and in the "world to come", that is, Jesus Christ of Nazareth, whom lived and died for the forgiveness of our sins, He was buried and He arose the third day to give us the hope and promise of everlasting life in His Holy name. He has come to give us life and life more abundantly (John 10:10). Alleluia and praise the LORD in the name of Jesus Christ of Nazareth. He lives and reigns forever and ever. Amen and Amen.

Conclusion

Matthew 24:15 says, "When ye therefore shall see the abomination of desolation, spoken of by Daniel the prophet, stand in the holy place, (whoso readeth, let him understand:)". Nebuchadnezzar had a statue he made for all to worship and he "…set it up…" (Dan. 3:1-7). There was a statue of Dagon, a god of the Philistines, that was set in that god's temple (1 Sam. 5:3). But the true and living God was able to knock over that statue, twice, and even break off its head and hands the second time miraculously (1 Sam. 5:1-4). The point is here, God is sovereign over all things, and can pay retribution to any and all for our works, however, as often and whenever He pleases. As He says, "Dearly beloved, avenge not yourselves, but *rather* give place unto wrath: for it is written, Vengeance is mine; I will repay, saith the Lord." (Lev. 19:18, Deut. 32:35, Rom. 12:19). Daniel speaks of the "overspreading" of this abomination, this would describe all kinds of evils in this world that have been allowed to come into places that are supposed to be Holy, this includes spiritual places as well, including our own mind (Dan. 9:27, Eph. 2:2, 3). Jesus said that if possible even the very elect would be deceived (Matt. 24:24). And I will testify; I have had my fair share of confusion, and deception in this lifetime. Jesus spoke about wolves in sheep's clothing, the wheat and the tares, etc., and the other apostles spoke of these things in detail as well (Matt. 7:15, 13:24-30; 2 Pet. 2:1, Jude 1:4). Daniel also spoke of the "…abomination that maketh desolate…" being "…set up…" (Dan. 12:11). I will say after doing much research for my books that I have written, I have found, as I have said in other parts of my writing, information regarding certain topics I have been writing about, where the information does not agree at all with what I thought, nor in some cases, with what the Holy Bible says. This is why we need to watch, pray, and listen to the Holy Spirit for all truth, because there is a spirit of error, that teaches lies (1 John 4:6). I am not going to judge why this has happened, but the Holy Bible does a perfect job of this, and it has everything to do with our disobedience to God, and His commandments, at least as of the date of writing this book in 2018 A.D. (Gen 2:17, 3:1-19). This is why we need to accept Jesus Christ of Nazareth, and His offering of forgiveness for our sins, by His Holy and righteous blood spilt on the cross, His death, His burial and His resurrection three days later for the hope and promise of eternal life in His Holy name. Alleluia and praise the LORD. Amen and Amen. This is the only way we can pass from our death in our sin, to life and everlasting life in the name of Jesus Christ of Nazareth, the only begotten Son of God, whom is life (John 14:6, Eph. 2:1-7). Alleluia and praise the LORD. Amen and Amen. Nevertheless, let us keep it simple, Jesus said, "…for that which is highly esteemed among men is abomination in the sight of God." (Luke 16:15). This all being said, the Holy Bible also associates desolation with rest of the land (Lev. 26:34, 35; 2 Ch. 36:21). So I will leave this for you to decide what to do with. Alleluia and praise the LORD. Amen and Amen.

On the flip side of the coin, we can look at this from the perspective of Jesus Christ of Nazareth fulfilling all Scripture, as He even said the Scriptures speak of Him (John 5:39). So the abomination then would be, man standing in place of God, doing God's judgement (Dan. 8:11, 2 Thess. 2). That is, man judged Jesus Christ of Nazareth, standing "…in the Holy place…", and "…set up…" His body on the cross at Passover 31 A.D. (Matt. 24: 15, Dan. 12:11). The overspreading of abominations is man's false witness against Jesus Christ of Nazareth, accusing Him of all kinds of evil, none of which are true, even betrayal and denial, including His own disciples, Judas Iscariot and Peter, respectively (Matt. 26:14-16, 33-35, 59-61, 69-75). Jesus Christ of Nazareth, is the Righteous Branch, the Holy One, the Just one, the only begotten Son of God, the Messiah and Saviour of the whole world (Jer. 23:5, John 1:14, 18; 3:16, 18; Acts 3:14, 15; 7:52; 1 John 4:9). Alleluia and praise the LORD. Amen and Amen. Daniel 12:10-12 says, "Many shall be purified, and made white, and tried; but the wicked shall do wickedly: and none of the wicked shall understand; but the wise shall understand. And from the time *that* the daily *sacrifice* shall be taken away, and the abomination that maketh desolate set up, *there shall be* a thousand two hundred and ninety days. Blessed *is* he that waiteth, and cometh to the thousand three hundred and five and thirty days.". This could describe the time of Jesus' ministry, about three and a half years, and could describe the forty days after His resurrection and ascension to the right hand of the Father, including the day of Pentecost in 31 A.D., ten days after His ascension, when the Holy Spirit was poured out, and could even include the days of His conception, birth, and some Biblical accounts of His childhood, and John the Baptist's witness of Him (Matt. 1:18-25; 2, 3, 11:7-15; Luke 2:42-52, Acts 1:2-4, 2:1-4). This would explain why Jesus said on the cross, "…it is finished…", it would also explain why He spoke of the work He must finish, that God, His Father, gave Him to do (John 4:34, 5:36, 17:34, 19:30). This would also explain the taking away of the daily sacrifice (Dan. 11:31, 12:11). Because Jesus came to heal us, to forgive us our sins, He said if we believe in Him we will never die (John 11:25-27). So these all indeed fulfilled the Scriptures in Christ Jesus of Nazareth's Holy name. Alleluia and praise the LORD. Amen and Amen. Nevertheless, Jesus also said, if a man asks you to walk a mile with him, walk with him two (Matt. 5:41). And in the book of Revelation, we are admonished to give "Babylon" double for all that she has done to us (Rev. 18:6). So as even Jesus spoke, there may still be yet to come a "great tribulation", to fulfill this Scripture as well, as of the date of writing this book in 2018 A.D. (Matt. 24:21, Rev. 2:22). But understand this, that Jesus has come to forgive us of all our sins (John 3:16). He died on the cross for the forgiveness of our sins, spilling His Holy and righteous blood on that cross. He was buried and arose the third day to give us the hope and promise of eternal life in His Holy name. Alleluia and praise the LORD. Amen and Amen.

With all of this being said, we can look at our salvation in two ways at the least, from a works based, "good" deeds, point of view or a faith based salvation by grace, which is a gift from God in Christ Jesus of Nazareth's Holy name (Eph. 2:8, 9). I am inclined to believe salvation by the grace of God, in the name of Christ Jesus of Nazareth, whom came full of grace and truth (John 1:14). Alleluia and praise the LORD. Amen and Amen. No matter, regarding this abomination, and it being setup, Jesus did say when these things start to come to pass to "…flee to the mountains…" (Luke 21:21). Now you may have your own way of understanding and interpreting the abomination of desolation, and God may have even revealed to you personally how it ought to be interpreted, and what to do about it, but in general there are a few examples in the Holy Bible, by Jesus of "mountain" experiences. The first one is the sermon on the mount, which is a very good start, and includes, "…Blessed *are* the poor in spirit: for theirs is the kingdom of heaven.", "…Love your enemies, bless them that curse you, do good to them that hate you, and pray for them which despitefully use you, and persecute you…", "Take therefore no thought for the morrow: for the morrow shall take thought for the things of itself. Sufficient unto the day *is* the evil thereof.", and "Judge not, that ye be not judged." (Matt. 5:3, 44; 6:34; 7:1). I would encourage you to read the entire sermon for an in depth understanding of who you are in Christ, and what we ought to do in this world (Matt. 5-7). Jesus prayed on a mountain alone (Matt. 14:23, Mark 6:46, John 5:15). He was on a mountain healing the multitude and did the miraculous increase of fishes and loaves twice (Matt. 14:15-21, 15:29-38). One of the more miraculous experiences was His transfiguration on the high mountain, where Moses and Elijah were revealed, speaking to Jesus about His crucifixion (Matt. 17:1-3; Mark 9:2-4, Luke 9:28-31). Then Jesus was on the mountain with His disciples after His resurrection, saying all power is given to Him, in heaven and in earth (Matt. 28:16, 18). God's kingdom is greater than the kingdoms of this world. Alleluia and praise the LORD. Amen and Amen. God is in full control of all things (Matt. 28:18, John 1:3, Rev. 4:11). The LORD omnipotent reigns. Alleluia and praise the LORD. Amen and Amen. So no matter, we must remember that ultimately, Jesus Christ of Nazareth came to earth, conceived by the Holy Spirit in the virgin, Mary, espoused to Joseph, born into this world as a child of Israel, of the tribe of Judah (Matt. 1:18, 2:20, 21; John 1:49, Rev. 5:5). He was raised with His brothers and sisters by His parents, He began His ministry in 27 A.D. at the age of about thirty and completed it by dying on the cross for the forgiveness of our sins at Passover 31 A.D., spilling His Holy and righteous blood on that cross, He was buried and the third day He arose to give us the hope and promise of eternal life in His Holy name. Alleluia and praise the LORD. Amen and Amen.

Reader's guide

This book was written with the idea of healing in mind. There may be some subjects in the end that are of more interest, or need more clarification, where you may desire to review them for a better understanding. Part of the reason why the "appendices" exist is to expand on some of the topics written about in this book, so referring to them may be preferred. When writing the book I had in mind I was reaching out to a "lost" generation, but the truth of the matter is we are all children of God, no matter what age we are. Some of the topics discussed are not usually talked about at least commonly weekly in Church or in the home, at least that I know of, so they may be new to the reader. And it may take some time to discern how to apply them to each of our daily lives.

The question section attempts to do this, at least in part, by opening back up the readers mind to the Holy Spirit of God. So that you can pray about, meditate on and discuss with others the subjects spoken about. Although the topics in this book have been spoken about and continue to be spoken about by various students of the Holy Bible, the reality of the subjects will only be fully known in God's timing. In order to better understand our place with God, in life, family and this world, we need to grow in our understanding of somethings. Hopefully, most of the subjects will be simple enough to understand that not much contemplation is needed, because God does desire us to become like little children in our relationship with Him and others (Matt. 18:3). So with that being said, pray about, meditate on and discuss the ideas that interest you with whom God wills and see if you can come to some peace in these matters. God bless and keep the faith!

Chapter One: Heaven on earth
Discussion: Salvation

> "The hill of God *is as* the hill of Basha; and high hill *as* the hill of Bashan. Why leap ye, ye high hills? *this is* the hill *which* God desireth to dwell in; yea, the LORD will dwell *in it* for ever. The chariots of God *are* twenty thousand, *even* thousands of angels: the Lord *is* among them, *as in* Sinai, in the holy *place.*"
> - Psalm 68:15-17

Some of us may never "see" or step foot in the "promised land", Moses saw it from a hill and many Israelites died in the wilderness without likely even seeing a glimpse of it literally. This may be a reality for many today who are not able to, for one reason or another, travel to these places of pilgrimage literally. But we must remember as Jesus said, "...I am with you alway, *even* unto the end of the world. Amen." (Matt. 28:20). And He said, "... the hour cometh, when ye shall neither in this mountain, nor yet at Jerusalem, worship the Father...the hour cometh, and now is, when the true worshippers shall worship the Father in spirit and in truth..." (John 4:21, 23). My point is God and Jesus Christ are with us no matter where we are here on earth, even to the "end", whether we "see" that far off "promised land" or not (Matt. 28:20). It is by faith we live in God and Christ, and this is a gift, not earned by merit of works, so that no man can boast (Eph. 2:8, 9). Glory be to God, the Father, Almighty and His only begotten Son, Jesus Christ of Nazareth. Alleluia and praise the LORD. King David lived in Jerusalem, and he still felt like a stranger from time to time (Ps. 39:12, 69:8). The apostles wrote about being a stranger on the earth, and a pilgrim (Matt. 25:35, Eph. 2:12, 13, 19-22; 1 Pet. 2:11, 12). And Jesus said Himself, that His kingdom was not of this world, or else His servants would fight for Him, albeit Peter did cut off the ear of a high priests servant, but Jesus healed the servant's ear, and Jesus spoke those words after that event (Matt. 18:10, 11, 36; Luke 22:50, 51). We must remember as Jesus Christ, Himself said, that God is a Spirit (John 4:24). So this means that His kingdom is a spiritual kingdom first and foremost. He inhabits our praise (Ps. 22:3). Righteousness and judgment are the habitation of His throne (Ps. 97:2). He inhabits eternity (Isa. 57:15). This is a God much greater than us, but merciful and loving enough to send His only begotten Son, Jesus Christ of Nazareth, to die on the cross for the forgiveness of our sins and to show us the way to salvation in His Holy name. It is by grace that we are saved, not by works, so that no man can boast (Eph. 2:8, 9). Praise the LORD God Almighty, and His only begotten Son, Jesus Christ of Nazareth. Alleluia and Praise the LORD. Jesus also said that God's kingdom does not come by observation, but that His kingdom is within us (Luke 17:20, 21). That is because God is a Spirit and all of creation exists by, through and for Him (John 1:1-3, Rev. 4:11). When reading through this chapter's discussion questions and meditating on any answers, consider that great gift God has given us in His only begotten Son, Jesus Christ of Nazareth, whom died on the cross for the forgiveness of our sins, He was buried and arose three days later to give us the hope and promise of everlasting life in His Holy and precious name. Glory, thanks and praise be to our God, in Jesus Christ of Nazareth's Holy name. Alleluia and praise the LORD. Amen and Amen.

Discussion Questions

1. What do you believe about salvation and being "born again"? Read Isaiah 46:3 & 4 and some other Biblical verses that may help you with your understanding of being born again.

a. Jesus and the man discussing being born again (John 3:1-21).

b. Born of water and Spirit (John 3:5). One is natural, physical, the other is from God (John 1:12, 13; 1 Pet. 1:23).

c. It is appointed unto men once to die and then the judgement (Heb. 9:27).

2. Have you accepted Christ's sacrifice for the forgiveness of your sins yet?

a. Encourage self-reflection and group discussion.

3. How seriously do you take your conversion, and what are some changes you can make today to better follow God's path for you in this life?

a. Encourage self-reflection and group discussion.

Chapter Two: Outer space
Discussion: Peculiarity

> "Prove all things; hold fast to that which is good."
> - 1 Thessalonians 5:21

God does not desire us to be blind, cookie cutter people (Ex. 19:5, 6; 2 Pet. 2:9, 10). He created Adam from the dust, and then created Eve from one of Adam's ribs (Gen. 2:21-25). This is the first example of God using two different "methods" to bring about the same result, human life. God does say that He does not change, and I am not suggesting anything otherwise, but we must remember that God created us all (Mal. 3:6). This is where a discernment of spirits comes in (1 Cor. 12:10). The apostle, John, admonishes to "try the spirits", as not all "spirits" are in Christ Jesus of Nazareth (1 John 4:1). We must remember that we each have our own spirit that dwells in us, and this spirit without Christ Jesus of Nazareth is naturally fallen, and rebellious towards God, as we "inherited" this nature from our ancestors in Adam and Eve first, after they ate from the tree of knowledge of good and evil (Gen. 3, Job 32:8). That being said, we can be redeemed from this fallen "nature" by the blood of Jesus Christ of Nazareth. Alleluia and praise the LORD. It is by His Holy and righteous blood that we are saved from our sins and we have the hope of our own resurrection and eternal life in His Holy name. Jesus did many miracles and a variety of them as well, healing the sick, the blind, the lame, the dumb, He walked on water and cast out unclean spirits, He also multiplied fishes and loaves (Matt. 4:24, 9:27-30, 11:4, 5; 12:22; 14:24-33; Mark 1:23-27, 6:35-44). Not only this, but He said, we would do greater things than Him, in His Holy name, because He went to the Father (John 14:12). Is it any wonder we live in the world we do today with all of its miraculous inventions? I think not, all for the glory of God in the name of His only begotten Son, Jesus Christ of Nazareth. Alleluia and Praise the LORD. We must remember that God created us to be like Him, He gave us a mind to think up and invent incredible things, but this same mind can be deceived, and be used to do evil as well. This is why we need Jesus Christ of Nazareth in our life, accepting the Holy Spirit, as God's Spirit to fellowship with us and teach us, and help us in our thoughts, plans and to fulfil our desires and "dreams" (John 15:5). Without God and His Holy Spirit we are nothing more than brute beasts, and eventually dust (Gen. 3:19, 2 Pet. 2:12, Jude 1:10). But with Christ Jesus of Nazareth, we have eternal life in His Holy name. Praise the LORD God Almighty and His only begotten Son, Jesus Christ of Nazareth. Alleluia and praise the LORD. When reading through this section, consider the offering in Christ Jesus of Nazareth, God gave for your sins on the cross so that you can have life and life more abundantly, in Jesus Christ of Nazareth's Holy name. And how you can use this precious life God has given you to glorify Him, in Christ Jesus of Nazareth, God's only begotten Son. Alleluia and praise the LORD. Amen and Amen.

Discussion Questions

1. What do you believe about your place in your relationship with God and others?

    a. Common salvation (Jude 1:3)
    b. Gifts, trials, desires and experience are not all exactly the same (Rom. 12:6-8)
        i. Some: Apostles, Prophets, Evangelists, Pastors, Teachers, Miracles, Gifts of healing, Helps, Governments, Diversities of tongues (1 Cor. 12:28, Eph. 4:11). These "jobs", speaking generally cover every task given to mankind here on earth, especially

"helps"; this could be volunteering or working in a paid job. If we are working for the kingdom of God all things are possible (Matt. 19:26).

    ii. Many members one body (Rom. 12:4, 5).

c. That being said, Christ understands all our difficulties (1 Cor. 10:13, Heb. 2:18, 4:15; 2 Pet. 2:9, 10)

d. The closest human being we may be able to compare ourselves with outside of Jesus Christ of Nazareth in this life, may be our spouse, if God has blessed us with one (Eph. 5, 1 Pet. 3:7).

2. Are we all created like robots or is there something different about each of us in Christ Jesus of Nazareth?

a. "Thou hast heard, see all this; and will not ye declare *it?* I have shewed thee new things from this time, even hidden things, and thou didst not know them. They are created now, and not from the beginning; even before the day when thou heardest them not; lest thou shouldest say, Behold, I knew them." (Isa. 48:6, 7; Jer. 31:22).

    i. New Covenant in Christ Jesus of Nazareth's Holy blood (Heb. 12:24).

b. Isaiah 28:21 says, "For the LORD shall rise up as *in* mount Perazim, he shall be wroth as *in* the valley of Gibeon, that he may do his work, his strange work; and bring to pass his act, his strange act."

    i. Strange act (Matt. 17:25-27, 25:35, 27:1-10, Luke 5:17-26)

    ii. Repentance, forgiveness of sins, and redemption through Jesus Christ of Nazareth, so God is all in all (1 Cor. 12:6, 15:28).

c. Jesus' disciples did not always agree amongst one another (Matt. 20:20-24, Luke 2:24). Jesus did not blindly agree with the religious authorities, etc. (John 2:24, 25). God gave us a mind to think, not to be a "robot", but the Holy Bible also says that rebellion is like the sin of witchcraft and stubbornness is akin to idolatry, so we must discern when our own attitudes, thoughts and desires, boarder on rebellion from God (1 Sam. 15:23). As the apostle, Paul, says, "...bringing into captivity every thought to the obedience of Christ..." (2 Cor. 10:5). Jesus Christ of Nazareth ought to be our standard of how to live life, because He gave up His own will to do the will of His Father (Luke 22:42). He died on the cross for the forgiveness of our sins, He was buried and the third day He arose to give us the hope and promise of eternal life in His Holy name. Alleluia and praise the LORD. Amen and Amen.

3. There is a long list of "jobs" inside of the Church of God, what gifts do you think you might have that you can use to glorify God?

a. 1 Corinthians 12:5, 8-10, 28

b. Ephesians 4:11

c. Gifts

    i. administration, operations, wisdom of words, word of knowledge, faith, gifts of healing, working of miracles, prophecy, discerning of spirits, divers kinds of tongues, interpretations of tongues, etc.

d. 1 Corinthians 12:11

    i. "...dividing to every man severally as He will."

4. Does God place any favour for men over women or women over men in the salvation plan?

    a. 2 Corinthians 6:18
    b. Matthew 22:30, Galatians 3:28
    c. God is not a respecter of persons (Acts 10:34, 35)
    d. On earth there may be some form of "hierarchy" as it would seem. But in reality, we are all one in Jesus Christ of Nazareth, and God, the Father, through His Holy Spirit (John 17:22, 23). Alleluia and praise the LORD. Amen and Amen.

> "In the beginning was the Word, and the Word was with God, and the
> Word was God. The same was in the beginning with God."
> - John 1:1, 2

It may be hard for us to wrap our minds around the concept of Jesus being God, but Him still having a Father in heaven. But I think of it this way, we can be both a father and a son in this life, so why cannot Jesus be the same? He said, "I and *my* Father are one." (John 10:30). God desires us to be one with Him as well (John 17:20-23). This is unity; this is walking with God in obedience to Him (2 Cor. 6:16, Gal. 5:16, 25; Eph. 2:10, 5:2). Our ancestors were made in His image, in His likeness in the beginning, through His Holy Spirit (Gen. 1:26, 27). So should we not be like Him also when we are redeemed by the blood of Jesus Christ of Nazareth, God, the Father's, only begotten Son? As Jesus said, "...with God all things are possible." (Matt. 19:26). God spoke with someone else, before Adam was created during the creation week, so there was obviously someone with Him in the beginning (Gen. 1:26). Was this Jesus Christ of Nazareth, the Word of God, likely so yes (Gen. 1:26, John 1:1-3). Was He born into this world in the flesh yet? Of course not, but as He said of Himself, "...Before Abraham was, I am." (John 8:58). Jesus Christ of Nazareth is our Creator; He existed with God even before we existed here on earth (John 1:1-3). So what does God have intended for us in this life and in "the world to come" (Mark 10:30)? Only God knows for certain, but while reading through these discussion questions and considering your relationship with God, the Father, Almighty and His only begotten Son, Jesus Christ of Nazareth, hopefully the answers you are looking for will come to you. As the Holy Bible, says, God is calling us to be peace makers (Matt. 5:9). He is calling us to know the truth, Jesus Christ of Nazareth is the truth, and the truth will make us free, so there is no reason why the truth of all things cannot be revealed to you and I as well (John 8:32, 14:6, 14:26). There is also the love of Christ that passes knowledge and the peace of God that passes all understanding (Eph. 3:19, Phil. 4:7). So keep these truths in mind while meditating on and answering any of this chapter's discussion questions. And remember that Jesus came into this world, conceived by the Holy Spirit of God, born of the virgin, Mary, espoused to Joseph (Matt. 1:18-25). He was raised as a child of Israel, of the tribe of Judah, with brothers and sisters (Matt. 2:1, 13:55, 56; Mark 6:3, Luke 2:42-52, Rev. 5:5). And He died on the cross for the forgiveness of our sins, He was buried and He arose the third day to give us the hope and promise of eternal life in His Holy name. To God be the glory in the name of His only begotten Son, Jesus Christ of Nazareth. Alleluia and praise the LORD. Amen and Amen.

Discussion Questions

1. Find some verses that describe God's way of seeing and thinking (Hint: Isa. 55:8, 9).

   a. "Now unto him that is able to do exceeding abundantly above all that we ask or think..." (Eph. 3:20).

   b. "For my thoughts *are* not your thoughts, neither *are* your ways my ways, saith the LORD. For *as* the heavens are higher than the earth, so are my ways higher than your ways, and my thoughts than your thoughts." (Isa. 55:8, 9).

2. The Holy Bible says, "...with God all things are possible." (Matt. 19:26). Find some other verses that are encouraging for you to persevere in your life, trials and challenges, and in time of peace.

    a. "...greater is he that is in you..." (1 John 4:4).
    b. "...according to the power that worketh in us..." (Eph. 3:20).

3. How have events and experiences in your life opened up your mind to thinking about doing the impossible? Think of an example and meditate on how God used that experience to prepare you for His path for you in this life.

    a. God will never give us more than we can endure (1 Cor. 10:13).

Chapter Four: Hell on earth
Discussion: Forgiveness

> "…Whatsoever ye shall bind on earth shall be bound in heaven: and
> whatsoever ye shall loose on earth shall be loosed in heaven."
> - Matthew 18:18

Forgiveness is the key to moving forward in our relationship with God and others. As Jesus said, "…whatsoever ye shall loose on earth shall be loosed in heaven." (Matt. 18:18). He also said, "And when ye stand praying, forgive, if ye have ought against any: that your Father also which is in heaven may forgive you your trespasses." (Mark 11:25). If we allow the blood of Jesus Christ of Nazareth to flow over us, cleansing us, forgiving us of our sins, and helping us to forgive ourselves as well as others, this will give us the freedom we are looking for in this life and forever more. When we no longer hold the grudges, the condemnation, the anger or the judgements that are at best by our own human standards and our understanding of how we believe God judges, then we are freed from the tyranny of God's wrath (John 3:36). As Jesus said, "Judge not, and ye shall not be judged: condemn not, and ye shall not be condemned: forgive, and ye shall be forgiven: Give, and it shall be given unto you; good measure, pressed down, and shaken together, and running over, shall men give into your bosom. For with the same measure that ye mete withal it shall be measured to you again." (Luke 6:37, 38). I realize for some this may be a hard "pill" to swallow, but if you as a believer spend more time thinking about the cross of Christ and meditating on what He did for you, you may find that the other stuff becomes less and less important. I have studied the Scriptures, both in the New and Old Testament, regarding Jesus' life, crucifixion and resurrection, and I have come to the conclusion, that it is only by the blood of Jesus Christ of Nazareth on the cross that I can forgive anyone, even myself. I am not saved by my own efforts, desires, prayers, or otherwise, it was by Jesus Christ of Nazareth's act on the cross that I am saved. When you realize this one simple truth for yourself as well, you may find your freedom that you have been looking for all your life. Here it is, ready for the taking, all for the glory of God, the Father, Almighty and His only begotten Son, Jesus Christ of Nazareth. Alleluia and praise the LORD. When reading through this chapter's discussion questions, consider how Christ died for you on the cross, He was buried and He arose the third day to give us the hope and promise of eternal life in His Holy name. And consider what this means for your relationship with Him and others here on earth, and forever more in His everlasting name. Alleluia and praise the LORD. Amen and Amen.

Discussion Questions

1. The apostle, Paul, admonishes in the New Testament to redeem the time for the days are evil, what does this mean for you?

   a. Walk in wisdom (Col. 4:5)
   b. Ephesians 5:15, 16
   c. Psalm 73:3
   d. Psalm 90:15
   e. Psalm 130
   f. Joel 2:25

g. For those who believe they have lost time with loved ones or are ageing and have lost time fulfilling dreams, God seems to give us opportunity to redeem it. A good example is a King of the Old Testament whom had fifteen years added to his life after repenting (2 Kings 20:1-11).

2. Sometimes life challenges can bring us to a spiritual place that is dark to say the least. Jeremiah wrote an entire book of the Old Testament about it called Lamentations. What are some things you can do, when you are experiencing your "...walk through the valley of the shadow of death..." (Ps. 23:4)?

   a. Lamentations 3
   b. "...fear no evil..." (Ps. 23:4)
   c. 1 Chronicles 28:9
      i. God understands all imaginations of our thoughts (1 Chr. 28:9).
      ii. He knows what we are thinking and knows what we are going through (Ps. 139:2, 4; Heb. 2:18, 4:15).
      iii. He knows what we need even before we ask for it (Matt. 6:8).
      iv. He can do abundantly more than we can ask or think (Eph. 3:20, 21).

3. Why are we subject to bondage?

   a. Fear of death (Heb. 2:15)
   b. We cannot serve two masters (Matt. 6:24).
   c. Jesus said, "...Whosoever committeth sin is the servant of sin." (John 8:34).
   a. Jesus came to set us free from bondage. He came to give us life and life more abundantly (John 10:10).

Chapter Five: Hell in the ground
Discussion: Purity

> "Marriage *is* honourable in all, and the bed undefiled: but
> whoremongers and adulterers God will judge."
> - Hebrews 13:4

Jesus Christ of Nazareth is "Faithful" and abiding in Christ gives us His "faithfulness" (Rev. 19:11). The apostle, Paul, said it is not a sin to be married (1 Cor. 7:28). Of course, this ought to be common sense, as marriage is spoken of often in the Holy Bible of God as a commandment of God (Gen. 2:24, Mal. 2:15, Matt. 19:4-6). But as the Holy Bible of God says, people would pervert the gospel message, as well as do evil things, against God's commands and knowledge, etc. (Dan. 11:35, 2 Tim. 3:1-5). God commanded man to "…leave his father and his mother, and shall cleave unto his wife: and they shall be one flesh.", from the beginning starting with Adam and Eve (Gen. 2:24). Throughout the Holy Bible, God's commands are used to uphold and protect the marriage institution as a sacred and Holy union. Jesus Christ of Nazareth confirms this during His ministry saying, "…What therefore God hath joined together, let not man put asunder." (Matt. 19:6). He does speak of eunuchs being either made so of themselves, of man, or some of God's choosing (Matt. 19:12). But on the whole, the Holy Bible makes clear that an "undefiled" marriage is a worthy goal to attain in this life, by and through God's Holy Spirit in Jesus Christ of Nazareth's Holy name, the only begotten Son of God, and God, the Father, Almighty and, as God wills it, forever more in Christ Jesus of Nazareth's Holy name (Heb. 13:4). Husband and wife are said to be "heirs together" (1 Pet. 3:7). Is it any wonder the adversary attempts to steal our reward, he is jealous of something he cannot attain by himself (John 10:10). This would be the reason for bodily perversions of all kinds. That said, our bodies are created as temples of the living God (2 Cor. 6:16). We ought to learn first to treat our own body with good health, in the soul, mind and physical body, before God will trust us with another human being. This is why our early childhood, and "teenage" years are important in developing our relationship with God, the Father, Almighty, and His only begotten Son, Jesus Christ of Nazareth, through the Holy Spirit of God, and mankind, as this sets the stage for our grown-up years. Nevertheless, Jesus Christ of Nazareth died on the cross to forgive us our sins, not to condemn us, He was buried and the third day He arose to give us the hope and promise of eternal life in His Holy name. So no matter where you may be at in life; married, divorced, unmarried, etc., you can always be forgiven in Christ Jesus of Nazareth's Holy name, first and foremost, and God willing He will open doors for you to move forward with a spouse, as He wills. Jeremiah says in Lamentations, "For the LORD will not cast off for ever: But though he cause grief, yet will he have compassion according to the multitude of his mercies. For he doth not afflict willingly nor grieve the children of men. To crush under his feet all the prisoners of the earth. To turn aside the right of a man before the face of the most High, To subvert a man in his cause, the LORD approveth not." (Lam. 3:31-36). God desires us to fulfill His purposes for us in this life, and He gives us the desires of our hearts (Ps. 37:4). So keep this in mind when considering the questions in this chapter's discussion section and where you stand in your relationship with your Creator and others here on earth, all for the glory of God, the Father, Almighty and His only begotten Son, Jesus Christ of Nazareth. Alleluia and praise the LORD. Thanks be to our God, and His only begotten Son, Jesus Christ of Nazareth, for all things. Amen and Amen.

Discussion Questions

1. What does God say about our bodies being His temple?

   a. Ephesians 2
   b. Ephesians 3
   c. 1 Corinthians 6:20
   d. Song of Solomon 8:6, 7
   e. Matthew 10:29-31

2. How are we cleansed?

   a. Understand that we are a threefold being made of body, soul and spirit and that our entire being God is calling into communion with Him, to receive eternal life in the name of His only begotten Son, Jesus Christ of Nazareth (1 Thess. 5:23).
   b. We need to cast off the old "man" and receive the Holy Spirit, in Jesus Christ of Nazareth's Holy name to renew our body, soul and spirit unto eternal life (Eph. 4:22-24).
   c. Mind
      i. Romans 8:6-9
      ii. "...carnal mind is enmity against God..."
      iii. "...ye are not in the flesh, but in the Spirit, if so be that the Spirit of God dwell in you..."
   d. Body
      i. Matthew 15:18-20
      ii. "For out of the heart proceed evil thoughts, murders, adulteries, fornications, thefts, false witness, blasphemies..."
      iii. Colossians 3:5-8
      iv. "Mortify therefore your members which are upon the earth..."
   e. Soul
      i. Luke 21:19
      ii. "In your patience possess ye your souls."
   f. Start by accepting Jesus Christ of Nazareth as your Lord and Saviour (Acts 4:12).
   g. And accept His Holy Spirit as your Comforter and helper (John 14:16-18, 26; Heb. 13:6).
   h. Lifelong conversion process; patience, prayer, praise and fellowship (Matt. 10:22).

3. How is our purity maintained?

   a. Lifelong endurance (Matt. 10:22)
   b. Speak with God in prayer
   c. Read God's Word, the Holy Bible of God
   d. Praise and worship God
   e. Fellowship with other believers
   f. Have faith. Without faith we cannot please God and faith is a free gift so just ask for it (Eph. 2:8, 9; Heb. 11:6). You will receive it.

g. Ultimately, it is not by our own efforts, but by God, the Father, that we are forgiven, protected and kept pure, by His Holy Spirit, through Jesus Christ of Nazareth's death on the cross for the forgiveness of our sins, His burial and His resurrection the third day to give us the hope and promise of eternal life in His Holy name. Alleluia and praise the LORD. Amen and Amen.

Chapter Six: Lake of fire
Discussion: Marriage

> "…I will have mercy, and not sacrifice…"
> - Matthew 9:13

One way to look at the "end" of the world is as a "burnt offering" to God (Gen. 8:20, 22:2; Isa. 28:22). But we must remember what the Scriptures say about our offerings to Him. He desires "…mercy, and not sacrifice…" (Hos. 6:6, Matt. 9:13). He says that all that are in the fields and forests are His (Ps. 50:10-12). There is nothing that we can give God that He does not already have. As the Holy Bible says, "…of thine own have we given thee." (1 Chr. 29:14). The point is God created this world to be inhabited, and He created it so that we can enjoy it (Isa. 45:18, John 10:10). The Holy Bible says, "…grieve not the holy Spirit of God…" (Eph. 4:30). As Jesus said of Himself, "…I am come that they might have life, and that they might have *it* more abundantly." (John 10:10). Jesus Christ of Nazareth is life; He is the way to become a child of God (John 14:6). He is life and life more abundantly (John 10:10). Praise the LORD God Almighty, and His only begotten Son, Jesus Christ of Nazareth. Alleluia and Praise the LORD. A spouse is a gift from God (Matt. 19:6, Rev. 19:7). For those whom have difficulty relating a relationship with God, to a marriage supper, Jesus used other parables to describe the Kingdom of God (Matt. 13, Luke 13:20, 21). The point is that God's kingdom has everything to do with marriage, but it can be related to in other ways as well. No matter what we choose to do here on earth in this life, we ought to put God first, and then He will direct our path for us (Prov. 3:6). To God be the glory in the name of His only begotten Son, Jesus Christ of Nazareth. Alleluia and praise the LORD. Amen and Amen.

Discussion Questions

1. What is the value of true love?

    a. Song of Solomon 8:6, 7
    b. Greatest form of Love (John 15:30).
    c. 1 Corinthians 13
    d. 1 Corinthians 6:20

2. What does it mean for two to become one flesh?

    a. Matthew 19:4-6
    b. Job 36:11
    c. At God's right hand are pleasures forever more (Ps. 16:11, Rev. 4:11).

3. Where does our faith and hope come from?

    a. Encourage self-reflection and group discussion.

Chapter Seven: What now?
Discussion: Conclusion

> "And I saw a new heaven and a new earth: for the first heaven and the
> first earth were passed away; and there was no more sea."
> - Revelation 21:1

This verse is probably the simplest verse for considering life here on earth, and what is to come. It says the "first" heaven and "first" earth, this should be a good indication that, as far as we here on earth are concerned, there was no "earth" or "heaven" before this one. This could be argued till the cows come home, but as the Holy Bible says, "The LORD preserveth the simple…" (Ps. 116:6). So it is much easier to take this verse for what it says, nothing more or nothing less. Revelation 21:4 says, "And God shall wipe away all tears from their eyes; and there shall be no more death, neither sorrow, nor crying, neither shall there be any more pain: for the former things are passed away.". This should be a great and simple promise for the "world to come", but not only that, God desires us to experience His kingdom today, here on earth now (Mark 10:30, Luke 17:20, 21). All that is required is that we accept His free gift of eternal life in the name of His only begotten Son, Jesus Christ of Nazareth. The conversion process, the "renewing" or "regeneration" of our soul, mind and body can and will be done today, in the name of Jesus Christ of Nazareth. He healed the sick, the blind, the dumb, and forgave sinners during His earthly ministry, and has been doing the same through His Holy Spirit, since then by His precious blood spilt on the cross for the forgiveness of our sins. Do you realize this? Then give God, the Father, Almighty the glory in the name of His only begotten Son, Jesus Christ of Nazareth. He died on the cross for the forgiveness of our sins, He was buried and the third day He arose to give us the hope and promise of eternal life in His Holy name. Alleluia and praise the LORD. When reading through this chapter's discussion questions, consider what has been done for you, in the name of Jesus Christ of Nazareth, and how you ought to move forward in His Holy name, as He wills you. Alleluia and praise the LORD. Amen and Amen.

Discussion Questions

1. Psalm 102:25-28 does a great job of explaining simply how the earth was established and what His plans are for it into the "future". Read the Psalm and meditate on how this truth affects your life here on earth and possibly your descendants after you.

   a. Psalm 102:25-28
      i. God laid the foundations of the earth of old and the heavens are the works of His hands (Ps. 102:25).
      ii. The earth and heaven shall perish, but God endures (Ps. 102:26).
      iii. The earth and heaven shall wax old like a garment. The earth and heaven shall change like a person changes their vesture (Ps. 102:26).
      iv. The Lord remains the same and He lives forever (Ps. 102:27).
      v. The children of God's servants shall continue, and their seed shall be established before God (Ps. 102:28).

2.   What does it mean to you, to be a "new creature" or "new man", in Jesus Christ of Nazareth's Holy name?

   a.   2 Corinthians 5:17
   b.   Galatians 6:15
   c.   Ephesians 2:15-17
   d.   Ephesians 4:24
   e.   Colossians 3:10, 11

3.   What part do you have to play in the new things God is doing here on earth and into eternity?

   a.   Isaiah 42:9
   b.   Isaiah 43:19
   c.   Isaiah 48:6-12
   d.   Jeremiah 31:11